The Magic Eye

The Magic Eye

The Cinema of
Stanley Kubrick

Neil Hornick

Sticking Place Books
New York

ISBN 978-1-942782-52-0

For Savka, Maya and Wangdak

and in fond memory of David Cronin

One more time…

CONTENTS

A NOTE FROM THE PUBLISHER

Even though it is only now being published, I have known about this book, which was written in 1969, my whole life.

I first read *The Magic Eye* more than thirty years ago, when Neil – my late father's oldest friend – passed me a copy, explaining that he had written *the very first book* about Stanley Kubrick, but that for various reasons it had never been published. I liked the book back then, and like it even more now, especially given that collectively, as best we can, Neil, scholar Filippo Ulivieri and I have attempted to piece together the background to events surrounding the un-publication of *The Magic Eye*.

For any number of reasons, one could argue that Neil's book is by now so out of date as to render it largely meaningless, not least because it was written before Kubrick's final five films were made. Moreover, research on Kubrick is today voluminous (is he – after Hitchcock – the most written-about film director in history?), made more so since his family handed his archives over to the London

College of Communication, where it is now accessible to all. In his book, Neil spends a few paragraphs on details that in more recent studies might be spread over an entire chapter. There are, by now, plenty of books about individual Kubrick films, and in the case of the director's early work as a photographer, for example, multiple illustrated volumes documenting those years exist. Neil's lengthy synopses of the films seem unnecessary until you realise that such detailed exposition was required because many readers might not have even seen the films being written about – such was cinema distribution of the late 1960s. No VHS tapes or DVDs. No internet. Film prints only.

So why publish *The Magic Eye* now, more than five decades after it was first written, and a quarter-century after the death of Stanley Kubrick?

From the perspective of 2024, it's worth reiterating that had Neil's book appeared in 1970, it would, indeed, have been the first published volume about Kubrick, pre-dating Alexander Walker's *Stanley Kubrick Directs* by a year, Norman Kagan's *The Cinema of Stanley Kubrick* by two years, and Michel Ciment's legendary interview book by nearly a decade. Only Jerome Agel's comprehensive study of *2001* (released in April 1970) would have pipped Neil to the post. In terms of its contribution to Kubrick Studies, to that historiography, *The Magic Eye* has value.

The book is also significant because, refreshingly, Neil isn't always gushing in his praise for Kubrick's films, and more importantly it's a prime example of how Kubrick attempted to do all he could to control his own image. Neil's book is the reality of Kubrick's image-control obsessions taken to their ultimate conclusion. He would redline the transcripts of his interviews and send them back to journalists. In the case of *The Magic Eye*, Kubrick didn't just make edits – he erased the entire project, and Peter Cowie's Tantivy Press, described in 1970 by the *Los Angeles Times* as "the world's only English-language publishing firm devoted totally to books about movies," never did issue a Kubrick volume.

Another merit of the book is that Neil was, and remains, a theatre man by training, a creative practitioner at heart, which is one reason why *The Magic Eye* is lucid, jargon-free and wholly readable. Unencumbered by the kind of language that has since infected film studies on campuses, Neil, in fact, is occasionally and endearingly hesitant in his analysis ("to stretch the point a little"). He offers up his opinions on the films, but is also anxious to pull together the most basic facts about their production, alongside biographical particulars of Kubrick. Much of those details are by now common knowledge, but at the time, where else would one have found all that information in one place? *The Magic Eye* is an excellent summary of what a diligent researcher with a British Film Institute library card and French language skills but no direct access to Kubrick or his archives-to-come, nor, of course, to the Internet or anything approximating it, would have been able to piece together in 1969. (There appears to have been no published English translation of one of Neil's key sources: Renaud Walter's lengthy *Positif* interview with Kubrick – so Neil did his own.)

Neil's empirical project included a hope that he might interview people who had worked with Kubrick, including Peter Ustinov, Peter Bull, William Sylvester, Douglas Rain and Leonard Rossiter. Peter Sellers expressed his openness to the idea ("If you would like to contact me again early in August we may be able to arrange a mutually convenient time and place to talk about Stanley's work'), Laurence Olivier begged off ("One smallish part in one film is not sufficient opportunity to study a man's methods"), Véra Nabokov wrote on behalf of her husband, acknowledging receipt of Neil's letter, noting that Vladimir didn't have the time to respond "in adequate detail," James Mason was hesitant ("perhaps you might coax me into supplying you with a few comments if you told me a little bit more about your book and yourself"), and John Trevelyan, secretary of the British Board of Film Censors (who, upon its publication, raved about Alexander Walker's book in the *Evening Standard*), prudently noted: "Since Stanley Kubrick is a friend of mine I think it courteous to ask him about this before I give you an answer." In the end, the only interview Neil conducted was with Rossiter – which, he said, yielded nothing of interest for the book.

At the end of this book is a timeline which offers context to the *Magic Eye* debacle. Everything hinges on the agreement – in the form of a letter written by Kubrick, dated 1 October 1969 – that Peter Cowie made with Kubrick, effectively giving the world-famous film director control over the project. Enquiries made this year reveal that no paperwork relating to Neil's manuscript of *The Magic Eye* appears to be held by the Kubrick Archive, which suggests that Kubrick either disposed of such things or perhaps handed over all relevant material to his lawyers. At one time, Neil thought about depositing any Kubrick-related paperwork he had into the Kubrick Archive. He told me that he liked the idea of somehow infiltrating that collection with illicit material – pages that Kubrick hadn't approved of. And the Archive was willing to take it. But in the end, it was decided that he should hold onto that documentation himself.

The filmography included in the original draft of *The Magic Eye* has been cut. A handful of minor changes have been made to the text, primarily the correction of spelling and some factual errors.

Paul Cronin
New York, March 2024

FOREWORD BY FILIPPO ULIVIERI

To the devoted Kubrick fan, Neil Hornick's lost book is the stuff of legend. Due to a series of obscure and frustrating events, what might have been the first-ever guide to the life and films of Stanley Kubrick became the book that Stanley Kubrick didn't want anyone to read.

While the manuscript had been in the British Film Institute library since 1972, its existence was brought into the open only in 1997, in John Baxter's biography of Kubrick. Baxter used Hornick's misadventure to illustrate Kubrick's control over the "attempts by writers to examine his life or career [which] were scrutinised and, more often than not, thwarted."

In fact, while Baxter's intuition that Kubrick was ruthless in controlling how he was portrayed in all sorts of publications was very much correct, Hornick's case is unique. His is the only known book that suffered from Kubrick's control to the extent of remaining unpublished. Only now, more than fifty years after the incident, is *The Magic Eye* finally reaching a wider public.

Hornick summarised his experiences in a statement that he wrote in 1972, when he had abandoned all hope of ever seeing *The Magic Eye* in bookshops. However, as with any story, there's another side to it. The history of Hornick's book can be unravelled in full only through archival research.

The Magic Eye was a commission handed in May 1969 to Hornick, who inherited from a previous author the promise from Kubrick of an interview. At that time, Kubrick still made himself readily available to those who wanted to write about him. He routinely allowed reporters to visit his sets while he was filming and invited selected journalists to his home to discuss the latest work at length when it was about to premiere. In 1969, he spoke to Joseph Gelmis for a chapter in his book *The Film Director As Superstar* and provided a running commentary to Jerome Agel's *The Making of Kubrick's 2001: A Space Odyssey*, published in 1970. In total, I have discovered 362 individual texts containing original quotes by Kubrick, a number that proves without any doubt that, contrary to popular belief, the director did engage with the press, and far from sparingly. In his 50-year career, with 12 films released during his lifetime, interviews with Kubrick average 25 per film, and 13 per year before 1972. The notion that he rarely granted interviews and never spoke to the press is, simply, untrue – a myth.

Kubrick, still committed to an interview, gladly accepted Hornick's request that, in the shared interest of factual accuracy, he vet the manuscript. He also facilitated Hornick's access to prints of some of his films. After receiving a first draft of *The Magic Eye*, however, his conduct changed completely: he endlessly postponed the interview and refused to be in direct contact with Hornick, using his assistant and lawyers as intermediaries. By enforcing a clause in the agreement he had made with Hornick's publisher, and threatening legal action, Kubrick stalled the project. What Hornick did not know, but in the end suspected, was that Kubrick had begun cooperating with someone else: Alexander Walker – journalist, film critic and friend of Kubrick's – who was writing his own book on the director's life and career.

In March and April 1970, Walker visited Abbots Mead, Kubrick's home on Barnet Lane, Elstree, near London, to view prints of the films in the director's own projection room, discuss each in detail afterwards, and take copious notes. On 25 May, Walker taped a lengthy interview with Kubrick, which was transcribed in July. Walker spent the remainder of the year writing his book, while Kubrick was busy preparing and filming *A Clockwork Orange*. Two days after principal photography wrapped, on 26 February 1971, Kubrick began vetting a draft version of Walker's typescript, primarily to check his quotes – which he edited, expanded, condensed, and sometimes rephrased entirely, going back to fine-tune each multiple times – and to correct factual errors or inappropriate interpretations of certain events, but also to tone down observations which he felt read too categorically, or to ask for more context to better explain hastily written passages.

The revision process took Kubrick more than a week, after which he went back to work on *A Clockwork Orange*. In June, while cutting the film, Kubrick found the time to answer a series of questions in written form, which Walker used for a Q&A section to conclude his introductory essay. *Stanley Kubrick Directs* was ready to be put on sale in American bookshops at the end of September 1971, to capitalise on the upcoming release of *A Clockwork Orange*, which was set for December. At the beginning of 1972, with the film about to open in the United Kingdom, the book was published in Great Britain. Soon afterwards, with a newly written final chapter on *A Clockwork Orange*, *Stanley Kubrick Directs* was republished both in the US and UK in an "expanded edition."

From an unused preface, we learn that it took Walker fifteen months and some thirty visits to Kubrick's home to write his book, and that he was allowed to attend the filming, on New Year's Eve 1971, of the fight between Alex and the Cat Lady in a large country mansion, which enabled him to see the director at work with his own eyes. A letter to Walker's publisher also reveals that Kubrick approved of the overall structure of the volume, which was focused primarily on

Paths of Glory, Dr. Strangelove and *2001: A Space Odyssey,* and gave his permission for the reproduction of frames from any of his films to be used as stills in the book.

Kubrick gave Walker unprecedented access to the inner workings of his art, cooperating with him fully and promptly in the creation of his book. Even though he would concede his time to other authors in the years following – notably, Gene D. Phillips, for his 1975 book *Stanley Kubrick: A Film Odyssey,* and Michel Ciment, for his lavish *Kubrick* tome, expanded twice after its first publication in 1982 – no book was favoured with such active participation as *Stanley Kubrick Directs.*

In his 1972 statement attached to *The Magic Eye,* Hornick hints at the notion that his book was deemed overcritical of Kubrick and therefore dropped to make way for a more positive appraisal. The same supposition is advanced by John Baxter, but more explicitly. Although it is certainly the case that Walker's book is full of praise for Kubrick – in fact, in its 300-plus pages I can find not a single clause which is less than glowing – I am not entirely convinced this was the reason behind the interdiction of Hornick's book.

To begin with, I don't agree that *The Magic Eye* gives the impression of a mixed reception of Kubrick's films, with the bad points always outweighing the good ones, as Kubrick, via his associates, lamented. I find Hornick's summary of the reception of the films in the US and UK not only accurate but also well balanced, overall admiring, and occasionally enthusiastic. True, it would have been the first book entirely about Kubrick to appear on the market, and perhaps the director wanted nothing short of a paean. But maybe Kubrick's real issue with Hornick's book, regardless of its positive or negative stance, was the simple fact of its existence. If published before Walker's book, it may have seemed as though Kubrick had resorted to a critic friend to safeguard his reputation; if published after, it was bound to divert some attention from it, thus dissipating its potential. After putting so much effort into *Stanley Kubrick Directs,* perhaps Kubrick didn't want to run the risk of a less than sensational impact, or of a harmful dynamic between authorised vs. unauthorised monographs.

I would like to advance another possible rationale behind the quashing of *The Magic Eye* – a provocative one.

The years 1968 to 1972 were critical for Kubrick. After the furore that *Dr. Strangelove* stirred in the US political debate and the astonishing success of *2001* in the cultural landscape, Kubrick faced his greatest setback when his planned epic *Napoleon* failed to receive financing from any of Hollywood's major studios. When, in 1970, he signed a multi-picture deal with Warner Bros., he needed a third hit to cement his position within the studio, his stature among film critics, and his reputation with the general public. In the years leading up to *2001*, Kubrick controlled how he was portrayed in the press by insisting on approval of his interview quotes before publication and through the promotional material included in his films' press kits and exhibitors' manuals, which he either wrote himself or supervised.

These texts spread stories about his masterful command of cinematic technique, his keen eye for detail, his extensive research before each new venture, his indomitable attitude… In short, they encouraged the emergence of his unique status amid the Hollywood crowd. The world began to see him as a director of rare breed, a virtuoso in the motion picture arts, an all-powerful perfectionist, a force of nature. What he still lacked was the final piece to complete his design: the critics' unmitigated approval.

Up until then, his films had been met with polarised reactions. Positive reviews usually exceeded negative ones, but a few scathing comments by prominent critics had stained their reputation. *2001* in particular suffered from the reaction of a handful of highly influential critics from New York who scorned it as an unimaginative, boring failure. Kubrick needed something to turn the critics around.

The Magic Eye was hardly the answer.

Although Hornick writes that Kubrick's "recent films are among the few big-budget productions today that are informed by individuality, intelligence, and taste; are not, in short, compromised en route from conception to realisation," he never hesitates to point out their flaws. The fact that he is greatly impressed by *Paths of Glory*, "a film of intoxicating visual sophistication, intelligent, abrasive, moving, and subversive," doesn't prevent him from noting that certain narrative choices occasionally overstressed the ironies in the story. Nor does his resounding praise for *Dr. Strangelove* – a socially impactful work of art "that belongs to the Swiftian tradition," bravely made and exhibited at a time when it was most agitational, yet timelessly relevant – cloud his judgement over less harmonious sequences.

Moreover, Hornick – an intelligent enough observer of the political aspects of moviemaking in Hollywood – uncovers some of Kubrick's tactics. He reports that when certain critics grumbled about Sue Lyon looking too old for the part of Lolita, Kubrick defended his casting by saying that the actress actually looked younger than her age, adding that girls of 13 do not look like babies. However, retorts Hornick, the point is not whether Sue Lyon looks younger or similar to many American teenagers, but whether she embodies the characteristics of a nymphet as defined by Nabokov in his novel. Kubrick's justification of Sue Lyon, writes Hornick, "does not really hold water." It was likely due to a censorship issue that Lolita was presented as a relatively mature girl in the film. This is not the sole instance in which Hornick challenges Kubrick's statements to the press. When he reports that Kubrick was enthusiastic about *Spartacus* at the time of its release, only to disparage it in the years following, Hornick notes that the statement was "perhaps best interpreted as discreet public relations talk." It is not hard to imagine how badly such comments might have gone down with Kubrick.

Hornick makes no mystery about the fact that he doesn't consider *Lolita* as successful as Kubrick's earlier work. What I find most damning in Hornick's criticism, however, is that the flaws he sees in the film tarnish perhaps the most coveted trait of Kubrick's image: his unique personality, which imbued everything he touched.

After an unsparing dissection, Hornick draws his analysis to a close and writes that Humbert and Lolita's relationship in the film "is not only normalised and sanitised

– it is also sentimentalised… Nelson Riddle's over-lush music surges up romantically… The film tends to invest their relationship with the quality of a conventionally doomed movie romance." The "mostly anonymous camera style," "disappointingly flat" photography, a series of "flatly conventional compositions" – all contribute "to the general air of theatricality," so that the film is "often as flat and static as a British second-feature thriller." Gone is Kubrick's previously lauded visual flair: *Lolita* has an "oddly impersonal style… that betrays the spirit of the novel and paralyses the film." Stanley Kubrick's *Lolita* suffers from "stylistic atrophy," "stylistic anaemia." A bland, unoriginal, sentimental movie – the opposite of what Kubrick wanted to make (and to be seen making).

At the end of his review, Hornick writes that *Lolita* is the only Kubrick film which can be described as "an actors' movie," that is, a film in which the actors' performances are the main or sole highlight, with all other elements, including direction, subordinate. When speaking with Walker about *Lolita*, Kubrick expressed his regret about the film by touching on precisely the points raised by Hornick, including the problem with the censors and Riddle's "overemphatic score." He concluded: "It's an actors' picture, if it's anything." It is impossible to know whether Kubrick saw his naked opinion mirrored in Hornick's book, or if *The Magic Eye* pushed him to admit his own failure, but it goes without saying that this frank view of *Lolita* was not included in Walker's printed book.

On the whole, *The Magic Eye* does not build up to a negative critique of Kubrick – far from it. The director's impressive achievements are described nowhere better than at the end of the chapter on *2001*. But the book is indeed a piercing and unbiased assessment of an artist, relentless in observing with rigour and acuity every single choice Kubrick made, and very honest in weighing up each.

It is also a book that contextualises Kubrick. Hornick always kept in mind the conditions under which the films were made, to see whether the director's will to maintain his creative independence had been strong enough. Hornick put his intent on paper in his first letter to Kubrick: "of any given film I would like the reader to know what pressures and restraints were contended with, if any, and how the finished picture was affected by them." When this was indeed the case, Hornick didn't shy away from indicating as such.

The problem is, Kubrick didn't need an even-handed and contextualised analysis of his films, however positive. He preferred that they be seen as absolutes. He didn't need reality, he needed (yet another) myth. He had already very artfully created the persona of a distinctive, powerful filmmaker, thus paving the way for him to become one. And now, by fostering a climate of approbation, Kubrick could hope to become a darling of the critics.

To that end, Walker's *Stanley Kubrick Directs* was most useful. The book opens with the lines: "Only a few film directors possess a conceptual talent – that is, a talent to crystallize every film they make into a cinematic concept. It is a skill that… transcends the need to find a good subject, an absorbing story, or an extraordinary premise to build on. Essentially, it is the talent to construct a form that will exhibit the maker's vision in an unexpected way… It is this conceptual talent that most strongly distinguishes Stanley Kubrick." What Walker meant was that Kubrick's films are not simply stories, but concepts, ideas, intellectual ventures. This rather abstract reading served to move Kubrick's work closer into the realm of film critics, who more than most people respond to the conceptual.

Sure enough, the second paragraph of Walker's book made his (and Kubrick's) operation clearer still: Kubrick "is a filmmaker who resists the customary critical approach that tries to distinguish strongly linked themes in a director's work" because "almost every film Kubrick has directed has entailed constructing a new concept." The implication is that, up until then, no one had succeeded in fully understanding Kubrick. *Stanley Kubrick Directs* calls for a new critical framework, and offers itself as the guiding example.

For the next thirty pages, Walker characterises Kubrick's by now well-known mythological image. Kubrick is so thorough in his preparations that he exhausts the area of research in question, and hence has no interest in repeating himself. He is thus freed from the standard demands of the film industry. At the same time, however, he understands the laws that govern success or failure in Hollywood and works within them. In performing this remarkable balancing act, he has succeeded in reconciling his own uncompromising requirements with those of the industry and made films which are admired both for their originality and box-office success.

Ever unpredictable, he strives for perfection in everything he does. He works as if possessed and demands the same level of focus and self-discipline from his crew. He knows more about photography than many veteran cameramen and doesn't consider any of his predecessors or peers to have been an influence on him. His curiosity is insatiable, his range of interests vast, even though he had no formal education. He is obsessive yet firmly rational, pondering his choices carefully before taking any action. He is one of the most elusive of filmmakers – his life style is self-sufficient, almost monastic. Living in the English countryside, a discreet environment that provides him with a highly favourable psychological climate in which he can function, Kubrick is remote from Hollywood, keeping his distance so that he can better plan his course of action and maintain total control of his work. Then, for the remaining 270 pages, Walker waxes lyrical about each of the films, casting light on their themes and the wondrous cinematic ways with which Kubrick brings them to the screen.

It isn't that Hornick fails to recognise Kubrick's influence on contemporary American cinema. At the beginning of Chapter 1, he writes that Kubrick "commands the power and respect to set up very expensive productions over which he exercises complete control as producer, director and co-writer," that "each new Kubrick film is a major cinematic event, each generates discussion in social sectors extending well beyond film circles," and that Kubrick "draws on rich creative, technical and organisational resources to realise projects of increasingly grandiose design," resulting in two masterworks which "have a quality of catharsis: each in its own way, they purge the world of its imperfections." But Hornick's book is certainly not Walker's gushing parade.

Moreover, some of Hornick's criticisms take issue with the foundations of Kubrick's mythology. For example, at odds with his reputation as a perfectionist, Hornick notes how occasional scenes look synthetic and poorly arranged. He even spots incongruous details, such as a Penguin book in *Lolita*, which is supposed to be set entirely in the US. Hornick opens *The Magic Eye* by saying that "Kubrick is less an innovator than one of the cinema's consolidators, a man who applies the inherited discoveries of the medium with enormous dynamism and flair." This view clashed openly with what Kubrick liked to see in press material, such as this example, from a studio release at the time of *Dr. Strangelove*: "Kubrick revels in making films that are controversial and off-beat... [he is] one of the most creative talents functioning on the Hollywood scene today."

Neither is there anything of the conceptual in Hornick's unpretentious book, which brims with a love of film technique. Before analysing a film's themes, Hornick pays attention to the staging and editing of the scenes, to camera placement and lighting effects, thus rooting all thematic and aesthetic effects in the mise-en-scène.

By closely comparing the two texts, I detected one more, possibly revealing, difference. Hornick describes the pivotal role played by Alexander Singer, a former high school friend of Kubrick's, at the beginning of the director's career. Even more attention is given to James B. Harris, his producing partner, who took on the financial and logistical burdens of filmmaking and enabled Kubrick to blossom as a director. Walker skates over these contributions, implying that Kubrick was able to reach the heights of Hollywood all on his own. Similarly, Hornick punctuates his text with quotes from people who have worked with Kubrick, which provides a broader picture of the director. Walker gives voice to no one but Kubrick.

With equal attention to the disowned works of *Fear and Desire* and *Spartacus*, a hard critical line on *Lolita*, its focus on the pressures and restraints of the film industry and its implicit blows to Kubrick's myth-making enterprise, *The Magic Eye* had everything to irk Kubrick at that particular moment in time.

The archival documents shed no light on whether the idea for *Stanley Kubrick Directs* emerged before or after Kubrick had read Hornick's manuscript. Could *The Magic Eye* have been a catalyst for Walker's book? In any case, the result is clear: *Stanley Kubrick Directs* is a reverential account of the heroic deeds of the great Stanley Kubrick, while *The Magic Eye* analyses the ups and downs of an artist's career, set within the productive and cultural frameworks of his era. Hornick never had a chance.

Kubrick's history with his collaborators shows that he was not keen on confrontation and open conflict. When disagreement arose, he usually went silent, left the opponent in the dark, and went on his way. The publication of Arthur C. Clarke's novel of *2001: A Space Odyssey* offers a stunningly similar case to Hornick's.

For more than a year, Clarke's literary agent had been trying to get the final draft of the novel from Kubrick, who was contractually entitled to read and amend it before publication, but kept insisting that he was too busy with filming to do so. In June 1966, with Clarke losing thousands of dollars on turned-down commissions, his agent bypassed Kubrick, sent the manuscript to Dell Publishing, and signed a six-figure deal. Kubrick protested but did not relent, still maintaining he had to check the manuscript first.

A year later, with no finalised text in sight, Dell cancelled the contract, even though they had begun typesetting and advertising the book, at a cost of $10,000. Fearing a potential lawsuit, Kubrick instructed his assistant to "discuss nothing… and just be totally dumb about the situation." Not until March 1968, a mere two weeks before the film's opening, did Kubrick sign off on the manuscript. The novel of *2001* was published three months after the film of *2001*, precisely what Kubrick had always wanted, but concealed, in order to prevent his film from being regarded as an adaptation of pre-existing literary material and not an original story.

The circumstances around *The Magic Eye* underscore Kubrick's guile to an even greater extent. He entered into an agreement with Hornick's publisher, giving himself the right to "examine the entire contents of the book prior to its publication" and to make amendments on it "as I shall in my absolute discretion determine." As an added measure, Kubrick granted himself the right to approve any foreign language version, should the book be sold and translated in other territories. Kubrick had no stake in Hornick's book, nor did he contribute anything, yet he demanded absolute control over it. He could kill the book on a whim – and he did. The publisher's ill-advised decision to sign such a preposterous agreement was the kiss of death for *The Magic Eye*. Kubrick, in blaming the author for a generally negative bias but without pointing to anything specific that he wanted amended, effectively rendered Hornick impotent.

It is unfortunate that *The Magic Eye*, a very stimulating text, was aborted. The book strikes a superior balance compared to Walker between critical assessment and the need to summarise the films' plots in an age in which old films were not readily available. Even if it does occasionally fall into what Kubrick derogatorily called "divining kinships" between films, Hornick does it with measure and purpose. And he was the first ever to do so.

Hornick also does an admirable research job. He wrote quite a bit about unrealised projects and even analysed two early drafts of *2001: A Space Odyssey*, introducing another innovative feature for its time: an analysis of the often bumpy creative process behind the writing of a screenplay – something else that surely didn't sit well with Kubrick, who famously reprimanded one assistant after he had rescued an early draft of *2001*'s script from the wastebasket and donated it to the British Film Institute: "One day, I'm sure you'll become a great director or a writer. And then you'll realise you don't want people seeing your first drafts."

The Magic Eye abounds with clever turns of phrase and well-written opinions, such as this line about *Killer's Kiss*: "It is possible to view the film as a succession of rectangular traps, the ultimate trap being the camera itself." Or this comment about the pace of *The Killing*: "a relentless ritualistic quality which becomes almost a visual manifestation of Fate." Hornick's prose is much more concise than Walker's, and more effective. It is also, in many cases, more insightful. For example, no other writer, before or since, has suggested why Bowman and not Poole was the man chosen for the extra-terrestrial rendezvous, or why the décor of the astronaut's final destination was coloured green. Most of all, and again contrary to Walker, Hornick clearly identifies the central concern of Kubrick's cinema, the unifying crucial issue that binds together his diverse body of work: control, its mechanisms, its failures and abuses.

While reading *The Magic Eye*, an intriguing question came to my mind: what if it had been published all those years ago? What would have happened to Kubrick's status among film critics had they heard Hornick's voice – a voice that is not negative, but realistic? With its down-to-earth, craft-oriented analysis of the films, would the book have chipped away at the myth of the all-powerful, never-failing director? Might it have humanised Kubrick? Would we today be witnessing the ripples of an often onanistic exegesis of Kubrick's cinema if Alexander Walker's *Stanley Kubrick Directs*, with its overinflated symbolic reading of the films, hadn't thrown the very first pebble in the pond?

While one can entertain such alternative reality, *The Magic Eye* is finally here to be read, thought upon, and savoured.

Filippo Ulivieri is a writer and lecturer, described by *The New York Times* as "Italy's leading Kubrick expert." He is the author of *Stanley Kubrick and Me: Thirty Years at His Side*, a biography of Kubrick's personal assistant Emilio D'Alessandro, which he adapted into the film *S is for Stanley*, winner of the David di Donatello award for Best Documentary Feature. His forthcoming book, which includes a comprehensive study of Kubrick's mythological persona, is *Cracking The Kube: Solving the Mysteries of Stanley Kubrick Through Archival Research*.

Neil Hornick at the Stanley Kubrick Archive,
London, February 2024.

RETURN ENGAGEMENT BY NEIL HORNICK

Once again I made my way along these
corridors and through these rooms in
this construction that belongs to the past...

Last Year in Marienbad

The book that Kubrick suppressed
When Paul Cronin expressed interest in publishing *The Magic
Eye*, my aborted book about Stanley Kubrick, I was at once
amazed, delighted and perplexed. What folly was this? Had he
taken leave of his senses? Or was it me who was finally losing
his marbles? Why on earth would anyone want to resurrect this
dead duck of a hot potato?

How Kubrick himself contrived to suppress the book's
publication way back in 1969 is explained in the statement I
included with the typescript that I deposited in the British
Film Institute library in 1972 (also included in this book).
And you can find a lot more about it here.

Of course, I was deeply disappointed by the book's suppression. It would have been my first published book, as well as the first ever to be devoted to Kubrick's entire oeuvre (up to and including *2001: A Space Odyssey*). However, I'd not been aiming for a career in writing about cinema and was too busy enjoying my activities in experimental theatre to allow the cancellation to plunge me into utter despair. Tantivy Press publisher Peter Cowie's offer of an alternative, less troublesome commission also helped soften the blow.

However, as I began researching a book about Elia Kazan, the subject Cowie and I agreed upon, I soon came to a stark realisation that stopped me in my tracks: much as I liked his films: *I had nothing original to say about him.* And it was taking *much too long.* After all, a great deal had been published about this prolific long-established stage and film director, whereas at that time there hadn't been an inordinate amount of stuff to track down for a comprehensive study of Stanley Kubrick's career. He was still relatively fresh thematic territory, and relatively accessible too since he lived in England and wasn't averse at that time to giving interviews. But now other creative prospects were seductively beckoning and I was raring to go. So I ditched the Kazan project, resigned from a not very fulfilling day-job as Lecturer in Drama at Hatfield Polytechnic (having worked there for only a year), and went for broke (sometimes literally) with what turned out to be an eventful career in alternative theatre.

The plot thickens

Given the sad fate of my book, I thought I'd finished with Kubrick. But, as I'm sure others before and after me have also discovered, one is never really finished with him. If you've once been bitten – or is the word "smitten"? – by the Kubrick bug, it kind of gets into your bloodstream and stays with you for life. Meaning that I remain interested in him to this day, much as Kubrick retained his interest in Napoleon long after he'd shelved his projected film about him. There are plenty of reasons for my interest, of course, but perhaps it all boils down to the powerful *mystique* of the man, a mystique that has grown immeasurably over the years since I wrote about him. Can it be 25 years since he died? His presence in the world of film was so distinctive that he still seems to be very much around. In 2019, you couldn't just walk into the major Kubrick Exhibition at London's Design Museum. It was so crowded that the only way you could be sure of getting in, I discovered, was to book your ticket well in advance.

So here I go once more, making my way along these same corridors and through this labyrinth, past these pillars, in a return engagement I could never have foreseen. Inspired by renewed interest in this, my relatively early contribution to Kubrick Studies, I'll now try, at the prompting of my quixotic publisher, to piece together and bring into focus some scattered recollections of my involvement, at the time my path crossed Kubrick's.

How did I get involved?

Sheer chance is the answer, as I didn't seek out the commission and my qualifications were meagre. I had no relevant professional track record and had never published an article, let alone a book, about film-making (though – fair's fair – I did once broadcast on the BBC World Service a review of a National Film Theatre screening of music-hall artistes on film).

True, I'd been a lifelong film fan and in younger days had been a keen reader of such popular film magazines as the sepia-toned *Picturegoer* (with its plentiful quota of starlet pin-ups), *Picture Show* and, later, *Films and Filming*, which came along just in time to satisfy my burgeoning adolescent interest in cinema as art, as distinct from pure entertainment (*Sight and Sound* was still a little beyond my reach). The cover of the first issue featured Marlon Brando and Eve Marie Saint in Kazan's *On the Waterfront.* Perfect choice. It was love at first sight.

I'd been a frequenter of "art houses" like the Hampstead Everyman and the Hendon Classic (in which local treasure, I was only quite recently amazed to learn, two of my uncles had been sleeping partners). True, my elder brother once worked as a travelling salesman for an obscure film distribution company and regularly brought home copies of the trade journal, *Kine Weekly*, which featured attractively glossy ads that enabled me to see what movies were on their way weeks before they were actually released. True, at 16 I was probably the youngest member of Hendon Film Society when it was run by Bob Cobbing (future sound-poet and manager of Better Books), as part of his local fiefdom, Hendon Arts Together, and had to decline an invitation to become the society's secretary because I was too busy studying for my A-levels. And true, I was in the habit of keeping lists and writing detailed notes and personal reviews of most of the films and plays I saw and the books I read – including books about films.

But perhaps my most relevant film-related credential and best claim to being a fully paid-up *cinéphile* was to have participated during my university days in Thorold Dickenson's pioneering Film Studies seminar at Slade School of Fine Art. It had been set up in 1960, conveniently close to University College, where I was reading Psychology. Other members of the first Slade seminar included future critic Ray Durgnat, film-maker Don Levy and, some time after I'd left, writer Joel Finler. The way it worked, basically, was that Dickenson showed his films and then we discussed them. Dickenson would also monitor any film projects that seminar members happened to be working on, and we may have viewed cuts of some of some of these. Did Dickenson's approach have any distinctive features that might have been reflected, years later, in my work on *The Magic Eye*? Not that I can think of.

Neither Joel Finler nor I can remember how we met, but thanks to our shared interest in cinema, we became friends and he went on to be *Time Out*'s first regular film critic, as well as the author of several scholarly film books, including *The Hollywood Story*, which won him the BFI Film Book of the Year award. He would often invite me to join him at film previews and press shows. And it was Joel (the "mutual acquaintance" mentioned in my 1972 statement) who was to recommend me to Peter Cowie as a possible replacement for David Austen, the original contracted author of the Kubrick book. Austen, a *Films and Filming* reviewer and feature writer – he'd published a review of *2001: A Space Odyssey* in the magazine – had to withdraw owing to illness. Joel himself didn't want the job, he told me, not so much because he was busy with projects of his own but rather because, unlike myself, he wasn't keen on Kubrick's films.

So when Joel asked me if I'd be interested to take over from Austen and write a book about Kubrick for the Tantivy Press paperback series, I jumped at the chance, especially as it entailed – and this was a major attraction – *interviewing Kubrick himself*. I signed a contract with Peter Cowie in May 1969 to deliver the finished book by the end of September and received an advance of £200. Soon after that, I met Austen, who passed on to me some preliminary notes he'd written and the beginnings of a Kubrick filmography that helped me get started. So far as I know, that marked the end of Austen's association with the project.

Research equipment

I find it hard to imagine today how I managed to research and write the book in only four months, while also involved in intensive performance work with the touring Wherehouse La MaMa company, for which I wrote, acted and directed. I can only assume that the bulk of the writing must have been carried out in the weeks before I joined La MaMa.

The pre-digital world of 1969 may have been primitive, but an intrepid researcher wasn't entirely without resources. There were, as now, splendid specialist archives and libraries. Principally, there was the highly congenial BFI library, where I probably did most of my research. I spent a day in the British Museum Library skim-reading an entire *Dr. Strangelove* novel. And I may also have made use of the Newspaper Archive in Colindale – hello again, *Kine Weekly* and other trade papers. Also pretty good was the reference section in my local library, which was very efficient at acquiring books from other libraries. It was at Hendon Library that I'd studied for my O- and A-Levels, ogled girls doing likewise, attended Hendon Film Society screenings, and borrowed gramophone records, some of which turned out to be relevant to the very book I was now researching (see, for example, my references in *The Magic Eye* to Howard Sackler, and "Daisy Bell," the song that's fused with HAL's sad dismemberment for all time).

And I wasn't exactly lacking in personal resources either. I'd got the makings of a database in the form of my growing home library of books, magazines and press cuttings. In fact, my film book section already included (and still includes) such early Tantivy Press publications as Robin Wood's *Hitchcock's Films* (1965) and Peter Cowie's *Swedish Cinema* (1966). And my own mind was nothing if not an overstuffed repository of occasionally useful film and showbiz lore. As for the copious reviews I wrote, until then strictly for my own information, they must have included detailed preexisting appraisals of most of Kubrick's films to date, from *The Killing* to *2001: A Space Odyssey*, released only a year before. Thus, I was able to prime my critical apparatus and bring a certain pre-emptive preparedness as well as pro-active energy to the task in hand. What's more, Kubrick himself helped me along the way.

The reel thing

Since DVDs had yet to be invented, the only way for an independent researcher to see particular films of the past – and see them in sharp focus – was by having them privately projected, assuming you were lucky enough to find prints of them or had access to the BFI's extensive collection. As mentioned in my 1972 preface, Kubrick was sufficiently supportive to have his editor and general factotum Ray Lovejoy deliver to my home 35mm reels of *Killer's Kiss* (which I'd never seen, probably because it had never gone on general release in Britain) and *Paths of Glory* (which I needed to see again). These films were to be transported by me, presumably by taxi since I didn't drive, to one of the small Soho viewing theatres you could hire for the purpose – probably the Warner screening room. On this or some other occasion Warner gave me as many stills as I wanted for the book's illustrations. I also watched *One-Eyed Jacks* (once a Brando-Kubrick joint project) in a viewing theatre, so it's likely that Kubrick arranged that for me too.

It was certainly a measure of his willingness to help that Kubrick entrusted his own film prints to a man he'd never even met. But the real point of this anecdote is to record that the film fan in me who'd been so impressed by *Paths of Glory* when I first saw it, aged 18, on general release, was thrilled to gaze upon the actual reels of the film, as supplied by the great director himself, incongruously stacked on the sofa in the living room of the flat in Golders Green that I shared with my future wife. I even felt a little nervous that I was responsible for their safekeeping, at least until they were due to be picked up by Ray Lovejoy.

This was privileged access indeed. But I was eventually outdone in the privileged access stakes by another participant in the Kubrick story.

A Walker steps into the frame

In March 1972, sometime after my book had gone under, I heard tell that Alexander Walker, the prominent *Evening Standard* film critic and, reputedly, a personal friend of Kubrick, was to publish a book about him. When it appeared later that year, it pretty well put paid to any lingering hopes I may have harboured of *The Magic Eye* ever being published. Yet, oddly enough, my response on first hearing about Walker's book was to write a friendly letter introducing myself to him as a former biographer of the director, and wished him luck with his own venture. All these years later I'm none too sure why. In fact, I'd completely forgotten about it until I recently came across a copy of the letter in my files. There's something perversely disingenuous about this cheery missive. What did I hope to achieve? But whatever obscure need it satisfied in me, Walker did not deign to reply.

When I eventually got round to reading Walker's book, *Stanley Kubrick Directs*, I admit to being peeved to find it generally more perceptive than my own – or so I thought at the time. Could Walker's insights, however, have benefited from an even more privileged access than my own? I could see well enough that while Walker was strong on analysis, there was nothing in his book that might have ruffled the director's feathers. I was therefore quite pleased when one reviewer dryly noted that the wording on the book's cover was so positioned that it could be construed in a way not intended by either its author or subject:

Stanley Kubrick Directs
Alexander Walker

It's been a long time since I read Walker's book. But I'm willing to believe it was a work of hagiography. Not that Walker was anybody's lackey. He was a forceful, idiosyncratic personality in his own right, a trenchant working film critic and author who cut a distinctive figure on the cultural film scene – not easily awed or swayed by others, I should think. In addition to reading his weekly column in the *Evening Standard*, I'd read and enjoyed several of his books.

As the author (or co-author) of *Kubrick Directs*, Walker may well have had his own interests at heart should he have privately welcomed the stifling of *The Magic Eye* at birth. Whichever way you cut it, you can't help suspecting that something fishy was going on, something like an *informal understanding* or *collusion*, fortified by strategic skills honed long ago in the chess battles of Washington Square Park. To have been the unwitting victim of such a collusion, if collusion there was, perpetrated by two such well-known public figures, I suppose confers a distinction of sorts. Or am I over-dramatising the situation?

Kubrick disapproves

I did the research. I wrote the book – without the benefit of the still unforthcoming interview. And I delivered the manuscript to Tantivy Press in (fairly) good time – 29 October 1969, just a month later than our contract stipulated. Cowie declared himself happy with the result and printed 12,000 covers, featuring a photo of HAL from *2001: A Space Odyssey*.

We were all set to publish – subject, of course, to Kubrick's contracted approval.

Unfortunately, it was never to be given.

What was it, then, that motivated him to withdraw his cooperation and block the book's publication? And was he justified in doing so?

We know that Kubrick objected to what he perceived to be the book's imbalance of "good" and "bad" points – an impression shared, we were informed, by no less a *consiglieri* than the ubiquitous Ray Lovejoy. As the reader will see, there were two films in the Kubrick canon that I wasn't keen on: *Spartacus* and *Lolita*. Even at the time, i.e. when Kubrick took against *The Magic Eye*, I was aware that my criticism of these films, notwithstanding Kubrick's own declared dislike of *Spartacus* and despite my enthusiasm for the Kubrick films I *did* admire, was enough to rile him, though not yet go so far as to take legal measures to thwart the book's publication. Could I have been too harsh, too "overly emphatic" in my criticism, as he claimed? I know from personal experience how painfully criticism can sting. Even the mighty Orson Welles once confessed that it was only the bad reviews that he remembered.

Was I too naively trusting that Kubrick would be tolerant of my more critical comments, given my high regard for most of his other pictures? Probably. Re-reading my appraisals of *Spartacus* and *Lolita* today, I do wonder whether it was necessary for me to chip away at them so doggedly. A few of my comments were not simply critical. They strike me now as downright disrespectful, even insulting – though surely not defamatory, nor beyond the ministrations of a competent external editor – a measure which Peter Cowie might have considered worth trying in order to save the beleaguered project. But perhaps as a matter of principle I'd have stubbornly refused to co-operate with such an intervention. Much like Kubrick himself.

I recently watched *Lolita* again for the first time in years to see how it strikes me now. In case any readers think I've been too repentant in my remarks, allow me to put the droogie boot in one more time and declare that I stand by my verdict in *The Magic Eye*. The scene in which Humbert Humbert attempts to erect a camp bed with the help of an elderly attendant in the hotel room where Lolita is sleeping is even worse than I recall – ill-conceived, over-long and stupefyingly unfunny. However generically wide-ranging Kubrick's cinematic expertise, it's clear that slapstick was not his – or James Mason's – forte. Moreover, I was aware that Kubrick might not wholeheartedly warm to some of my speculations in the final chapter about his psychological make-up and thematic concerns.

Today, I would add that my occasional recklessness in expressing my views the way that I did could have had something to do with an irreverent, provocative strain in my character that may have served me well in my performance work, but in this case at least was self-defeating.

Who then could blame the distinguished and busy film director for wanting to swat this annoying upstart who presumed to pronounce negative judgment on some of his films? Who could blame him for not wanting to waste any more of his precious time dealing with this distraction when his lawyers could dispose of the problem as quickly and efficiently as in fact they did?

At the same time, who could blame Peter Cowie for wanting to avoid placing his successful film publishing venture in jeopardy because of a possibly costly legal battle that he might lose, therefore consenting to sign a ridiculously one-sided but legally binding agreement with Kubrick that effectively placed the fate of the book – without even the long-promised interview that was supposed to have been its centrepiece – wholly in Kubrick's hands?

It was a stitch-up, of course, a monstrous bluff. But Cowie could not challenge Kubrick too forcibly if he still wanted the interview – and the book, in which Tantivy Press had already invested a fair amount of money – to happen. And if Cowie was complicit in his own entrapment by caving in and allowing his hands to be tied, so too was I – up to a point.

In fact, I was separately threatened with severe retribution by Kubrick's lawyers if I proceeded with publication elsewhere, even though *I* was not bound by any signed agreement with the man who was now, to my increasing dismay, my adversary. Who could blame me for not wanting to rock the boat and antagonise him further? But who could blame me, likewise, for not wanting to prolong the agony, giving up on the whole sorry imbroglio, and getting on with my own creative life, which, in contrast to *The Magic Eye* assignment, was going great guns, since it entailed TV appearances and an upcoming European tour which included a play I'd devised and directed for Wherehouse La MaMa.

But wait – maybe all was not lost. Maybe another publisher would be bold enough to take the book on. Perhaps the very difficulties it was in would prove to be a promotional asset (Roll up! Roll up! Would *you* dare to read "The Book Stanley Kubrick Tried to Suppress!")

My relationship with Cowie was still cordial, by the way. I bore him no ill-will, though I suppose I had good cause to complain about his handling of the situation, for which, to give him his due, he sincerely apologised. We were in this together, were we not? It came down, though, to Cowie presenting me with a simple choice: either give up my efforts to somehow salvage the book and keep my £200 advance, or return my advance and be released from my contract with Tantivy in order to try my luck elsewhere.

For better or worse, I chose to cut myself loose. My contract with Cowie was terminated and I submitted *The Magic Eye* to several other publishers. In so doing I felt obliged to play fair and explain the unusual background circumstances in case any interested publisher were to be suddenly clobbered from left field by injunctions. And guess what, would you believe it? Not a single publisher I submitted it to thought well enough of the book to take it on.

Who could blame them?

At least that's how I remember the way it all ended. Peter Cowie may remember it differently. Or have another story to tell.

Envoi: Binden to the rescue

Sometime in 1974, I was among a select few invited by Roy, once a fellow member of Wherehouse La MaMa, to afternoon tea at David and Angie Bowie's smallish London pied-à-terre (or perhaps the word is pad-à-terre, in keeping with the patois of the day). That's David Bowie of "A Space Oddity" fame, not to be confused with David Bowman of *2001: A Space Odyssey*.

A former soldier, professional burglar and smuggler as well as an actor, Roy was now involved in the rock music scene and it seemed that he and Angie Bowie were an item.

Disappointingly, neither of the Bowies were there to greet me and the other half a dozen or so invitees. David, we learned from Roy, was abroad, and Angie, evidently a free spirit in more ways than one, was otherwise engaged that day. But I was impressed by the luxurious fluffy white wall-to-wall carpeting in their flat and – the very latest thing – an early video camera lying to hand in the living room. And it was there that I met a friend of Roy's, another actor-cum-criminal called John Binden. As yet, I was unaware of his fearsome reputation as a hard man and gangster (in Donald Cammell and Nic Roeg's seminal British gangster film, *Performance*, you can see him posing roguishly, if not Roeg-ishly, in the nude).

Binden mentioned that he'd recently returned from a weekend trip to Ireland to play the small part of a recruiting officer in Stanley Kubrick's *Barry Lyndon*. Naturally I was eager to hear more. According to Binden, he'd been flown to Ireland at short notice as a replacement for an actor so nervous at being in the great director's presence that he kept fluffing his lines, until Kubrick lost patience, fired him on the spot, and had him replaced by Binden. Not a man to be easily intimidated by anyone (as is testified by his association with the Kray and Richardson gangs, as well as Princess Margaret), a word-perfect Binden – he learned his lines on the plane coming over – nailed his two-minute recruitment speech without mishap.

So what was Kubrick like, I asked? Whereupon Binden told me that during a break in shooting, Kubrick confided that he'd been preparing a film about Napoleon and asked Binden who he thought should play the leading role. Unhesitatingly, Binden replied, "Why, you, Stanley. *You* should play Napoleon."

Epilogue/Prologue
More time – about fifty years of the stuff – has just passed in an instant, thanks to the magic of the written word. It's 2024. And – hey presto! – here I am again, obliged to recall past humiliations in order to put together a few no doubt error-strewn afterthoughts about this painful episode in my life,

instead of doing the sensible thing and letting sleeping dogs, as well as dead ducks, lie. Who knows what will come of such meddling? Could Kubrick have made secret provision beyond the grave to prevent publication of *The Magic Eye* in perpetuity, abandoning me once more to ply my way through these endless labyrinthine corridors, these same deserted rooms, in this construction that belongs to the past…

I wouldn't put it past him. Perhaps I'll stick around the planet a bit longer to find out.

Neil Hornick
London, March 2024

1972 STATEMENT

This manuscript has a very chequered history. It was originally commissioned by Peter Cowie of Tantivy Press, but the author, David Austen, fell ill during the early stages of preparation and had to withdraw. Knowing I was enthusiastic about Kubrick's work, a mutual acquaintance suggested me as a replacement author, and Cowie agreed.

Since Austen had planned on devoting a central section of the book to an interview with Kubrick, he had informed Kubrick of the project, and Kubrick replied: "I am deeply appreciative of your interest in my work and I can only say that I hope my schedule will let up, within the next few weeks, sufficiently so that we might get together for a chat."

Kubrick and Austen never met, although Kubrick did reply to some preliminary questions of fact submitted by Austen.

When I took over the book, I informed Kubrick of the change of authorship, expressing my desire to hold to the interview idea and also the hope that he would assist me in clearing up any factual problems arising from my research. Kubrick at this stage was so far agreeable as to send me for viewing prints of *Killer's Kiss* and *Paths of Glory*, which were otherwise inaccessible.

I received no reply to subsequent letters in which I raised questions of factual detail. In fact, Kubrick was never to contact me at all, except indirectly through his intermediary, film editor Ray Lovejoy.

However, through his lawyer, Kubrick did draw up an agreement with the publisher Peter Cowie that the book would not be published before he – Kubrick – had vetted it for factual errors.

Cowie was enthusiastic about the manuscript and had already spent £800 printing the covers (I have one of them as a wan souvenir of the experience). Suspecting that the wording of the agreement left it open to Kubrick to veto publication on *any* grounds, Cowie queried the wording with Kubrick's lawyer, who replied:

"Although I appreciate that you have tried to provide an objective standard in relation to 'valid criticism,' I feel that, as a lawyer, the sentence poses more problems than it solves. Clause 1 should therefore remain as drawn by myself since I am sure that we both appreciate that a man of Mr. Kubrick's intelligence and integrity can be relied on to treat this matter responsibly."

Cowie could not but concede to this graciously worded rebuttal.

In due course Kubrick received the manuscript. Cowie received the news that Kubrick could not allow it to be published. *No explanation was given.* Efforts were made to elicit from Kubrick the nature of his objections so that factual errors could he corrected. Eventually Cowie ascertained from Ray Lovejoy (and I quote from Cowie's account to me of their conversation) that "Kubrick objects to the manuscript not so much because of any factual errors (there are just a few which he will correct) but because your chapter on each film gives him (and Lovejoy) the impression of a 'mixed review,' a summary of the bad points, which, in his view, always outweigh the good on account of the overly emphatic way in which criticism is presented."

I leave the reader to judge whether or not this is in fact the case. The point is: if this verbal summary of Kubrick's objections is to be relied on, then it is clear that they lie precisely in that area of "criticism" as distinct from "fact" which Kubrick's lawyer strongly implied would not be his concern.

I wrote to Kubrick expressing my willingness to reconsider and revise substantial sections of the book in the interests of greater accuracy and correct emphasis, so long as the critical integrity of the book was not jeopardised. There was no reply from Kubrick. His lawyer, however, informed Cowie that Kubrick would be "prepared to consider a re-edited draft of the manuscript if one were resubmitted." But despite further entreaties by Peter Cowie and myself Kubrick would not provide any further indications on the basis of which I could make the revisions that might render the manuscript more acceptable to him. The conclusion was inescapable: remove or mute adverse criticism or – no dice.

I could not see my way to doing this. Cowie, held by the agreement, was regretfully obliged to reject my manuscript. I was subsequently threatened with litigation if I attempted to publish the book elsewhere, although *I* had not entered into legal agreements with Kubrick. I attempted to get the book published elsewhere, with no success.

Early this year a book appeared on Kubrick by his friend Alexander Walker. I feel now that the best thing I can do with this manuscript, on which I spent a year of my life, is to place it in the thesis section of the BFI Library, where at least it might find a small public.

I believe Kubrick to be one of the most distinguished film directors of our time. I also believe that clearly emerges from my book. But I believe that what also clearly emerges from my book is why a man of such stature and reputation would trouble to prevent publication of a book which ventures both to criticise and understand him.

Neil Hornick

PREFACE AND ACKNOWLEDGEMENTS

One problem in writing about Stanley Kubrick is that the issues he tackles are of such public import that any full discussion of them must go well beyond the limits of film aesthetics. The operations of a military hierarchy; the waging of revolution; nuclear catastrophe; the future of mankind – these are hardly matters to be lightly despatched in a paragraph or two. I have tried in this book to strike a balance between information and exposition, analysis and evaluation of the films, and brief discussion of some of the issues in their social context.

I hope the background information will make the book useful as a work of reference. In my critical analyses I have tried to keep in mind the conditions under which the films were made, a factor of great importance in an industry where the artist is subject to so many pressures – commercial, censorial and otherwise. This approach is, I believe, especially useful in the case of a director like Stanley Kubrick who, from the beginning of his career, has tried to maintain his creative independence. Since Kubrick is an adaptor as well as a director (most of his films are based on novels), I should also forewarn the reader that I pay fairly close attention to details of adaptation. I say "forewarn" because I know that in some critical circles such attention is considered completely irrelevant. I hold to the view, however, that evaluation of any film remains at best incomplete and at worst misleading without reference to the way source material has been reworked for the film medium.

Wherever possible I have let Kubrick speak for himself through the infrequent but generally revealing interviews he has given. Translations of quotations from the French are my own.

2001: A Space Odyssey really requires a book in itself. And it has got one. Jerome Agel's *The Making of Kubrick's 2001* is a fascinating anthology of background information, comment, interviews, reviews and pictures, worth reading if only for a remarkable analysis of the film by a fifteen-year-old American girl. Unfortunately it's not yet published in this country, and I read it only after completing my own manuscript. I've resisted expanding my interpretation of the film to include all the stimulating ideas in the Agel book, but I am indebted to it for various factual details.

The present book is the first to be devoted to all of Kubrick's work. It was originally undertaken by David Austen, who had to withdraw owing to illness. I am very grateful to him for providing some invaluable information and for illuminating comments on Kubrick's work. He also compiled the filmography [not included in this edition] and the basis of a now extensive bibliography. Joel Finler read the manuscript and made many helpful suggestions. I must add my appreciation to that of other film researchers for the excellent friendly services provided by the British Film Institute. And thanks are due to Elizabeth Swenson, Jean Sullivan, Cathy Haynes and Alexandra Jones, who, at various stages, slaved like Spartacus deciphering and retyping my all but illegible manuscript. Special acknowledgments are due to the authors listed in Part B of the Bibliography, whose interview material I have liberally plundered.

The Magic Eye

1. Still Life, Movie Life

In 1952, Stanley Kubrick, a 24-year-old former photo-journalist, left New York for California to shoot his first feature film. It was made on a shoe-string budget with his own savings and money borrowed from his family and friends. Technical equipment was hired by the day, and the small cast of actors was virtually unknown. The film, *Fear and Desire*, was exhibited on a limited art-house circuit in the U.S.A. and soon passed out of circulation.

Now aged 41, Kubrick enjoys an international popular and critical reputation, and commands the power and respect to set up very expensive productions over which he exercises complete control as producer, director and co-writer. Each new Kubrick film is a major cinematic event, each generates discussion in social sectors extending well beyond film circles. In Ira Levin's novel, *Rosemary's Baby*, Rosemary's struggling young actor husband hurries to a screening in the hope of meeting a director (who in fact does not show up). It is Stanley Kubrick. The name is dropped casually into the novel in passing – Kubrick's eminence is taken for granted.

Passionately dedicated to film-making, Kubrick draws on rich creative, technical and organisational resources to realise projects of increasingly grandiose design. But he is sometimes disparaged for his so-called "clinical detachment," for being more interested in machines than human beings. I shall argue that this judgement is as partial in Kubrick's case as it is in the case of Antonioni, a director often similarly accused. Kubrick's films, far from being impersonal, are direct, powerful and revealing expressions of his very individual way of viewing the world. His subjects, while socially and politically charged, are at the same time audacious public projections of his own psychological landscape. It is the purveyors of trivia – cute sex comedies for jaded commuters, glossy slug-them-with-a-smile melodramas, Big Liberal Statements signed with a solemn flourish by a Preminger, a Kramer, a Zinnemann – who are truly impersonal.

Kubrick tends to relate his own work to the European rather than to the American cinema.* At the time of making *Paths of Glory*, a *Cahiers du Cinéma* interviewer tried to coax him into praising American directors, but he preferred to talk about Ophüls and Bergman.† Other directors he is known to admire are Fellini, Truffaut and David Lean. He recently commented: "I can't say I have any particular taste for the old Hollywood directors of the thirties like Vidor and Hawks. I'm not particularly influenced by European directors, rather by everything I've seen. But European films are the first to try and tell stories that don't compromise, unlike films whose only object is to create a universe of happiness, an unreal picture of the world and men."[1]

Kubrick does have qualities in common with other American directors: he has something of Kazan's brusque editing style, Wilder's sardonic humour, Frankenheimer's concern with politico-military machines, Huston's ease in the world of interlocking male relationships, and the American cinema's (or should one simply say "the cinema's"?) traditional preoccupation with physical violence. This kind of affinities game is all too easy to play. But the one American director with whom comparison is inevitable is Orson Welles. Both Welles and Kubrick are preoccupied with themes of power and its attendant anxieties. Both employ a style which can be broadly described as "baroque" in its emphasis on dramatic lighting chiaroscuro and unusual in-depth compositions. Both men are expatriates who have virtually abandoned America to finance and retain artistic control over their productions. Both are avid readers, reputed to require very little sleep each night.

In certain important respects, of course, the two directors are very different. Welles is a cosmopolitan exile, expansive

---

* Kubrick does not regard himself as an expatriate. In a recent interview (4) he says there is nothing permanent about living and working in England, that it is quite possible he will make a film in the U.S.A. in the future, and that in any case he commuted back and forth several times a year. Yet in the same interview he states: "By the time I decided to do *2001* I had gotten so acclimatized to working in England that it would have been pointless to *tear up roots* and move everything to America." [my italics]

† Max von Sydow, incidentally, has recently expressed a desire to work for Kubrick.

and mercurial, a bon vivant and raconteur with strong roots in the theatre. Kubrick, who has never worked in the theatre, remains an intensely private, even reclusive individual, who is seldom, if ever, to be seen in public outside the film studio. Those few journalists who have interviewed him agree in finding him unusual among American directors in his complete lack of flamboyance – self-effacing, diffident and elusive. More fundamentally, Kubrick is less an innovator than one of the cinema's consolidators, a man who applies the inherited discoveries of the medium with enormous dynamism and flair. Perhaps this is why Welles once said: "Kubrick is a great director who has yet to make his great film." He may well have revised this appraisal after seeing *2001: A Space Odyssey*.

Kubrick is now settled in Hertfordshire, England, a short drive from M-G-M's (now defunct) Boreham Wood Studios, where he shot *2001*. With him are his third wife, Christiane, a former actress who played the German girl in *Paths of Glory*, and his three daughters, one of whom appeared as Dr. Floyd's daughter in *2001*.

Let's now consider how Kubrick became a film director.

*

Stanley Kubrick was born in New York, in the Bronx, on 26 July 1928. He comes from a Jewish family of Austro-Hungarian origin, resident in the U.S.A. for several generations, and he has one sister, Barbara, six years younger than himself. He grew up in comfortable middle-class surroundings. His father, an eminent doctor still in practice, was a keen chess-player and amateur photographer. Dr. Kubrick fostered an enthusiasm for these hobbies in his son and gave him his first camera, a Graflex, for his thirteenth birthday.

An indifferent scholar at William Howard Taft High School in the Bronx, Kubrick failed English outright one year. His favourite subjects were the sciences, but physics was the only subject he was any good at. He spent most of his spare time wandering around the neighbourhood taking pictures and watching movies. Having no particular ambition, although he had once considered becoming a jazz drummer, he went through a rather confused adolescent period. "I never learned anything at school," Kubrick comments, "and I didn't read a book for pleasure until I was nineteen."[2] Photography became his primary means of self-expression; he was the official photographer on his high school newspaper and his pictures began to appear in exhibitions.

It was while he was in his final year at Taft that he snapped the picture that was to begin his professional career. On his way to school one morning in April 1945, his attention was caught by the grave face of a news vendor, framed by newspapers announcing the death of Franklin D. Roosevelt. Kubrick took the picture and sold it to *Look* magazine for $25 – ten dollars more than he was offered by the *New York Daily News*.

By the time he graduated from Taft, he had sold three complete photo-stories to *Look*, including a study of his English teacher at work in the classroom. But he was intent on continuing his education. Unfortunately his graduation average of 67 and the flood of ex-servicemen seeking college places after the war prevented him from getting into university, so he registered at the City College of New York in the hope of achieving the averages he needed to transfer to undergraduate courses. Hearing of his academic troubles and impressed by his work, Helen O'Brien, the picture editor of *Look*, offered him the job of apprentice staff photographer. Kubrick gladly accepted. He was 17 years old.

He was to stay with *Look* for four and a half years, working on literally hundreds of photo-stories, to become by the time he was 21 one of America's outstanding magazine photographers. He enjoyed a reasonable degree of independence since he was not assigned to subjects but submitted his own ideas which, if approved, he went ahead and shot. His subjects tended to be socially oriented stories rather than topical scoops, and his early preference for "candid" camerawork is indicated by the fact that he carried his camera concealed in a shopping bag to avoid being identified as a journalist or tourist. His work enabled him to travel widely through the United States, Mexico and Canada, and as far afield as Portugal. Relieved from the pressures of the school curriculum, he became a copious reader. Although he does not regard any of his early journalistic work with particular satisfaction, he feels that joining *Look* at that stage in his life was the best thing that could have happened to him.

In 1949 he and his first wife, Toba Metz, a Taft classmate whom he had married when he was 19, moved to Greenwich Village. Here Kubrick supplemented his income by playing for quarters in the endless open-air chess games that took place in Washington Square – sometimes making as much as $3 a day. About this time, he renewed his friendship with another former Taft classmate, Alexander Singer. Both were compulsive movie-goers. Singer had at 18 written a vast scenario for a proposed film version of *The Iliad* (he was to direct his first film in 1960, *A Cold Wind in August*, which deals, one year before Kubrick's *Lolita*, with the hopeless relationship between a middle-aged woman and a teenage boy). Together, Kubrick and Singer would discuss film theory, visit the Museum of Modern Art film shows as many as five times a week – Kubrick saw the entire Museum collection at least twice – as well as keeping up with the new Hollywood films. They were able to see sometimes eight of these a week in double-feature programmes playing twice weekly on the two main circuits. Even in the annals of advanced movie-mania this is a sobering record.

Singer was employed as an office-boy at the *March of Time* documentary film company, and had seen his employers dispensing $40,000 a time for short eight- or nine-minute documentaries. Dissatisfied with the limitations of still photography, and encouraged by Singer, Kubrick decided to make a short documentary film for a tenth of the *March of Time* budget. Significantly, his first film dealt with physical combat.

Day of the Fight was a 16-minute narrated study of Walter Cartier, a young middle-weight boxer who had been the subject of one of Kubrick's *Look* photo-stories, "Prizefighter." Concerned with the crucial hours just before a big fight when training is over, the film culminates in Cartier's second-round knockout of his opponent, and incidentally touches upon conditions in the fight game in general. A musical score was provided by Kubrick's fiend, Gerald Fried, who was to work on every Kubrick picture up to and including *Paths of Glory*. The film was shot with a rented spring-wound 35mm Eyemocamera. Made with Kubrick's own savings for $3,900, he tried to sell it for $40,000 but the best offer he could get – the open-handed *March of Time* having gone bankrupt in the meantime – was from RKO Pathé, to whom he sold the film at a profit (or loss – versions differ) of $100.

The story goes that when he saw *Day of the Fight* projected as a supporting featurette with a Mitchum-Gardner movie, *My Forbidden Past*, he was so impressed that he determined there and then to give up his job at *Look* and devote all his time and energy to film-making. When RKO advanced him $1,500 for another short, he promptly resigned from *Look* and went off to New Mexico to make *Flying Padre*. The subject, which just happened to be easy to arrange at the time, was the day-to-day routine of one Rev. Fred Stadtmueller, who piloted his own Piper Cub plane to get round the eleven mission churches in his parish of four thousand square miles in north-eastern New Mexico. Like the earlier film, it was scripted, directed, photographed and edited by Kubrick, with music by Fried, and released – one week earlier than *Day of the Fight* – in March 1951 in RKO's *This is America* series.

Kubrick, who describes the film as "a silly thing," barely broke even with *Flying Padre*. But the transition from stills to movies had been made.

---

1. Walter, Renaud. "Entretien avec Stanley Kubrick," *Positif*, December 1968-January 1969.
2. Agel, Jerome (editor). *The Making of Kubrick's 2001* (Signet, 1970).

2. Battleground of the Mind
Fear and Desire (1953)

No doubt Kubrick could have gone on successfully turning out documentary shorts just as he had turned out magazine photo-stories – had any more offers been forthcoming. But being given no further commissions, he went back to playing chess in Washington Square. He was, in any case, now eager to make a feature film. In this he was encouraged by Joseph Burstyn, a distributor and exhibitor who was virtually the innovator of the "art-house" concept at a time when foreign and experimental films were rarely to be seen in the U.S.A.

Kubrick commissioned a screenplay from a Greenwich Village poet friend, Howard Sackler. Sackler was, years later, to specialise in the production of star-cast recordings of classical plays and in 1968 achieved a Broadway success with his own play *The Great White Hope*, about the Negro boxer, Jack Johnson. (Sackler is currently writing the screenplay for a film version by Martin Ritt for 20th Century Fox). The film, *Fear and Desire*, was financed by relatives and Kubrick. Reports of the total cost range from $9,000 to $50,000, which makes it a very low-budget production.*

Although he intended to make the film in New York, winter was upon him by the time he had raised the necessary cash and he was obliged to shoot the film in California. After signing up three members of his cast from the Off-Broadway theatre circuit, Kubrick, his wife and Sackler spent six weeks in California scouting suitable locations and completing the cast – Virginia Leith, who had one line as a peasant girl, and Frank Silvera. The rest of the cast and the small technical crew then joined them in California. "Our 'crew' consisted of three Mexican laborers who carried all the equipment."[1]

Wherever possible he rented shooting equipment, the most expensive item being a 35mm Mitchell camera costing $25 a day. The owner of the hiring company spent a morning showing him how to load and operate it. To stretch his meagre

---

* Kubrick's own estimate, in a recent interview: "The dubbing was a big mistake on my part; the actual shooting cost of the film was $9000 dollars but because I didn't know what I was doing with the sound-track it cost me another thirty thousand."

budget, Kubrick resorted to such ingenuities as filming twilight scenes in broad daylight with filters over the camera lens and underexposing the film. Because a Hollywood fog-spraying machine was too expensive to hire, he used a large insecticide crop-sprayer to create fog effects, nearly asphyxiating his cast and crew in the process. He was still a long way from the multi-million-dollar budgets of *Spartacus* and *2001*.

Whereas most Hollywood directors at that time often shot 500,000 feet of film to produce a feature length movie, Kubrick limited himself to 50,000 feet, from which 5,940 feet of useable film was obtained – every scene that was shot appearing in the final edited version. All the dialogue and background music was post-synchronised in New York, a process which cost as much as all the other production expenses combined. Editing and dubbing, completed in November 1952, took nine months – Kubrick's painstaking approach to editing was in evidence at the very beginning of his career.

The film was turned down by every major distributing company and was finally distributed by Joseph Burstyn on his art-house circuit, receiving its premiere in April 1953 at the Guild Theatre in New York. Initially a commercial failure, it eventually broke even and has long since passed out of circulation in the U.S.A. It has never been shown in Great Britain.

The luridly titled *Fear and Desire* is a story of men in war, but unlike Kubrick's later studies of military combat, it has an abstract setting; neither the nationality of the soldiers nor the location of the war is identified, but as the opening narration indicates, the men fight "on the battleground of their own minds." Four soldiers have crashed in a transport plane behind enemy lines: the pilot – an intellectual lieutenant seeking "meaning," two privates – an inexperienced youth and a middle-aged man, and a tough sergeant (Frank Silvera). Led by the pilot, they make their way warily through the woods, attempting to reach their own lines. At nightfall they attack and kill some enemy soldiers whom they surprise at supper in a shack. Next day they are forced to hide from a group of peasant women, but one of them sees the men and they take her prisoner. She is tied to a tree and the youth is left on guard while the others go down to the river to construct a raft that will carry them downstream to their own lines. The youth attempts to befriend the girl and convince her of his innocence, but her fear and incomprehension so unnerve him that he kills her and runs down to the river babbling dementedly.

The others, meanwhile, have discovered an enemy command-post in a farmhouse occupied by a general and his aide. Outside there is a light aircraft. After some debate about courses of safety, duty or ambition, they resolve to kill the general and his aide and escape in a plane. Their plan requires the sergeant to create a daring diversionary attack which he sees as his chance for glory. The pilot kills the general and makes his escape with the older private. In safety they await the sergeant, who arrives by raft with the youth whom he has found babbling in the shallows. However, the pilot finds it has all been pointless: the private's madness, the sergeant's heroism, and his own murder of the general have left them just where they started. While they have escaped their physical enemies, the mental conflict that remains precludes their achieving peace of mind.

Certain features of Kubrick's individual style were already apparent in his first feature film: a documentary-like use of natural light sources, sometimes shining directly into the camera; dramatic lighting contrasts; and rapid cutting from scene to scene. The economy of technique is exemplified by his treatment of the killing of the enemy soldiers: a blast of gunfire is followed by close-ups of a bowl of spilled stew dripping upon the heads of the slaughtered men. The background of the San Gabriel Mountains and river was used anthropomorphically to reflect the mental state of the men: brightly lit when optimistic, gloomy and ominous when frightened, while in the final scene of groping uncertainty the river is blanketed in fog.

Kubrick, who is happy that *Fear and Desire* has fallen out of circulation (it's possible that he still retains a print of his own), regards his first film as pretentious and amateurish, despite some good touches. "I knew nothing about directing. I didn't even know that I knew nothing. The film was shown only because it had been shot in 35mm and had cost too much to be hidden away in a drawer."[2]

All the same, the film was not badly received by the few critics who reviewed it. While, on the whole, critical of the film's content, they acknowledged its visual flair. Mark van Doren described it as a "brilliant and unforgettable film... beautiful, terrifying and weird." *The New York Times* called it "A powerful study of subdued excitements... it augers well for the comparative tyros who made it." The *Motion Picture Herald*, not usually lavish in its praise of obscure non-commercial subjects, commented: "A fragment of war, tense and taut, is etched out in this documentary-flavoured drama. Its theme, the animalisation of man through the devil's chemistry of war, is gotten across with moving eloquence and conviction. Shot on location in Southern California, the picture has the mark of quality and sincerity."[3] And Parker Tyler was struck by the psychological surprise awaiting the soldiers at the end: "It shows the subtlety and profundity at the heart of *Fear and Desire*, and is a bull's eye in the universal area of the soldier's psychology, his bad conscience as a killer. *Fear and Desire*, a most impressive might-have-been, comprises an abstract of what serious inspiration and thought could accomplish in the film medium but actually accomplishes so seldom... It may be inept and make-shift but it doesn't resort to cheapness and romantic stereotype."[4]

To what extent Howard Sackler's screenplay was written according to Kubrick's prescription is not known, but it was this aspect of the film which critics found most unsatisfactory. Iris Owens, who provides an interesting account of its making in an issue of *Modern Photography*, concludes: "Dramatic facial close-ups, symbolic action, rapid cuts from one scene to another – all create a feeling of tension and expectancy which the story itself does not always fulfil."[5] Jackson Burgess puts it less gently: "The script by Howard Sackler is embarrassingly banal – a virtually incomprehensible story tricked out with vague, adolescent pessimism masquerading as Deep Thought."[6] He quotes a typical line from the film: "We spend all our lives seeking our real selves, our permanent addresses."

Burgess, whose analysis of *Fear and Desire* is the most detailed I can find, continues:

> The post-recorded sound is terrible: the sound level doesn't vary throughout, a character sounding exactly the same in an interior close-up as he does in an exterior

medium-long shot, and all of them sounding muffled and at the same time elocutionary. The actors are inexperienced (although the screenplay might have challenged the most seasoned players) and production details have a painfully homemade quality not far above the *mise en scene* of a junior high school play…

Cinematically, *Fear and Desire* shows some of the rag-bag quality one expects from a novice director who has studied his art: a couple of *Rashomon* shots, a Renoir shot. But on the whole it is surprisingly personal and original. Despite its several particular badnesses and its general fuzziness, the film has a striking purity and honesty and is unmistakably the product of a single man's striving. Its processes are governed by decisions of thought and feeling rather than by formulae or the councils of caution…

[A] powerful and complex vision is conveyed, and a vision of the vexing conflicts of virtue and authority and the uncertainty which swathes every moral choice. It is a vision of clarity (despite the vapidity of the lines assigned the lieutenant) and depth and dignity, and it is conveyed by means of image. This vision, in fact, is more effectively and simply stated by one central shot from the film than by any possible paraphrase or declaration, and that is in the scene of the shooting of the general, who is the type of authority and age, by the lieutenant, the type of youth, rebellion and moral yearning. The wounded general drags himself on his belly to the door of the farmhouse – a slow, painful, suspenseful progress. He crawls out onto the porch, to the edge of the circle of light falling from within, and raises his head to confront his attackers. The lieutenant, standing in the darkness, raises his pistol, and the eyes of the two men meet. There is another agonising hesitation, then the lieutenant fires and the general's head falls forward, his face striking the boards with a sickening thud.

The same actor, Kenneth Harp, plays both the general and the lieutenant, casting reminiscent of Poe's *William Wilson*-like identity of the moral types, and which perhaps anticipates the multiple roles of Peter Sellers in *Dr. Strangelove*. Burgess concludes: "the very badness of the film, its baldness, makes its basic images particularly accessible, and when those same images are recreated in later Kubrick films the vision of moral dubiety as man's tragic burden becomes more and more central to the director's work."[7]

Still only 24, Kubrick's debut in feature films thus earned him a certain amount of critical attention, but failed to make any impact on the production companies from whom he vainly awaited offers of work.

1. Gelmis, Joseph. *The Film Director As Superstar* (Doubleday, 1970).
2. Walter, Renaud. "Entretien avec Stanley Kubrick," *Positif*, December 1968-January 1969.
3. Uncredited. "*Fear and Desire*," *Motion Picture Herald*, 4 April 1953.
4. Tyler, Parker. "A Dance, a Dream and a Flying Trapeze?" *Theatre Arts*, May 1953.
5. Owens, Iris. "It's movies for me," *Modern Photography*, September 1953.
6. Burgess, Jackson. "The 'Anti-Militarism' of Stanley Kubrick," *Film Quarterly*, Fall 1964.
7. ibid.

3. Big City Blues
Killer's Kiss (1955)

Kubrick earned his living from 1952 to 1954 as a second unit director on a television *Omnibus* series about the life of Abraham Lincoln, based on a scenario by James Agee, and he also helped in the production of a short sponsored film for a trade union. Agee had seen *Fear and Desire*, as Kubrick relates: "I have always thought that James Agee made one of the kindest remarks anyone has ever made to me. After seeing my first film, *Fear and Desire*, which was really a very inept and pretentious effort, Agee... said to me, with a very pained and strained expression on his face, 'There are too many good things in the film to call it arty.'"[1]

Kubrick realised that if he was to advance his career as a feature film director, he must get the backing of a major distributing company before shooting.

New York had been one of his favourite photographic subjects and he had always been dissatisfied with the way it had been depicted by Hollywood, so he devised a list of action sequences that could be shot on location in New York and persuaded United Artists to distribute the picture (and, according to one account, part-finance it); the bulk or all of the money was raised from Kubrick's own savings and loans from family, friends and business acquaintances. Within a week, Kubrick had shaped his sequences into a reasonably coherent screenplay, and spent three weeks scouting locations. A few scenes only were shot in a small studio.

Killer's Kiss was once again a closely knit personal venture. It was written, directed, photographed and edited by Kubrick, co-produced by Morris Bousel, an uncle of Kubrick's who owned a drugstore in the Bronx, and music was again by Gerald Fried. The leading male role was played by a friend of Walter Cartier's, Jamie Smith, who was a former Golden Gloves finalist and had considerable acting experience, including a spell at the Actors Studio. The female lead, Irene Kane, was a model, introduced to Kubrick by his friend, Bert (*Jazz on a Summer's Day)* Stern, who had photographed her for *Vogue*. Frank Silvera, of *Fear and Desire*, played the heavy. And a ballet sequence was danced by Ruth Sobotka of Balanchine's City Center Company; she was to become Kubrick's second wife shortly after the production, and later worked on the art direction of *The Killing*.

Post-synchronisation (skilfully done this time) and editing took ten months. Released in September 1955, the film is 67 minutes, three minutes of which were cut by the British censor. Although its final cost was only $150,000, *Killer's Kiss* proved to be another commercial flop, partly no doubt because it had no stars in the cast. The film is hardly known in Britain. In recent years it has re-emerged only once, so far as I know, for a week's run in one of the Classic repertory cinemas.

In 1964, when a homage to Kubrick was arranged at the Museum of Modern Art, Kubrick declined to present *Fear and Desire* and *Killer's Kiss*, both of which he regarded as amateurish works, regretting in particular the phoniness of their dialogue. In an interview for *Positif* film magazine, Kubrick explains:

> It is better than *Fear and Desire* but it's rather a silly film. From the direction point of view there are some good sequences, but it's a foolish subject. The acting is very bad, and what's a film worth that has a silly story and poor acting?... In both *Fear and Desire* and *Killer's Kiss* I was my own director, cameraman, assistant cameraman. It was very good for me, because although this was a dissipating factor and I paid dearly for not giving enough attention to such things as directing the actors and the treatment of the story, I nevertheless learned a lot about the technique of everything that goes into film-making. I had to get everything going myself: every revolver shot, every axe-blow.

Asked if it was made in reaction to the traditional Hollywood gangster film, Kubrick replied, "I no longer remember what I had in mind. At that time I was much more interested in editing, photography, etc... I thought that if one had good shots and editing, that was enough to justify a film and I don't believe I even took that very seriously. I was so happy to make a film, no matter what the subject, that the rest didn't concern me… I didn't know much about directing the actors and I didn't have the time."

He agreed that in a certain sense it was a documentary on New York. But "it's not a very profound vision of New York. It's simply the standard decor of a thriller set in New York. It's an imitation documentary. The streets, the neon ads flashing on and off… one doesn't really sense New York. The only notable fact about *Killer's Kiss* is perhaps – but I'm not sure about this – that it's the first time that a film produced out of private finances went out on general distribution. I can't vouch for it. From this point of view, if the film has any value at all, it's for that, and that's about all."[2]

Killer's Kiss is set in the Manhattan loft district of New York. It concerns the relationship between a young boxer, a dime-a-dance girl, and the middle-aged dance hall proprietor for whom she works. The credits open against a sustained shot of Davy Gordon, the boxer, waiting at Penn Station for the train that will take him home to Seattle. As he waits, he narrates on the sound-track the events of the last two days. "It's crazy how you can get yourself into a mess sometimes," the narration begins, setting the general level of the dialogue. The rest of the film consists of an extended flashback, the camera returning from time to time to the image of the waiting man to prepare us for the reconciliation scene with which the film ends.

While preparing for a fight, Davy makes the acquaintance of Gloria Price, who lives across the courtyard of the tenement where he lives. She works as a taxi-dance girl for Rapallo, the proprietor of a sleazy dance hall off Times Square. Watching Davy's defeat on television, Rapallo becomes sexually excited and makes advances to Gloria which she reluctantly reciprocates (whether or not she is actually his mistress remains unclear). That night Davy is awakened by the sound of Gloria screaming and hurries to investigate. In her room he learns that she has been molested by Rapallo, who, frightened by her screams, has made a quick getaway. Davy and Gloria are attracted to each other and agree to go away together. Davy has to collect his fee from his manager, and Gloria her week's salary from Rapallo, so they arrange to meet outside Rapallo's dance hall. Gloria goes upstairs to get her money but Rapallo furiously refuses to pay her and tells her to get out. When she returns to the street, she finds Davy gone. His scarf has been playfully stolen by two drunken conventioneers and he has run after them to retrieve it. Davy's manager meanwhile appears with the money. Rapallo sends two of his thugs downstairs to beat up Gloria's companion but they mistake Davy's manager for Davy and lure him into an alley, where they beat him to death.

Gloria and Davy unknowingly return to their respective rooms to pack before leaving. But when Davy goes over to collect Gloria, she is missing. Through the window he observes the janitor letting two policemen into his own room and realises that they want him for the murder of the manager. Immediately suspecting Rapallo, Davy waylays him and compels him at gunpoint to take him to the deserted warehouse where Gloria is being held prisoner by the thugs. There Davy is overpowered by a trick and is shocked to see Gloria desperately embrace Rapallo and plead with him for her life. Davy escapes by jumping out of a window and is chased over the tenement roofs by Rapallo and one of his thugs. Davy and Rapallo fight it out in a mannequin factory, armed respectively with fire-axe and fire-pole. Davy kills Rapallo but is acquitted on grounds of self-defence, and in the closing shot of the film he and Gloria are reunited at the station.

There is a curiously inept use of the intermittent narration. At one point Davy tells us how he goes over to see Gloria in the morning: she greets him "all smiles and yawns" and they go for a walk before breakfast. But this information is conveyed against shots of Davy and Gloria already sitting at breakfast. And there are two clumsy flashbacks within the main flashback, both inserted by means of old-fashioned dissolves. In the first, Gloria tells Davy of Rapallo's attempt to molest her but although this is supposed to have happened "an hour ago," what we see lasts only a few minutes of screen time and might with less awkwardness have been inserted in chronological sequence. In the second sub-flashback, Gloria tells Davy something about her unhappy family background, a story concerning her father's relationship with her successful ballet-dancer sister. The story is narrated by Gloria in a literary tone of voice against an extended sequence of a girl dancing on stage. Though the sequence is competently directed, with a characteristic use of reflected lights from spotlights and footlights, it distracts the viewer from the content of the story and goes on too long. Conceivably intended as an experiment in mood imagery, it looks more as if it were gratuitously inserted to display the uninteresting talents of Ruth Sobotka.

The clumsiness of the film's construction is matched by the banality of the plot and what little there is in the way of dialogue. Beginning in a mood of low-key realism the film develops into a routine melodrama, involving the standard ingredients of romantic triangle, chase, rescue and fight-to-the-death. However, there is one unusual feature: all three protagonists are depicted as pathetic, defeated people. Davy leads a lonely loser's life. Gloria is a haggard-looking gamine who barely resists the advances of the odious Rapallo and at first responds cynically to Davy's love. Rapallo is no less pathetic. A small-time operator, frustrated and perverse, he is given to such declarations of self-pity as "All my life I've always spoiled the things that mean the most to me – all my life." All three characters have family photographs pinned to the walls of their dingy apartments. But the characters are not explored in sufficient depth for us to care about them, and it's not surprising that the actors can do little with their schematic roles, although Jamie Smith gives hints of ability. Gerald Fried's music is mostly as trite and mechanical as the plot: a romantic theme when young love is blooming, a vaguely Western lilt as Davy's uncle's letter from the country is read over the sound-track. Only in the final chase and fight sequences does it become more than conventional cinemuzak.

Yet despite these serious defects, the film remains today vividly cinematic, fresh and interesting to look at in a way that *Lolita*, for instance, is not. This is due to its unerring photographic style, a style compounded of both the realistic and the bizarre, or rather a style which searches out the bizarre within a texture of meticulous realism.

One is struck first by the immediacy of the location shooting, so far removed from the studio-bound artificiality of most of the Hollywood films of the period. In this, no doubt, *Killer's Kiss* was influenced by those few films which made use of authentic street locations – Dassin's *Naked City*, for example, Kazan's *Panic in the Streets*, and possibly *On the Waterfront* (released a year earlier than *Killer's Kiss*). The influence of Italian neo-realism, apparent in these films, is evident also in *Killer's Kiss*, with its use of natural settings and ordinary, socially oppressed people as heroes, played by relatively unknown or non-professional actors.

Kubrick achieves this sense of documentary realism in the settings by using concealed and/or hand-held cameras and generally relying on natural lighting, although all the action and dialogue were prearranged with characteristic precision. Thus the station scenes were shot with a telephoto-lens camera at a distance of a hundred yards from the actors with no light sources other than the natural light from the station roof. To obtain the shots of the electric signs and cinema marquees of Times Square, Kubrick hid his camera in a baby carriage with the lens pointing upwards. For the fight scene he hired a group of boxing handlers and a referee from Stillman's gym, blocked out the fight in detail with two professional fighters, and shot the sequence with four hand-held cameras in the Laurel Garden Arena in Newark New Jersey, adding some footage from *Day of the Fight*. No visitors were allowed on the set. The groggy quality of the low-angle images and the overhead lighting shining into the camera give the fight a feeling of painful immediacy, enhanced by the amplified sound of the blows (obtained by striking a sheep's head with a mallet). This may have been one of the scenes by the British censor. The drunken conventioneers careering down the street in their fezzes, the gym where the boxers work out, Davy's preparations for the fight (his body oiled and prepared like the gladiators in *Spartacus*), the neon-lit streets, the dismal seedy apartments – all have the look of recorded reality; and in the quiet observation of Davy and Gloria in their rooms there is something of the tenderness of the early Visconti. One impressively atmospheric scene has Davy moving around Gloria's room as she sleeps, fingering her stockings, smelling her perfume, and examining her belongings.

Kubrick in this early film already displays an intuitive grasp of how to compose and angle interesting shots and create a sense of texture and perspective. But there is more to *Killer's Kiss* than outstanding photographic craftsmanship. Firstly, one recognises what is to become a characteristic Kubrickian irony: a dime-a-dance girl is jealous of her successful ballerina sister; Davy misses his manager because of a harmless prank; his manager is murdered by mistake; halfway down the flight of steps leading from Rapalla's dance hall to the street where the fatal mistake occurs is a sign bearing the words "Watch Your Step." Secondly, strong elements of the bizarre and surreal are present. A remarkable close-up shot of Davy feeding his goldfish, his face distorted by the concavity of the bowl and the rippling water, uncannily resembles the light-flecked helmet-enclosed head of the astronaut in *2001*. A brief nightmare sequence, processed in negative, the camera subjectively zooming in fast-motion down endless tenement-flanked streets, anticipates the pursuit camera movements of *Lolita* and *Dr. Strangelove* as well as David Bowman's trip through the Stargate in *2001*. It is also the first hint, so far as I know, of Kubrick's taste for symmetrical set-ups. The final climactic fight in the mannequin factory, a brilliantly eerie conception, has the two protagonists apparently hacking the dummies to pieces and hurling the dismembered parts at each other. I say apparently because further butchery by the British censor has prevented British audiences from seeing the major part of this scene.

Neo-realism was not all Kubrick had assimilated. The emphasis in the film on doors, windows, mirrors and stairways, together with the dogged lateral tracking shots across the dance hall, denote the influence of Max Ophüls, whom Kubrick admired at the time above all directors, and of Orson Welles. There is also something of the oppressive atmosphere of Bergman's *Port of Call* (another director much admired by Kubrick) in the depiction of working-class youngsters struggling against the big city environment.

If one adds to doors, windows and mirrors, the tenement buildings, the television and the boxing ring, it is possible to view the film as a succession of rectangular traps, the ultimate trap being the camera itself; for at one point, Rapallo, photographed in reflected image, furiously smashes a glass against a mirror which in fact corresponds with the recording camera. Shades of Poe's *William Wilson* again, if this is not stretching interpretation too far. But consider that *Killer's Kiss* is a film concerned with voyeurism (defined for the moment as observation from a distance). Davy watches Gloria through their parallel windows, Gloria watches Davy, Davy watches the police, Rapallo works himself up into a sadistically sexual state watching Davy's defeat on television. And the man behind the camera, of course, watches them all – in what way, we'll consider in the final chapter.*

While not wishing to make any great claims for an apprentice work which is more a pretext for a film than a finished work of art, I would still consider Kubrick's dismissal of his early film as unduly harsh. Its narrative banality and clumsiness is amply compensated by the powerful sense of relish in the making which is conveyed. It is crude in its total design but the individual strokes are vividly imagined and firmly controlled. *Killer's Kiss* is best appreciated as a sketchbook of a film, recording the ideas of a man let loose in an exhilarating medium and discovering just what can be done with it.

1. Agel, Jerome (editor). *The Making of Kubrick's 2001* (Signet, 1970).
2. Walter, Renaud. "Entretien avec Stanley Kubrick," *Positif*, December 1968-January 1969.

* There was a good deal of window voyeurism going on in the American cinema of the early fifties, for example in *Don't Bother to Knock* and *Rear Window*. The function of windows in the cinema would furnish an ample thesis.

4. Against the Odds
The Killing (1956)

> Fifteen years as a court stenographer had given him
> frequent opportunity to see what usually happened
> when men placed their faith in luck in opposition
> to definitely established mathematical odds.

> Lionel White, *Clean Break* (1955)

After *Killer's Kiss*, United Artists offered to back Kubrick in the making of $100,000 quickies, but he declined the offer because Alexander Singer had just introduced him to James B. Harris.

Harris, the son of a millionaire, had since 1949 been involved in the running of Flamingo Films, a very successful production and distribution company specialising in the buying of film rights for television during the boom years of the medium. Harris's career was interrupted by army service in the Signal Corps where he worked as a script clerk, assistant director and cameraman on short army training films. On his discharge he returned to Flamingo Films to produce and direct a series of 75 fifteen-minute television shows. But he had become eager to produce feature films.

Singer had met Harris in the Signal Corps, told him of Kubrick's low-budget efforts, and eventually arranged for Harris to see them and meet Kubrick. Harris thought *Killer's Kiss* a great improvement on *Fear and Desire*, though "it looked as if the story had been made up in a hurry with little attention being given to anything other than going into production. I felt that if someone could relieve him of the responsibility of acquiring stories and getting scripts, and give him a chance to relax and concentrate on direction, he could become great."[1] Kubrick and Harris, both aged 26 at the time, both jazz and baseball enthusiasts, both keen to work outside the restrictive mould of the big Hollywood studios, hit it off and formed Harris-Kubrick Pictures Corporation. Harris was to take care of all the business arrangements, Kubrick was to direct. Their successful partnership, perhaps unique in the film industry, was to last through three films: *The Killing*, *Paths of Glory* and *Lolita*.

Seeking a congenial – and commercially viable – property with which to make their debut, Kubrick proposed a film version of a crime thriller, *Clean Break*. "I had seen the book mentioned in a column of Jimmy Cannon, a very good sportswriter in the States. He said it was the most exciting crime novel he'd ever read. Just out of curiosity I went into a bookshop and bought it."

Harris bought the property and went to United Artists, who offered to back the project for $200,000 if they could find a star. They found Sterling Hayden. He was not exactly a big box-office name but Harris insisted he was perfect for the leading role, and added $150,000 of his own to the budget to give Kubrick more shooting time. This still made it a low-budget production by Hollywood standards.

For his first deal with a major distribution company, Kubrick managed to retain his artistic independence.

> Because I had no conventional film financing and no contact with any film companies [on my previous films] nobody interfered with me, and I became accustomed to doing exactly what I wanted to do. So that at the time I made *The Killing*... it seemed inconceivable to me that I could work in any other way. Even though I didn't have the position at the time to warrant insisting on this, my persistence got Jimmy and myself artistic control of the film, within an agreed upon budget, providing that the Motion Picture Production Code Seal could be gotten and the film would not be condemned by the Catholic Legion of Decency and would not exceed a certain length.[2]

Kubrick wrote the screenplay, with additional dialogue by Jim Thompson, a crime-novelist friend. Formerly announced as *Sudden Death* and *Bed of Fear*, the title of *The Killing* was finally settled on, with the association of death and a gambling haul. For this, his first film to obtain a full circuit release, Kubrick worked for a percentage of the profits, which meant, as it turned out, that he worked for nothing. In England the film was badly handled by the distributors. It was put out as a second feature on the Gaumont circuit without benefit of a press show or West End screening. However, when a number of critics drew favourable attention to the film, it was rushed into the West End. A box-office failure, losing $120,000 on its investment, *The Killing* was an outstanding critical success and made Kubrick's name as a director. It was picked as one of the ten best films of the year by the *Saturday Review* and by *Time*, the latter breathlessly declaring: "At twenty-seven writer-director Stanley Kubrick, in his third full-length feature, has shown more imagination with dialogue and camera than Hollywood has seen since the obstreperous Orson Welles went riding out of town on an exhibitor's poll."[3] In England, Alan Brien said: "Anyone who wishes to be in at what may be the birth of a new screen master cannot afford to miss a visit,"[4] and the *Manchester Guardian* described Kubrick as "a young man who is certainly going to leave his mark on the American cinema."[5]

Kubrick regards *The Killing* as his first really professional work. In his *Positif* interview he states: "There again the subject was bad but I took more care over the direction. All the same it was shot in only twenty days. The editing – I edit all my films myself – took much longer… *Clean Break* is a very good suspense novel. The break of time chronology is already there in the book. That's why it's more interesting than a straightforward crime story. The time overlaps that we utilised in the film already existed. That's what attracted us, apart from the fact that the story was intelligent." Elsewhere in the interview he remarks: "The sole interest of *The Killing*, I believe, is to show just what point one can make a good film out of an unimportant story."[6]

Clean Break, written in 1955 by Lionel White, who also wrote the novel on which Godard's *Pierrot le Fou* is based, is a terse, functional thriller. It owes a good deal to W.R. Burnett's superior, more substantially written *The Asphalt Jungle*, which was filmed by John Huston in 1950. Another film influenced by *The Asphalt Jungle*, *Rififi*, was made in 1955 by Jules Dassin. All three stories deal with an ex-convict who gathers together an ill-assorted band of accomplices to carry out his master-plan for a big robbery. In each case the robbery succeeds only to be scotched by double-crossing, and ends in a blood-bath. By now, of course, this plot basis has become a distinct thriller sub-genre. At the time, Kubrick had not seen *Rififi* but he must certainly have seen *The Asphalt Jungle*. Roger Tailleur makes a trenchant (and sympathetic) remark: "*The Killing* is the film of an ex-adolescent who, one fine evening in 1950, saw *The Asphalt Jungle* and dreamed about it for a week."[7]

The characterisation in White's gangster yarn, and to a lesser extent in the film, is rudimentary to the point of stereotype – the bored vindictive wife with expensive tastes, the ex-con out for the big haul, the tough crooked cop, etc. But three elements invest the story with more than routine interest. Firstly, the fact that the men involved are mainly amateurs badly in need of a break. Secondly, the satisfying ingenuity of the robbery itself; and finally, the suspense generated on the day of the robbery by the disruption of chronological time.

Johnny Clay, released after a four-year prison sentence, plans a daring robbery: the lifting of $2 million dollars from the heavily guarded teller's office of a big race-track. He intends afterwards to fly off to Mexico with his girlfriend, Fay. To carry out his plan he gathers together a group of non-professional accomplices: Marvin Unger, who provides the meeting place and stake money for the operation; Randy Kennan, a tough corrupt cop, heavily in debt; George Peatty, a nervous little track cashier, hopelessly in love with his bored, unfaithful wife, Sherry; and Mike O'Reilly, a track bartender, who needs money to pay the doctor's bills for his bed-ridden wife. Johnny brings in two others to create diversions: Maurice Oboukhoff, a Russian wrestler fakes a fight with the bartender to occupy the teller's office guards, and Nicki Arrane, an expert marksman, who shoots the leading horse as the big race is run.

The plan is successfully carried through, but Peatty's wife has discovered the plot and informed her gangster lover, Val. Val turns up with a henchman at the hide-out and a shooting match ensues. Just as Johnny arrives with the money, he sees Peatty staggering out with blood streaming from his face. Peatty, mortally wounded, goes back home and kills Sherry, before dying himself. Johnny meanwhile transfers the money to a suitcase and leaves at once for the airport with Fay. They are not allowed to carry the case themselves and as it is being transported by trolley to the plane's baggage compartment a small dog runs into the trolley's path, the driver swerves, the case falls and bursts open, and the money is scattered by the propellers of the plane. Fay tries to get the stunned Johnny away from the airport but they are intercepted by the airport detectives.

The film sticks very closely to the novel's starkly related events and characterisation until the end. In the novel the dying Peatty, suspecting Johnny of having made advances to Sherry, looks for him at the airport and sees him embracing Fay whom he mistakes for Sherry. He shoots Johnny dead before expiring.

Kubrick's ending, by stressing the element of chance in Johnny's final failure, is visually and thematically an improvement on the original, although the scattered proceeds image has been seen before. (It occurs at the end of Lang's *Dr. Mabuse, Der Spieler* [1922], Clair's *À Nous la Liberté* [1931], and of course, there is the wind-blown gold dust at the end of Huston's *The Treasure of the Sierra Madre* [1948], that other tale of ill-assorted adventurers out for an easy fortune, ending in double-cross and slaughter. The idea reappears in Losey's exercise in the genre, *The Criminal* [1960], which has the gangsters frantically digging up a vast snow-covered field in the vain hope of finding their buried loot.)

The other minor changes in the film interpretation are also improvements. Sherry's further double-cross by transferring her charms from Val to Randy the cop, and her subsequent torture by Val, are cut. The character of Unger is changed from that of a condescending misanthrope to a friendly fellow with a dubiously fatherly interest in Johnny. (In the original screenplay, Marvin Unger, who suggests that he and Johnny travel together after the robbery, is

specifically 35-years-old. Was Kubrick obliged to muffle
the hint of homosexuality in Unger's interest by casting the
elderly Jay C. Flippen in the role?)

The bar-fight brawler in the novel is simply a boxer
called Tex. Kubrick turns the character into a philosophical
Russian wrestler with a taste for chess, who, in a fine scene in
the Academy of Chess and Checkers is allowed to strike, for
a gangster movie, an unusually literate note: "In this life,"
he genially rumbles, "you have to be a perfect mediocrity...
Individuality is a monster that must be strangled in its
cradle to make your friends feel comfortable. I have often
thought the gangster and the artist are the same in the eyes
of the Master. They are admired but there are always those
who wish to see them destroyed." The idea may not be
very profound but in its context of general skulduggery it
gives one a distinct lift. Later, the wrestler tells the story of
a goatherd who seeks the true nature of the sun by staring
at it, and goes blind – a parable that might well apply to the
astronauts of *2001*.

A further improvement over the original novel
occurs in the Nicki sequence at the car park. To get into
an advantageous position for plugging the horse, Nicki
pretends to be a paraplegic and bribes the car-park
attendant. In the film, the attendant is a Negro, so grateful
for Nicki's kindness that he continues to plague him with
little attentions until Nicki is compelled to get rid of him by
calling him "nigger." In the novel, incidentally, Nicki gets
away safely, but in the film he is shot dead by a policeman.
Was this because the Production Code could not tolerate
even one of the criminals escaping without retribution?

The credits of the film are set against documentary-
style shots of the Lansdown track during preliminaries
for the big race of the day, shots to be repeated later in the
picture. As the credits conclude and the horses are released
from the starting gate, so too is the mechanism of the plot
unsprung, a plot which can be identified with the racing
situation itself: the gangsters are runners who must follow
certain prescribed courses during the day. They are taking a
long chance against the odds with a huge prize as the stake

which they must win if they are to break out of the ruts of poverty, debt, frustration – and crime – in which they are trapped. It is not the only time in a Kubrick film that men are implicitly identified with animals in the vagaries of their behaviour.

The action is framed by the flat impassive voice of a *March of Time*-style commentator who keeps us briefed on the time and place in which the otherwise confusing movements of the gangsters take place. This "dossier" approach contributes to the narrative's documentary flavour. It is almost as if we are witnessing a reconstructed case out of authentic FBI files. As Marvin Unger is introduced, making contact with his two race-track accomplices, the commentary speaks of him as a single piece in a jigsaw puzzle in relation to a final, as yet unknown, design, and later Johnny Clay is referred to as the thread in an unfinished fabric. The metaphors aptly convey the structure of the film, the action weaving back and forth in space and time, crossing and double-crossing its threads. Another appropriate metaphor would be that of chess; for each man is brought into position, only to be temporarily abandoned while another piece in the game is deployed.

It is this sense of strategy and meticulous timing, the awareness that a single miscalculation can upset the whole operation, that gives the film something of its tremendous urgency and drive. And Kubrick goes one better than the novel by repeating certain key images at different points, notably that of the track team of white horses hauling the starting gate into position while the track announcer's voice repeatedly announces the crucial race. This disjunctive time device, arguably the most effective in an American film since *Citizen Kane*, not only generates tension but invests the film with a relentless ritualistic quality which becomes almost a visual manifestation of Fate. One is held in rapt fascination as the mechanism is exposed. The outcome of the game may not be completely foreseen but one knows, if not from the requirements of the Hollywood Production Code, then certainly from the terse commentator's voice, that it is lost from the beginning.

Shades of the prison-house loom over the characters. Johnny has just come out of prison and his girl speaks of having felt locked out as much as he felt locked in. She is hardly any better off now, since she is locked out of the robbery operation, and remains locked out at the end by Johnny's paralysing sense of defeat that prevents him from making a run for it. The film is accordingly full of prison-bar imagery – characters photographed through bedrails, bar-like reflections of window-frames, the bars of Peatty's cash-counter, the parrot's cage on which the camera momentarily dwells after Peatty bites the dust.

Extreme chiaroscuro effects, finely angled compositions, low ceilings, deep focus photography and incongruity tending to the bizarre – all relate the film stylistically to Welles and, to a lesser extent, the early Huston. Characters are mostly shot from above or below, magnified or dwarfed by the camera. Natural lighting from low overhead ceiling lamps and table lamps is evident here, as in other Kubrick films. All this helps to create a sinister claustrophobic atmosphere.

Kubrick is fond of tracking his characters laterally with people or objects intruding, as in life, between the character and the observing camera (cf. Kurosawa). One scene is particularly enriched by deep-focus photography. Nicki is discovered practising his marksmanship on fairground gangster cut-outs. The cut-outs occupy the foreground, Nicki and Johnny occupy the middle ground, and in the background, clearly seen in deep focus, is Nicki's roadster, parked outside a shack.

The most Wellesian scene is the return of the fatally wounded Peatty to his apartment. With blood streaming down his face he totters into the room to greet Sherry, who is packing in expectation of her lover, Val. The apartment is weirdly shadowed, and Peatty's parrot cries, "Watch out!" – recalling the "Watch Your Step" sign of *Killer's Kiss*. Sherry says, "George, you'd better go on and go – you look terrible." George shoots her and as she falls she says: "It's just a joke without a punchline." She is quickly followed to the floor by Peatty, whose collapse knocks the parrot-cage towards the camera. It is a scene of macabre, baroque imagination.

Black irony runs through the film. When George arrives home early in the film he complains of a stomach-ache. "Maybe you've got a hole in it," Sherry drily remarks, and he humourlessly replies: "How could I get a hole in my stomach?" Nicki, the horse assassin, is first seen fondling a puppy, and it is a small dog running in front of the airport baggage trolley which blows Johnny's chances for good. The airport clerk automatically comments to Johnny: "Thank you for flying American, sir." Nicki's fairground cut-outs anticipate the appearance of the detectives at the end, advancing guns in hand towards Johnny, while Johnny wears an absurd clown's mask for the robbery itself.

The punchline to Sherry's bad joke is provided at the airport when thousands of bank-notes whirl and scatter, an image of disaster and futility that is dramatically equivalent to the H-bomb explosion at the end of *Dr. Strangelove*. There are two visual anticipations of this final catastrophe: the money spills over the floor as the clerk crams it into the mailbag; and some of it scatters over the ground as Johnny transfers it from the bag into the suitcase.

It's a pity that two scenes look synthetic in this otherwise impeccably textured film: Nicki's gun is aimed at a very phoney back-projection of the big race; and the staged bar-room brawl becomes a bit of a "turn" for Kola Kwariani as Maurice, with his shirt ripping off picturesquely and a singularly unconvincing crowd of spectators neatly lined up to watch the show.

The cast of *The Killing* is like a Who's Who of Hollywood gangster movies. The fact that this gang of amateurs is played by familiar bit-part actors somehow defines the social level of the crime, as well as evoking a certain nostalgia by association. Sterling Hayden, the strong-arm man of *The Asphalt Jungle*, is promoted in *The Killing* to the brains behind the plot. He has the right grim, disenchanted look for Johnny but his inexpressive delivery makes one understand why he never got any satisfaction out of acting. Ted de Corsia, fleeing crook of *The Naked City*, appears here as the corrupt cop, and Joe Sawyer, Jay C. Flippen, Marie Windsor and Colleen Gray, all thriller veterans, are on hand. While most of the players perform competently, the film is distinguished by two outstanding presences, Elisha Cook Jr. and Timothy Carey. Cook, uneasy gunman of *The Maltese Falcon*, *The Big Sleep* and *Dillinger*, may not be much of an actor but he rivets the attention with his pale, scared yet homicidal eyes. He is given surely one of the most searching close-ups in film history when, the camera training on his face as Sherry hints that Johnny made a pass at her, his staring eyes grow aghast and his hand grotesquely pulls down the skin on one side of his face. And Timothy Carey, with his slurred speech, sleepily lowering eyelids and heavy dark features, embodies every law-abiding citizen's idea of malevolence.

When I first saw *The Killing* at the age of 17, I found it stunning. Has the film's cutting authority and economy of technique been so assimilated by the cinema of the sixties as to make it look dated? Well, inevitably knowledge of the exact outcome of the robbery means, where characterisation is so thin, some slight loss of tension but not so much that one still doesn't stay riveted to the screen.

It is the scenes between the couples that seem particularly trite today. Those between Peatty and his wife (having something in common with the Humbert-Lolita relationship) are grotesquely amusing for a while but tend to go on a little too long; Johnny's girlfriend, Fay, is required to say "I'm not pretty and I'm not very smart" when she is evidently very pretty indeed; and the scene between the bartender, Mike, and his ailing wife is as sentimental as that between Sherry and her strong-arm lover Val is routine Hollywood corn. There is also rather too much music in the film, especially the cool jazz cocktail music which unfailingly accompanies Sherry's appearances.

But *The Killing*, with its tightly organised screenplay and grippingly ingenious plot, is a great improvement on *Killer's Kiss*. Although it lacks some of the impressive quieter moments of the previous film, the world it portrays is still consistently a sad and sleazy one of shabby lives, botched opportunities and chance mishaps. Kubrick has made no more gangster films (unless his current film, *A Clockwork*

Orange, be so regarded). But his contribution to the genre is permanent. With Robert Aldrich's *Kiss Me Deadly*, *The Killing* is my candidate for the best American crime thriller of the fifties.

1. Uncredited. "Talking about People: James Harris," *Film*, Winter 1962.
2. Kohler, Charlie. "Stanley Kubrick Raps," *Eye*, August 1968.
3. Uncredited. "*The Killing*," *Time*, 4 June 1956.
4. Brien, Alan. "*The Killing*," *Evening Standard*, 26 July 1956.
5. Uncredited. "*The Killing*," *Manchester Guardian*, 28 July 1956.
6. Walter, Renaud. "Entretien avec Stanley Kubrick," *Positif*, December 1968-January 1969.
7. Tailleur, Roger. "Les Enfants de Huston," *Positif*, September 1958.

5. The Inevitable Hour
Paths of Glory (1957)

> The boast of heraldry, the pomp of power,
> And all that beauty, all that wealth e'er gave,
> Awaits alike th'inevitable hour,
> The paths of glory lead but to the grave.

> Thomas Gray,
> "Elegy Written in a Country Churchyard" (1750)

> "There's a rumour around there's going to be some executions."
> "Oh, balls! This isn't the cinema."

> Humphrey Cobb, *Paths of Glory* (1935)

Among those impressed by *The Killing* was Dore Schary, then head of production at M-G-M. Kubrick and Harris accepted a 40-week contract at Culver City Studios to find a congenial project to write, produce and direct together. It took them two weeks to get through the alphabetised synopsis cards alone but they could find nothing to interest them among M-G-M's voluminous files of scripts, novels and plays, and Kubrick filled in his time running old movies. However, he did write, with Calder Willingham, a screenplay of Stefan Zweig's novella *The Burning Secret*. "It was rejected," says Kubrick, "because it didn't appeal to them. At that time I didn't want to direct the film myself. But it would have made a very good film. It's an interesting story."[1]

Given Kubrick's admiration for Max Ophüls, it's significant that *The Burning Secret* comes from the same collection of short stories, *Kaleidoscope* (1936), from which Ophüls' *Letter from an Unknown Woman* was taken. Set mainly in an elegant Austrian hotel, the story is based on a triangular relationship which is a kind of inverted Lolita situation. A young Austrian nobleman on holiday by the sea, befriends a lonely twelve-year-old boy with the object of seducing the boy's mother. When he wins the mother's interest, his designs are frustrated by the now hateful intrusions of the boy whom the couple try unsuccessfully to keep out of the way. The story is chiefly concerned with the boy's awakening to the moral complexities of adult life, but the resemblance to the early part of *Lolita* is unmistakeable.

When eventually Kubrick did find a project he was interested in directing it was not among the M-G-M properties. "I remembered a novel of Humphrey Cobb that I'd read when I was fifteen and which left a deep impression on me, less for its literary qualities than for the disturbing and tragic situation of three of its characters – three innocent soldiers, accused of cowardice and mutiny and shot as an example."[2] "It was one of the few books I'd read for pleasure at high school, I think I found it lying around my father's office."[3]

Harris bought the film rights, hoping M-G-M would back it, but neither Schary nor anyone else at M-G-M could see the commercial possibilities of a story which had in any case, according to Hollis Alpert, been turned down in the past by every other major studio.

With twenty weeks of their contract still to run, Kubrick and Harris left M-G-M in the wake of Schary's departure in a big studio shake-up. They tried to interest other companies in their project but none would consider it without major modifications in the story-line – mainly the addition of love-interest – and without the commitment of a box-office star. The script was sent to every available actor they could think of, including Kirk Douglas and Gregory Peck, but no one would agree to play the part of Colonel Dax as it was written. Kirk Douglas, however, liked the subject and, either at his suggestion or on Kubrick's own initiative, Kubrick decided to have the screenplay rewritten to make it more acceptable to Douglas and to United Artists, the company least unreceptive to offbeat subjects. (Kubrick attributes UA's receptiveness in this case to the fact that other companies may have balked at offending their interests in France – through theatre holdings, etc. – whereas UA is not committed to exhibiting films in this way.)

Calder Willingham, whose novels Kubrick much admired, was hired to write the second draft, and additional dialogue was contributed by Jim Thompson. Willingham had earlier that year adapted for the screen his own novel and play, *End as a Man*, a bizarre and scathing account of life in a Southern military academy.

United Artists were still reluctant to back a film of such pronounced anti-militarist feeling. They agreed, it is said, only under pressure from Douglas, whom they did not want to lose from their fold of independent producers, and only on condition that the film be made on a low budget in Europe. United Artists put up $935,000 for the film to be made by Bryna, Douglas's own production company, of which a handsome proportion, $350,000, went to Douglas himself. Kubrick worked, as on *The Killing*, without salary, for a percentage of the profits. Again, the film was only to break even at the box office.

Kubrick and Harris wanted to shoot the film in France, where the story is set, but assumed (rightly, as the film's reception was to prove) that they would never get permission to make it there. They found the exteriors they needed, as well as the magnificent chateau setting, not far from Munich, where supplementary studio scenes were shot. *Paths of Glory* was therefore made entirely in Germany with a German production crew.

Kubrick could not speak German and his cameraman could not speak English, but the collaboration worked. "It was incredible how little we spoke to each other. Only things like 'brighter,' 'darker' – but there's nothing of importance in the film that isn't what I wanted."[4] All the same, the technical crew were apparently outraged that Kubrick chose his own camera angles and even operated the camera himself at times, notably in the attack sequence, when he handled the camera equipped with a zoom lens.

The sixty-day shooting schedule ended in May 1957, and the film took another sixty days to edit. It was further edited by Kubrick shortly after its premiere in November 1957. In England, in order to qualify for an "A" certificate, cuts were made which included Lieutenant Roget finishing off the executed men with bullets through their heads, and, incredibly, when the film was televised a few years ago by I.T.V., the famous cockroach scene was missing. It seems to me disgraceful, I must add in passing, that films are shown both in cinemas and on television without the public being informed whether or not cuts have been made.

*

Paths of Glory, published in 1935, was the sole literary work of Humphrey Cobb, a former soldier in the Canadian army who had been gassed and wounded on the French front and died in 1944. He also worked as a Hollywood script-writer, for his name turns up as co-scenarist of *San Quentin*, a Humphrey Bogart-Pat O'Brien prison movie of 1937.

The novel is set during the period of stabilised trench warfare in the First World War. The war had resolved itself into a slow brutalising affair of assault and counter-assault conducted from two great parallel lines of trenches zigzagging from Switzerland to the English Channel. Generals were obsessed with mass frontal attacks based on obsolete Napoleonic principles. Since both sides were equipped with machine-guns, such attacks were decimating. As the film's opening commentary puts it, "Advances were measured in hundreds of metres and paid for in lives by hundreds of thousands." Tired battle-shocked troops were prematurely ordered back to the front and morale was very low. In this terrible war of attrition, France suffered the most casualties.

Paths of Glory concerns an ambitious general who, lured by the bait of promotion, orders a war-weary division to launch an attack on an impregnable enemy position. The attack is a failure, and when the general sees from an observation point that the men are falling back or simply unable to leave their trenches, he orders a captain to fire on his own men to get them out. The order is rejected since it has not been put into writing, whereupon the infuriated general puts the whole division under collective arrest. He wants a section from each of the four companies shot, but finally settles for one man from each company.

The novel is a work of fiction based on a number of factual, documented incidents. A General Réveilhac actually ordered fire on his own trenches and only retracted when a Colonel of Artillery demanded a written order. Lillian Gish quotes D.W. Griffith on the making of *Hearts of the World* in the front-line: "Sometimes a barrage was dropped on our own trenches, which were supposed to be already empty – just to make certain our troops were moving ahead."[5] In April 1934, five men were "rehabilitated" after a court case; a despatch in *The New York Times* was wryly headed: "French Acquit 5 Shot for Mutiny in 1915: Widows of 2 Win Awards of 7 Cents Each." No sanctions could be taken against General Réveilhac as the affair had been struck from the records of the Chambre Française in 1921.

Paths of Glory is less concerned with the rights and wrongs of the First World War than with the terrible injustices which are made possible within the rigid hierarchy of the military caste system. Writing in a style that is neither emotionally overcharged nor too coolly detached, Cobb exposes the diabolic mechanism in which three men are trapped and slaughtered. Within this mechanism there is room for courage, decency and compassion. But once set in motion the machine is inexorable. For every act of comradeship there is one of betrayal. Officers are privileged, protected by their rank and their influential connections; the footsloggers are mere cannon-fodder; human lives are bargained over like cattle; death is such an ever-present reality that feelings are anaesthetised and men are reduced to accepting indifferently the slaughter of their comrades.

Individuality can have no place in such a system. Where such social stratification of leaders and led exists, the power-hungry, the incompetent and the vicious can destroy lives with impunity, and human relations are squalidly degraded. The novel is deeply anti-militaristic: "'Silly,' Dax thought, 'but the mere issuing of a command always inspires confidence. It doesn't matter whether it is a necessary command, or even a correct one." Then, a little later, an afterthought came to him: "It inspires self-confidence even in the man who issues it." There are some moving and horrifying evocations of feelings in the face of death. Cobb's grim point of view is that "the world's an immense graveyard, getting perpetual care from the survivors who are living off it."

However, the novel – and, by extension, the film adaptation – is misleading in one important respect. One would never guess from the treatment that before long half the French army would be in a state of mutiny. From May to August 1917, after the Battle of the Marne, the demoralised units of no fewer than 54 divisions were in open rebellion, deserting, demonstrating, attacking officers, brandishing red flags, distributing anti-war leaflets and threatening to march on Paris. During this period alone, 412 men were sentenced to death, of whom 55 were actually executed. (It is said that about 2,000 Frenchmen in all were shot during the First World War "pour encourager les autres.") The French censors managed somehow to hush up the situation; if the Germans had realised what was happening the whole course of the war would have been affected.

Paths of Glory is significantly set in 1916, before this immense wave of rebellion. Its central incident is in no way related to the general growing malaise. In fact, the story avoids all revolutionary implications by concerning itself with troops who are physically unable to carry out their orders, rather than with men who actively choose not to advance to the front line.

The novel was well received on publication and classed with Remarque's *All Quiet on the Western Front* and Barbusse's *L'Enfer*. In September 1935, in a *New York Times* review of an indifferent stage adaptation by Sidney Howard, Brooks Atkinson remarked that "some day the screen will seize this ghastly tale and make a work of art from it."[6] That it was not seized earlier than 1957 is because Hollywood is traditionally resistant to anti-establishment films, and because the anti-militaristic mood of the novel ill-suited the prevailing mood of the years preceding the Second World War, understandably enough if one considers the headline in the same issue of *The New York Times*: "LEAGUE DECIDES TO INVOKE SANCTIONS IF ITALY RESORTS TO WAR ON ETHIOPIA; NEXT MOVE IS NOW UP TO MUSSOLINI."

*

Like *The Killing*, the film of *Paths of Glory* is notable for its tight, spare, narrative style, and a script and editing geared to telling the story as starkly and economically as possible. The novel's somewhat discursive narrative line has been condensed and simplified. It has no leading reader-identification figure but explores the situation through all the ranks involved. Colonel Dax's relatively minor part in the novel is expanded in the film so that he not only argues with the jingoistic General Mireau but also leads the main attack, and survives to conduct the defence of the three men. In the novel he is a much-decorated professional soldier; in the film his civilian status is revealed early on as "the foremost criminal lawyer in France," which perhaps tends to throw his failure at the court martial into too emphatically ironic relief. He is also persuaded to carry through the attack when threatened with enforced leave, as he wants to remain with his men.

All this tends to glamourise Dax into something dangerously near to a stock movieland goodie, just as the expansion of General Mireau's villainous role establishes him as a familiar movieland heavy – especially as George Macready plays him with glowering manic ruthlessness. Similarly, it is Mireau's aide who in the film also conducts the prosecution and reads the execution statement, Richard Anderson's performance knowingly tuned to ironic mockery. By having Dax and Mireau confront each other early in the picture, the issues tend to be personalised and polarised for easy audience sympathies: liberal humanist versus unscrupulous opportunist. Nevertheless, this early scene is finely written; Dax responds to Mireau's "Show me a patriot and I'll show you an honest man" with Dr. Johnson's "Patriotism is the last refuge of the scoundrel," an exchange not present in the novel.

The film is so stylistically pared as to be invested with tremendous sinewy drive, but, after having read the novel, one regrets the omission, in the interests no doubt of narrative economy, of certain interesting details. We don't learn from the film that the unfortunate division is an exhausted mixture of veterans and raw recruits who have to break their leave to make the attack on the Ant-Hill. We don't learn that General Mireau is persuaded to accept only one scapegoat per company by the argument that the more men who are executed, the more chance is there of an influential connection making an unwelcome scandal of the affair. While it's inevitable that the film should omit much of the novel's detailed dialogue on death and observation of men in combat, it's curious that at no time does the film depict the physical horror of bloodshed. There is nothing in the film to compare, for instance, with the novel's sickening description of a lieutenant dying alone in a trench, and in the film's attack sequence men drop more like flies than human beings. Is this avoidance of the physical agony of war intended to ensure that we are not somehow titillated or distracted from the central moral issue? Whatever the reason, it is a curious reticence.

One major omission is the account of how the sacrificial victims are actually selected by their company commanders. In the film, only the background of Corporal Paris's selection is shown in detail. His "commander," the incompetent and cowardly Lieutenant Roget, hates Paris for not paying him the respect he thinks his superior rank deserves. When Paris witnesses Roget killing a comrade in the panic of a bungled reconnaissance mission, Roget is only too glad to choose Paris as his company's scapegoat. How the other men are chosen are among the most vivid passages in the book. Private Arnaud is selected by means of a grotesquely inept lottery. Private Ferol, the "undesirable," is selected by his Captain as a cool intellectual exercise by a process of elimination: the list is reduced to the two social incorrigibles of the company, both, incidentally, distinguished for their bravery in battle; since the other man is Jewish, the Captain chooses Ferol to avoid the possibility of another Dreyfus scandal. In the novel but not in the film, a fourth man is to be chosen, but the Captain simply refuses to carry out the order on the grounds that none of his men were cowardly, and goes off riding for the day.

On the other hand, there are some useful additions in the screenplay. Corporal Paris's mention of a cockroach in a letter to his wife is turned in the film into a bitterly moving exchange between Paris and Ferol in the guardhouse. "You see that cockroach?" says Paris. "Tomorrow he'll have more contact with my wife and child than I will." Ferol crushes the cockroach and indifferently remarks, "Now you've got the edge on him." It's a pity, however, that Corporal Paris, in the novel adamant to the end against taking confession, does in the film agree to take it – a sop perhaps to the Legion of Decency. Another effective addition – General Mireau's morale-boosting tour of the trenches – is weakened by having him enquire "Ready to kill more Germans, soldier?" of two of the very men who will be executed, an example of the way the film occasionally over-stresses its ironies.

The novel simply ends with the execution of the three men.[7] The film goes on to show Dax revealing to General Broulard, who has initiated the whole affair, that General Mireau ordered fire on his own troops. But the foxy Broulard, instead of reprieving the condemned men, decides to have Mireau face a public enquiry to demonstrate the integrity of the army. "I have only one last thing to say to you, George," Mireau responds on hearing the bad news. "The man you've stabbed in the back is a soldier." He proudly stalks out. Broulard remarks to Dax, "Well, it had to be done. France can't afford to have fools guarding her military destiny." Dax realises that Broulard approvingly thinks he is simply after Mireau's job, turns on him, and calls him a "degenerate, sadistic old man." Broulard, in turn, accuses him of being an idealist. Since Dax has earlier put the cowardly Lieutenant Roget in charge of the execution squad, the three villains of the piece are all, one way or the other, meted out punishment by Dax, which may be very satisfying for the audience but somewhat blunts Cobb's sterner more unremitting conclusion.

The ending of the film version of Calder Willingham's *End as a Man* undergoes a similar softening-up process. In the novel, the sadistic cadet, Jocko de Paris, is expelled from the Military Academy, but it's clear that the brutal hypocritical systems and his fellow cadets remain unchanged. In the film, the Academy is supposed to be purged of its single bad element when de Paris is run out of town by his upright fellow cadets.

And yet the scene in *Paths of Glory* is not just there for the purpose of allocating a little punishment here and there. One can see in Dax's blackmailing Broulard with the possibility of exposure and scandal a table-turning reversal that might appeal to the chess – or military – strategist. And when Broulard explains that the whole futile attack was initiated in response to pressure from civilian newspapers and politicians, a disclosure not in Cobb's novel, we are given a revelatory new perspective on events. While Mireau takes the war game seriously, the jauntily cynical Broulard knows and plays it as a game. "These executions," he blandly declares to Dax before receiving the news of Mireau's blunder, "will be a tonic for the division. Few things are more stimulating than seeing someone else die. Troops are like children. A child craves discipline… so do the troops. And one way to maintain discipline is to shoot a man now and then."

In any case the film does not end with Mireau's exposure. It adds the critically much disputed sequence in which a frightened German girl is dragged on stage in a bistro to entertain the jeering cat-calling troops with a song. Dax, still depressed after his encounter with Broulard, grimly watches this unfeeling spectacle, but gradually the whooping whistling men fall silent, touched by the nostalgia and simplicity of her song. Some hum the song with the girl, others weep, all are deeply affected.

A sergeant approaches Dax and reports: "We are ordered to move to the front immediately," and Dax replies, "Give the men a few more minutes, sergeant." Despite a too photogenic German girl (played by Susanne Christian, who was to become Kubrick's third wife), this final scene is genuinely moving, partly owing to Kubrick's tender sensitive photography of the men as they become subdued and nostalgically affected.

The scene is hardly gratuitous, as some critics have suggested, for it shows what is thematically central to the novel and the film, that these men are so used to living with death that they seem incapable of being affected by the wasted death of their comrades and are still ready enough to inflict cruelty on others. Yet at the same time they are victims, like their dead comrades. General Mireau regards the men as scum. If the war sometimes reduces them to the level of animals, they are still capable of feelings of loss and loneliness.

This final scene is less equivocal than deliberately ambiguous; it has the indefiniteness of real life, the sense that these men are, after all, vulnerable human beings, worthy of compassion. The ending implies that Dax is finally neither totally disheartened nor totally reconciled. All the same, one wonders how he might have responded a few months later to open rebellion from the ranks.

Placing Dax's personal crisis at the centre of *Paths of Glory* tends to resolve the drama into the trial of faith of the humane civilian idealist confronted with the cruel realities of unfeeling military expediency. Perhaps one's misgivings about this shift of emphasis from the novel would be less if it had been taken further, if Dax's crisis had been explored more thoroughly and convincingly.

One might just accept the ingenuousness of "the foremost criminal lawyer in France" saying at the court-martial, "I don't believe the noblest impulse of man – his compassion for another – is completely dead here." Or even that he should ask each of the generals in turn whether he really believes the terrible things he is saying. But such acceptance is hard when Colonel Dax is played by an actor with such a contemporary air of hard-headed pugnaciousness as Kirk Douglas. That the film was made at all was no doubt thanks to Douglas, probably, however, on condition that the role of Dax be expanded. Ironically, the expanded role needs a more subtle and reflective actor to make it work.

The film has a splendid visual surface, although at least one French critic has complained that details of trenches, uniforms and saluting procedures lack authenticity. This bothers me less than the jarring American accents and occasional use of American idiom such as "You're kidding."

While Adolphe Menjou and George Macready – supplied with a prominent duelling scar – make reasonably convincing Frenchmen, it's hard to take the accent emerging from behind the beard of the burly sergeant; and although it was a mischievous idea to have the priest played by Emile Meyer, a familiar Hollywood bit-part heavy, his broad Brooklynese does come over a trifle discordantly. The tavern scene is very nearly scotched by having the men whistle and applaud as no Frenchmen ever would; and the actor playing the cafe proprietor, Gallic beret and waistcoat notwithstanding, behaves gratingly like a slick American TV compere.

Ralph Meeker plays sympathetically as Corporal Paris. But the two outstanding performances of the film are those of Peter Capell as the President Judge of the court-martial, something of whose restrained impersonal "reasonable" quality might better have suited the interpretation of General Mireau; and Timothy Carey as Private Ferol, whose long slack face disturbingly suggest the pathological. His indifferent squashing of the cockroach – "Now you got the edge on him" – is superbly delivered, and his pitiful sobbing in the execution scene, praying and hanging on the arm of the priest who evasively reads from his prayer book, is at once grotesque and moving.

If one did not know Ophüls to be the director most admired by Kubrick at the time he made *Paths of Glory*, one would still have to invoke the name of the director whom Kubrick once described as the 'master of the analytic shot in movement, although Kubrick denies his specific influence on the picture. "Certain techniques," he says, "seemed suitable, for certain things." In *The Killing* and *Paths of Glory* "the technique in the end is rather simple. I tried to use technique as economically as possible."[8]

"It moves like a drumroll": what Cocteau said of Chaplin's *Shoulder Arms* is also true of *Paths of Glory*. Underlined by Gerald Fried's relentless drumbeat score, the mechanism we see unfold is in fact one sustained execution process, unpunctuated by conventional climaxes and pauses. Editing is characterised by very swift cutting from scene to scene without benefit of fades or dissolves, and the minimum of establishing shots. This technique, used to similar effect in the mid-fifties films of Elia Kazan, gives the film great tension and drive as well as keeping the viewer constantly on the alert.

The camerawork is marvellously fluent in this, the most Ophülsian of Kubrick's films, while retaining a basically documentary quality. The characters are constantly on the move, literally walking themselves into their various impasses or graves; and the camera observes and records their movements like an intruder. It dogs and pursues the characters as they pace to and fro, tracking laterally across the ballroom in long takes, pursuing and retreating before Mireau and Dax in their respective tours of the trenches.

Shooting from between the silhouetted shoulders of the judges in the court-martial scene both establishes a newsreel flavour and makes admirable compositions in depth to focus the viewer's attention. Low-angle shots, enabling us to see ceilings, and symmetrical frontal set-ups are much in evidence. The execution scene is brilliantly photographed. The hand-held camera at once observes the condemned men led to their posts and then shifts to their subjective viewpoint; we see Ferol blubbering upon the arm of the impassive priest, the unconscious Arnaud borne on a stretcher, Paris grimly resigned. The camera glimpses silent anonymous dignitaries turned out for the occasion and a press photographer manipulating his primitive equipment. Many of the shots are so centred and formalised as to emphasise the terrible ritual nature of the executions.

Kubrick's use of lighting is impeccable – the low-lying electric and candle sources of light in the dug-outs; daylight streaming through the vast windows of the chateau. In the night reconnaissance scene, a flare brilliantly reveals an object in the foreground as a dead body; when the flare dies we see that we could have identified it as such if we'd only looked hard enough.

Perhaps the most strikingly original camerawork occurs during Dax's interview with General Broulard in the library. Broulard, impatient to get back to the ball, leads Dax away from the static camera towards the library door, and just as the door is opened in distant long-shot Dax casually tells Broulard that Mireau ordered fire on his own men. As Broulard slams the door shut again, Kubrick's jump-cut to a close-up of the two men provides a superb emotional jolt.

The most disappointing sequence in the film is the long attack led by Dax. Conceived as a sustained virtuoso montage of slow lateral tracking shots, exploiting hand-held and zoom lens cameras and an eerie whining sound-track, the sequence comes over as strangely synthetic and contrived. This is partly because too much attention is paid to Dax himself, partly because the Ant-Hill objective looks suspiciously like a painted back-drop, but mainly because only a few men are actually seen to fall in what is supposed to be a decimating defeat, and those that do fall, drop to instant unagonised death as in any Hollywood Western. There is absolutely no sense, as I think there should be in such a sequence, of the ugliness, agony and horror of mass slaughter.

*

Much critical discussion has centred on what *Paths of Glory* is really about, whether it is, as some have maintained, one of the greatest anti-war films ever made, or an anti-militarist film, or even a beguiling fraud. Some have criticised it as a period piece so far removed in its simple issues from present-day complexities that it is irrelevant, others for its apparent inconclusiveness. For instance, Richard Lester has stated: "The thing in *Paths of Glory* that is sinister is, as I've said so many times, that it does seem to leave you with the feeling that if only Kirk Douglas had led our troops in the beginning, we would have been able to go out much more efficiently and kill the Germans at the Ant-Hill. How this could ever be considered a pacifist film, I'll never know, because it patently is not. It's 'What we want are more humane killers,' a line from *How I Won the War* which was to me a direct reference to the film."[9]

It is true that *Paths of Glory* is an exposé film rather than one that explores moral complexities and it would be foolish to claim for it great profundity. All the issues are crystal clear, the goodies and baddies are clearly identified, our emotional responses, except in the final scene, are accordingly simple and straightforward. It should be remembered, though, that Kubrick did not decide to make a war film and then look around for a subject so suitably distant in time as to make safe uncontroversial material. Rather, he chose to film a novel which had impressed him as a boy and which he believed, justifiably, to hold out great cinematic possibilities.

As he puts it: "Obviously war creates a very dramatic and very visual situation for a scenario. In a war, in a short period of time, people go through a fantastic period of tension which in peacetime would appear really artificial and forced because everything happens too quickly for one to believe in it. The war film, then, enables one to describe with extraordinary conciseness the evolution of an attitude of a character. Thus the problems come to a head more rapidly."[10] And again: "The soldier is absorbing because all the circumstances surrounding him have a kind of charged intensity. For all its horror, war is pure drama, probably because it is one of the few remaining situations where men stand up for and speak up for what they believe to be their principles."[11] One is reminded of Hemingway's remark that war provides the best subject for fiction because it offers the "maximum material combined with maximum action."

At first sight this may look as if Kubrick was cannily exploiting a well-tried genre to engineer some emotional excitement. But, of course, there are war films and war films. As a boy Kubrick preferred war films above all others, and in particular *Hell's Angels*, *The Dawn Patrol*, *The Fighting 69th* and *Sergeant York*. In *The Dawn Patrol*, a squadron leader has the terrible responsibility of reconciling apparently inhuman orders from H.Q. with the needs of the young ill-equipped pilots whom he must send out on suicide missions. *The Fighting 69th* is concerned with raw recruits coping with discipline and cowardice. And *Sergeant York* tells the real-life story of a First World War hero who captured or killed thousands of Germans while retaining his naive idealism and remaining at heart a pacifist. These subjects relate directly to Kubrick's own thematic preoccupations.

Kubrick, who does not consider himself a pacifist, was certainly not consciously trying to make a pacifist film. He regards the First World War as "tragically senseless,"[12] an absurd irrational war as distinct from the war against Hitler. *Paths of Glory* is not concerned with the physical brutality of war like *The Unknown Soldier* or *Fires on the Plain*. "I believe a film with anti-war pretentions," Kubrick says, "in which everything is ugly, scandalous, horrifying, doesn't show the whole truth in all its aspects. People who haven't been wounded or mutilated remember the war nostalgically as the greatest experience of their lives. In fact, I don't remember having seen a great war film. The only extraordinary war story is *The Iliad*."[13]

Nor does *Paths of Glory* stress what the two opposing sides have in common, like *La Grande Illusion* or *My Way Home*, except, of course, by implication in the final scene. Despite Kubrick's denial that it is for or against the military, *Paths of Glory* seems to me to be clearly about the operation and abuses of power in a military setting and reflects upon the whole concept of military honour, justice, sanity and authority.

In showing how individuals are destroyed by the machinery of an authoritarian system it illustrates Clausewitz's dictum that "war is the continuation of politics by other means"; and it demonstrates that militarism is an extension of the repressive element in social organisation. In this respect *Paths of Glory* is an anti-bastard movie, and hence in the mainstream of the American war novel. But the sense of human waste and futility relates the film also to such plays as Allan Monkhouse's *The Conquering Hero* and O'Casey's *The Silver Tassie*, which dwell bitterly on the appalling individual suffering in war. Kubrick has himself described *Paths of Glory* as "a rather cynically romantic film."[14]

It doesn't give one a fresh viewpoint or change one's mind about anything. But in denouncing false patriotism and opportunism, and in its revelations that the whole futile attack was carried out under pressure of newspapers and politicians at home, it to some extent de-mystifies the operation, as any "anti-war" film must to be worthy of the description. The fact that the status quo is basically preserved at the end hardly implies that Kubrick is in favour of it.

✳

If, as a minority of film critics think, *Paths of Glory* is so evasive, unaffecting and/or irrelevant, one would expect it to have made no impact outside critical film circles. But, on the contrary, the European reaction to the film was explosive.

Paths of Glory has never even been submitted by United Artists to the French censors, and François Truffaut stated that he thought it would never be shown so long as the Ministry of War had anything to say about it, even though *Le Canard enchaîné* published letters confirming the veracity of the incidents depicted. Kubrick wrote to *L'Express*: "I must express a certain surprise at the severity of reaction towards this film in your country. I have the profoundest respect for France, but I can't agree that a film be totally suppressed for political reasons. I can't think of another Western power which, at this time, would ban a film on this side of the Iron Curtain for political reasons. Eroticism and violence are the only censorship problems one hears about, and they can always be dealt with by cuts here and there. Perhaps my conception of political liberty is a little naive, but I think it must include absolutely freedom of expression in the arts."[15]

Perhaps it was a little naive. *Paths of Glory* was banned in Israel. Switzerland banned it as incontestably offensive to France, its justice and its army – this of a film depicting *true* incidents which took place *forty* years ago. Disturbed by the political reaction to the film, United Artists invited Belgian critics before its release in Belgium to comment on whether it should be shown or not. Only one critic advised against it; yet the head of United Artists publicity in Belgium, a Frenchman, was threatened with having his visa withdrawn, and the manager of the Brussels cinema showing the picture persisted in showing it under threats to his life.

Many incidents and demonstrations by patriotic pro-French groups occurred during projection, and eventually the film was withdrawn in Brussels on the intervention of the French Ambassador. Critics and students protested – there was actually a 2,000-strong demonstration by young people in the streets, but to no avail. It was shown elsewhere in

Belgium with the addition of a pre-credit disclaimer, which has since turned up in the English print: "This episode of the 1914-18 war tells of the madness of certain men caught up in a whirlwind. It is an isolated case, in total contrast to the historic courage of the vast majority of French soldiers, champion of the ideal of liberty which at all times the French people have made their own."[16]

As for its reception in Germany:

> Stink bombs and riots have followed in the film's wake in Germany. When it opened in the British sector, a dozen French soldiers were thrown out of the house after tossing stink bombs into the audience. French authorities threatened to quit the Berlin Film Festival unless the objectionable film was withdrawn from play during the time of the Fest. And in an unprecedented move, the French commandant of Berlin invoked Allied Occupation Statute 501, forbidding any action which might harm the reputation of one of the occupying powers of Berlin, and withdrew the film from all theatres in the French sector of Berlin. After French servicemen demonstrated at the preem during the Berlin Film Festival, the pic was also withdrawn.

More significant still, *Paths of Glory* was banned from playing on the U.S. Army and Air Force Military Motion Pictures Circuit in Europe.[17]

Kubrick in his *Positif* interview maintained his disbelief that *Paths of Glory* was banned in France simply on political grounds. "One doesn't ban a film just for political reasons, especially when the events took place so long ago. Even for a government, that doesn't seem very sensible... I don't believe it was just because it was against war... and also I don't think films have so much effect on people, unfortunately. They can at most participate in a general ideological movement, but I don't know of any films which have had a real influence on political events."[18]

As Robert Hughes has pointed out, the difficulty of making war films other than the usual guts-and-glory type, which often enjoy free production values by courtesy of the Pentagon, are manifold: box-office pressures; governmental restrictions; the tendency to involve the audience in the drama and heroics of battle (warfare is cinegenic); the distaste at the popular level for films of despair and defeat; and the participation of star actors whose charisma always survives whatever defeats the characters suffer.

Rather than berate Kubrick for not overcoming some of these problems, I remain impressed that he was able to achieve as much as he did in the teeth of the difficulties. In his taste for symmetry and lateral tracking, his black-and white-lighting contrasts, the ironic counterpoint between dark cramped dug-outs and spacious chateau, the fascination with the strategy of destruction, and the schematisation of character, it's possible to discern the common binding force of Kubrick's powerful chess mentality. But this would be itself to over-schematise what is in fact, for all its simplifications, a film of intoxicating visual sophistication, intelligent, abrasive, moving, and best of all – subversive. It would unfortunately be six years before Kubrick would make such another.

1. Walter, Renaud. "Entretien avec Stanley Kubrick," *Positif*, December 1968-January 1969.
2. ibid.
3. Bernstein, Jeremy. "How About a Little Game?" *The New Yorker*, 12 November 1966.
4. Renaud. "Entretien avec Stanley Kubrick."
5. Gish, Lillian, with Pinchott, Ann. *The Movies, Mr. Griffith, And Me*, W.H. Allen, 1969.
6. Atkinson, Brooks, "*Paths of Glory*," *New York Times*, 27 September 1935.
7. The script approved by United Artists actually had the three condemned men reprieved at the last moment. But in preparing the script for the shoot, Kubrick could not go through with this compromise, and as it turned out UA executives did not remark on the changed ending.
8. Renaud. "Entretien avec Stanley Kubrick."
9. Cameron, Ian and Shivas, Mark. "Interview with Richard Lester," *Movie*, Winter 1968-69.
10. Renaud. "Entretien avec Stanley Kubrick."
11. Young, Colin. "The Hollywood War of Independence," *Film Quarterly*, Spring 1959.
12. Bernstein. "How About a Little Game?"
13. Renaud. "Entretien avec Stanley Kubrick."
14. ibid.

15. Kubrick, Stanley. "*Paths of Glory*," *L'Express*, 5 March 1959.
16. Translation of the French disclaimer.
17. Uncredited. "Military Bans 'Glory' from U.S. Armed Forces," *Variety*, 16 July 1958.
18. Renaud. "Entretien avec Stanley Kubrick."

6. Revolution as Entertainment
Spartacus (1960)

> Success can't hurt that boy. Stanley always knew he
> was good.
>
> Kirk Douglas,
> after completing *Paths of Glory*

> He'll be a fine director someday, if he falls flat
> on his face just once. It might teach him how to
> compromise.
>
> Kirk Douglas,
> after completing *Spartacus*

After *Paths of Glory*, various projects were announced by
Kubrick and Harris: another war film with Kirk Douglas
for United Artists; an adaptation of Martin Russ's Korean
war novel, *The Last Parallel*; Richard Adam's *The German
Lieutenant*, a novel partially based on the author's experience
as a Korean War paratrooper, to be adapted to a Second
World War setting; an adaptation of *I Stole $16,000,000*,
the autobiography of ex-safe-cracker Herbert Emerson
Wilson; a Civil War epic, starring Gregory Peck, based on
the adventures of Confederate Cavalry leader John Singleton
Mosby. In April 1958, Columbia disputed Kubrick and
Harris's registration with the Motion Picture Association
of America of the alternative titles of *7th Virginia Cavalry*
and *The 7th Virginia Cavalry Raiders* for the Peck film,
whereupon Kubrick and Harris registered the titles *1st
Cavalry*, *2nd Cavalry*, *3rd Cavalry*, *4th Cavalry* and *5th
Cavalry*. But neither this nor any of the other projects was
to materialise.

However, one of those impressed by Kubrick's work was
Marlon Brando. He hired Kubrick to direct his production
of *One-Eyed Jacks*, which was already in process of being
scripted (by Sam Peckinpah). According to Kubrick: "I
worked with [Brando] and Calder Willingham for more than
six months on the scenario. And then everything deteriorated.

The story was bad, we weren't listening to each other anymore and my rapport with Brando wasn't very good. So I left."[1] In a more recent interview, Kubrick says: "Our relationship ended amicably a few weeks before Marlon began directing the film himself."[2]

Not much more is known about this abortive collaboration, so one can only conjecture why things fell through. Kubrick may have thought the screenplay was becoming too lengthy (the original rough cut of *One-Eyed Jacks* has been variously reported as running from 8 to 35 hours); he may have objected to the sentimentality of the love scenes; or he might simply have wanted to reduce Brando's prominence in the picture, for *One-Eyed Jacks* is nothing if not a psycho-dramatic documentary on its star.

How much of Kubrick's contribution remains in the completed film is difficult to guess. But apart from the fact that it is co-scripted by Calder Willingham and includes in its cast three Kubrick players (Elisha Cook Jr., Timothy Carey and Slim Pickens), *One-Eyed Jacks* does have something of a Kubrick flavour; or rather the flavour of *Spartacus*, the film Kubrick was to make next and which was released before *One-Eyed Jacks*.

Artistically the two films are about on the same level – authoritative handling of the action sequences, maudlin treatment of the love interest. There is even a scene more or less common to both pictures: the heroine consoles the condemned hero with inspiring words about their baby. And, of course, there is the theme itself – admittedly not uncommon in Hollywood – of the implacable outsider pitting himself against the forces of corrupted law and order.

During this period, Kubrick subsisted on loans from his partner, James Harris. While his career appeared to be foundering, Kirk Douglas's Bryna/Universal production of Howard Fast's *Spartacus* was running into trouble. Originally announced in May 1958 to star and be directed by Sir Laurence Olivier on a budget of $4 million, Olivier had to withdraw from directing owing to other commitments, and the direction was eventually assigned to Anthony Mann.

In April 1958, Yul Brynner announced that his own production for United Artists of Arthur Koestler's *The Gladiators*, starring himself as Spartacus and directed by Martin Ritt, would begin shooting in Rome in the Autumn. Douglas and Brynner became involved in a title dispute. By July 1958, Brynner had won from the Motion Picture Association of America the right to use the title *Spartacus and the Gladiators*; then somewhere along the line decided to abandon the project, leaving the field free to Douglas. But Douglas's troubles were still not over.

Shooting had been in progress for one, two or three weeks (reports vary) before Mann had artistic disagreements with Douglas and left the picture (he was to work again with Douglas on *The Heroes of Telemark*). According to Mann, Douglas "wanted to insist on the message angle. I thought that the message would go over more easily by showing physically all the horrors of slavery. A film must be visual, too much dialogue kills it… Look at *The Fall of the Roman Empire*."[3]

Despite his experience with Brando, Kubrick accepted Kirk Douglas's invitation to take over the direction of *Spartacus*, thus becoming at 31 the youngest director ever to be entrusted with a multi-million-dollar Hollywood spectacular. The offer represented a welcome opportunity to direct again and to make some money, but it proved to be a painful experience. Kubrick explains:

> I believe there are some good things in *Spartacus*, but it was a bad subject. This film came after the long period which followed *Paths of Glory*. I had written a scenario for Kirk Douglas, which he didn't like, and then I did a rough outline scenario for a film set during the Civil War, which was dropped. I had worked with Marlon Brando for six months, and almost two years had passed since my last film, with nothing accomplished. So, when Kirk offered me the direction of *Spartacus* I thought, 'Perhaps I can make something of it.' But experience proves that if it's not explicitly stated in the contract that your

decisions will be respected, they won't be. I thought
that many things in the scenario would be changed in
the course of shooting, but they were not... Dalton
Trumbo wrote the scenario and Kirk Douglas said
Yes or No. I don't think the film has any political
significance. I believe that it's a bad rather summary
treatment of a historical personage.[4]

Kubrick has commented elsewhere on the film:
"*Spartacus* was the only film on which I didn't have absolute
control. I was the director they hired, almost in the old
Hollywood tradition. Kirk Douglas was the executive
producer; he and Dalton Trumbo, and his producer Eddy
Lewis, who worked for Kirk, did what they liked with the
scenario and the choice of actors... Obviously I directed the
actors, composed the shots and cut the film, so that, within
the weakness of the story, I tried to do the best I could."[5]

So Kubrick did not have complete artistic control over
Spartacus, but just how much control he had remains uncertain.
For instance, it was reported that on joining the production
he promptly replaced the German actress Sabina Bethmann
with Jean Simmons as Varinia, and then went to work with
Trumbo, changing the scenario, as Kubrick puts it, echoing
Anthony Mann, "to a more visual conception, and removing
all but two lines of Kirk's dialogue during the first half-hour of
the film's three hour-plus running time. We fought over that
one, but I won."[6] That Kubrick sometimes had his say over the
script certainly bothered Trumbo: "I prefer not to talk about
my relationship with Stanley Kubrick, which was very cool.
We disagreed over the conception of Spartacus's character, in
particular in the film's last scene which is very equivocal... In
my scenario, as in the book, Spartacus dies in combat and is
then crucified,* but Stanley Kubrick shot Spartacus dying on
the cross, an unfortunate allusion that has nothing to do with
the revolt."[7]

In fact, Howard Fast had been the first to work on the
screenplay. He claimed to be directly responsible for at least half

---

* Actually, Spartacus is not crucified, alive or dead, in the book. He simply
disappears.

of the finished script of the film version of the book and sought appropriate credit. But so substantially had Trumbo revised or bypassed Fast's original screenplay that the Writers Guild ruled against Fast and Trumbo received sole credit for the adaptation.[8]

Trumbo was one of the famous Unfriendly Ten jailed in 1947 for refusing to answer questions about their political affiliations put by the House Committee for Un-American Activities. A prolific screenwriter since 1936, he continued on his release from jail, like many other black-listed writers, to earn a living under pen-names; until in 1957 the Motion Picture Academy of Arts and Sciences was embarrassed to discover that under the pseudonym of "Robert Rich" he had been awarded an Oscar for his screenplay of *The Brave One*. In January 1959, the Academy publicly declared its ban to be "unworkable and impracticable" (not, notice, as "wrong"). Kirk Douglas wanted Trumbo to sign his real name to *Spartacus* but Universal Pictures was against the idea, so that as late as January 1960 the screenplay was being credited to "Sam Jackson" and Trumbo could not set foot on the set. According to Trumbo himself[9] it was only when Peter Ustinov and Charles Laughton leaked the writer's real identity to the press that Universal agreed to put Trumbo's name to the picture, thus becoming the first major studio to "defy" the ban. The studio was consequently attacked by the American Legion. Meanwhile, Otto Preminger, taking advantage of the change of mood in Hollywood, boldly announced that Trumbo as Trumbo would write *Exodus*. The blacklist was not broken by any means, but *Spartacus* and *Exodus* certainly marked an improvement in the situation. Trumbo's next script for Douglas, *Lonely are the Brave*, dealt with the last stand of a lone rogue cowboy against the legal encroachments of modern life – a variation, like *Spartacus*, on the theme of the politically oppressed outlaw.

In all these dealings, incidentally, Stanley Kubrick took no part. From the purchase of Howard Fast's novel to the world premiere took 33 months – 165 days being spent shooting. In 1960, *Spartacus* was the most expensive film ever made in Hollywood. It cost $12 million, of which it is said $4 million went to cover the cost of a six-minute battle scene shot in Spain. It took $14 million at the box-office, thus becoming the second most financially successful film of 1960 and, according to a 1962 *Variety* poll, the ninth biggest money-maker in the history of Hollywood.

Production details – according to publicity blurbs – were aptly astronomical: more than half a million dollars' worth of statues, military equipment, household furnishings, Roman army uniforms and assorted properties; 150 labourers simultaneously working on set construction, occupying four of Universal's largest sound stages and sprawling over the back-lot; Libyan desert scenes shot in Death Valley, California; 8,000 Spanish soldiers executing full-scale classical battle manoeuvres on a vast plain 40 kilometres outside Madrid. Even the seven versions the screenplay went through were cited in publicity as evidence of the film's lavishness.

The original cut of the film reputedly ran 4 hours 20 minutes. It was released in America at 196 minutes, including a 14-minute interval. Since, for distribution purposes, it had to have an "A" certificate, about three minutes were cut by the British censor. I understand that the same shots were cut in the U.S.A. to earn it an A3 (Adults Only) rating. The cuts included shots of limbs being hacked off in battle and of Crassus's face spattered with the blood of the Negro slave whose throat he has slit. In France the cuts included the oblique homosexually tinged scene between Crassus and Antoninus, his slave. Even after cutting, the film's brutality was noted by several reviewers, although by 1969 the scenes of violence strike one as relatively innocuous. *Spartacus* won three Academy Awards: for Colour Art Direction, Colour Cinematography, and Best Supporting Player – Peter Ustinov. Critical reaction, on the other hand, was very mixed.

Anthony Mann, who went on in 1963 to make an even more expensive Roman epic, *The Fall of the Roman Empire*, claims: "I worked nearly three weeks on what can properly be called the direction, and the entire prologue is mine: the slaves on the mountain, Peter Ustinov examining Douglas's teeth, the arrival at the school of gladiators and the antagonism with Charles McGraw... For the rest, and up to the escape, the picture is very faithful to my direction. Curious thing,

Kirk considered that Stanley Kubrick went a little too far with *Dr. Strangelove*."[10] Reports conflict as to whether Mann directed all the scenes in the gladiators' school (except those involving Jean Simmons) or whether he only prepared these scenes. Kubrick himself claims that none of Mann's footage appears in the completed film.

It's hardly surprising that a film of such chequered and disputed origin should have struck so many critics as an unsatisfying melange of the intelligent and the crass. On the whole, those who praised the film did so as a superior example of a genre generally reserved for brainless diversion and/or hollow edification, while those who were disappointed in the film viewed it rather in the context of Kubrick's artistic development.

Since *Spartacus* is in fact such a hybrid collaborative work, I propose to discuss it initially as a Hollywood phenomenon, before considering it as a possible expression of Kubrick's art. In fact, Spartacus offers a most instructive example of how a subject of revolutionary import becomes more and more diluted and compromised as its potential audience grows larger. After Arthur Koestler's 1939 novel about *Spartacus*, the subject undergoes progressive popularisation through Howard Fast's 1951 novel, and the Hollywood film version, until it reaches its ultimate (?) degeneration in the Italian sword-and-sandal pics, such as *Son of Spartacus* and *Revenge of Spartacus*, which exploit the subject for the sake of a strictly commercial relay of picturesquely violent fun and games.

※

What little is known about the real Spartacus is derived mainly from two differing second-hand accounts in the 2nd Century A.D. by Plutarch and Appian. Plutarch described Spartacus as a man "in understanding and gentleness superior to his condition." Of Thracian origin, he deserted the Roman army and became a brigand, only to be recaptured by the Romans and sold into slavery. He became a gladiator at the Imperial training school at Capua, and in 73 B.C. organised a break-out with 70 fellow gladiators armed with kitchen knives.

This isolated incident developed into the most serious of the internal challenges faced by Rome. With his fellow leaders, Crixus and Denomaus, he established his force in the then quiescent Mount Vesuvius crater and cleverly defeated the Consul sent on what was believed to be a minor mopping-up operation. The rebel band was soon joined by herdsmen, vagabonds, runaway slaves and released slaves until it reached the proportions of an army 12,000 strong which ravaged the countryside. Spartacus strove to restrain its savagery, but there was a perilous division in the high command. Seeing no hope of victory against Rome, Spartacus planned to move northwards and cross the Alps, thus enabling his followers to disperse to their own countries and homes. Crixus wanted to continue plundering in Italy, broke away with his Gaulish and German followers and was killed in battle soon after. Instead of proceeding north, Spartacus for some reason went south. But the Mediterranean pirates who were to have carried him out of Italy betrayed him, and Spartacus was trapped by a shore-to-shore line of earthworks laid down by Crassus, a millionaire politician seeking to steal political limelight from his rival, Pompey. Spartacus broke through the fortifications into the north again but after further battles and splits in high command finally succumbed to Crassus, although Pompey managed to take some of the credit for the victory. Six thousand prisoners were crucified along the Appian Way from Rome to Capua. In this, the first great popular uprising in history, Spartacus succeeded in defeating the Roman army nine times, gravely threatening Roman power.

The Spartacist movement founded in Germany in 1919, out of which developed the German Communist party, was inspired by the revolt of 73 B.C. Spartacus's great struggle has also inspired, prior to 1960, at least one ballet (by Khachaturian), one play, three Italian films and two novels. In 1931, the distinguished American tragedian, Edwin Forrest, played Spartacus in *The Gladiator* by Robert Montgomery Bird, the first play in English ever to have a thousand performances during its author's lifetime. In 1913 the Pasquali Film company made *Spartacus, or the Gladiator of Thrace*, following it up a year later with *Spartacus, or the*

Revolt of the Gladiators. At least one of these silent films is still shown at the Cinémathèque française and apparently includes a spectacular Mount Vesuvius sequence. In 1952, Riccardo Freda made *Spartaco* with Massimo Girotti (called in England *Spartacus the Gladiator* and in the U.S.A. *The Sins of Rome*).

The novels are both by ex-communists. Arthur Koestler's *The Gladiators* (1939), sticking closely to the known facts, is a tough, unsentimental and finally pessimistic analysis of the causes of revolutionary failure. Drawing on Koestler's own experience of both Russia and Spain, it is a compelling imaginative feat. It attributes the failure of Spartacus's revolt in particular and, by implication, of revolutions in general to the lack of a coherent programme and creed, and to internecine conflicts. Incidentally, the novel includes a scene reminiscent of *Paths of Glory* (written three years earlier), in which Crassus orders every tenth man in the regiment that fled Crixus's army to be flogged to death in full view of his comrades.

Howard Fast's novel is very different in approach. Written in 1951 at the height of McCarthyism, Fast failed to find a publisher and was obliged to publish the book at his own expense and sell it on subscription. It has by now sold three million copies in 45 languages. It's hard to understand today how this innocuous romance could ever have been considered subversive. Heavily – too heavily – researched, written in a woolly epic-romantic style, and full of facile aphorisms, the book tells us a good deal about a decadent society organised on the basis of slave labour. But where Koestler is cool, piercing and unsentimental, Fast is effusive, romantic and misty-eyed. Spartacus becomes an idealised Christ-like figure, enjoying a beautiful relationship with a tall, full-breasted, golden-haired German maiden, Varinia, who fights beside him, idolises him and remains faithful to his memory. Unlike Koestler, Fast's interest in the question "why did we fail?" is merely rhetorical, or rather he believes that the revolt did not fail insofar as it took place. The slave army is consistently unified and aims at nothing less than the overthrow of the entire world system. Despite Fast's understanding of the commercial basis of gladiatorial combat, his awareness of the processes of political mystification and his undoubted compassion, it is clear that for him the revolt is a simple confrontation between good and evil, the rebels consciously standing for brotherhood, equality, solidarity, respect for life, common ownership – and strict monogamy!

It's unfortunate – but perhaps inevitable – that this inspirational best-seller version of the Spartacus story, with its pseudo-religious elements and copious love interest, should have been filmed rather than Koestler's biting novel (although what Brynner and Ritt might have made of it is open to question). The flavour of the whole enterprise is conveyed by Kirk Douglas's revealingly homespun statement: "*Spartacus* has been the most exciting challenge of my career. The production as a whole and the character of Spartacus in particular. Don't think of him as an action hero. Somehow, people seem to think that men with muscles have no brains. But Spartacus was a good general and a human being who had a dream he wanted to accomplish. The spiritual side of his character is even more important than his physical side."[11]

In the film version, nearly everything is appropriated to the requirements of a specific commercial genre: the Hollywood star-vehicle multi-million-dollar costume spectacular. To say that a subject is appropriated to a genre means that there must be a thorough readjustment of emphasis on character, situation, and narrative line, in order that certain conventional values may prevail over others. If, as in *Spartacus*, one is dealing with the explosive subject of revolution, then the subject must be so processed and "cleansed" that it can be experienced in a way that is stimulating but not really disturbing. After all, the picture has to make money. The problems and implications of revolutionary activity are shorn of danger and challenge, the subject is rendered safe and harmless. This is achieved in *Spartacus* by the classic sterilising techniques of (a) distancing, (b) personalising, (c) simplification, and (d) rhetoric.

Distancing is attempted by the opening commentary which informs us that what we are about to see took place before the coming of a new faith called Christianity put an end to slavery. Thus we are enjoined not to think of the Spartacus revolt as having any political relevance to our own times, times in which, of course, slavery does not exist. For all its blurring of the issues, Fast's novel does attempt to relate the revolt to contemporary industrial society; he provides a brief account of how political mystification works in a democracy, and also contrives a scene in the best naturalist tradition in which after the revolt Crassus takes some aristocratic visitors around his perfume factory, and dismisses the suggestion that the condition of his factory workers could be equated with those of the slaves... Naturally, there is no hint of this in the film version.

Personalising and simplification function to distract the viewer from the real revolutionary issues and make the story more wholesome. In the Fast novel (as in Koestler's), events are seen refracted, as it were, through the recollections and thoughts of several Romans who came into contact with Spartacus; the novel proceeds by a series of linked un-chronological flashbacks, not unlike the structure of *The Killing*. Spartacus is thus glimpsed obliquely as a rather enigmatic rebel spirit. The film, on the other hand, resorts to conventional chronology, fixing our attention from the beginning on Spartacus as the man to watch out for, a rebellious and dangerous character inclined to help a fallen comrade rather than get on with his back-breaking labour in the salt-mines. Arriving at the gladiators' training school, he is again immediately singled out as a probable trouble-maker. Is it Spartacus or Kirk Douglas, the star, one wonders, who is being brought well into focus as a hero-figure? And what is consequently being defocussed?

Spartacus is represented as unique not only in his rebelliousness but in his ability to inspire love, for he alone of the gladiators develops a romantic attachment with a slave-girl, Varinia (her nationality changed in the film from German to British, eighteen years before Caesar invaded Britain). The growing love between this underprivileged pair is dwelled upon at the same time as Crassus, on a visit with his entourage to witness a privately arranged combat, registers his sexual interest in Varinia, buys her, and arranges to have her sent to him the following day. Thus, the relationship between the military protagonists, Spartacus and Crassus, is tightened more closely even than in the novel, providing an emotional framework through which the revolt can be easily understood: sexual rivalry. It is when Spartacus hears that Varinia is to be sold that he launches his crucial attack on the guard that precipitates the outbreak; the rebellion is therefore triggered by the threat of romantic separation. When at the end, Gracchus, the demagogic politician, remarks to Varinia, "So this is the woman it took eight [sic] Roman legions to conquer" we are left in no doubt as to what all the bloodshed was really about.

This is not, of course, to suggest that Spartacus is not also shown to be motivated by hatred of Roman oppression and compassion for his fellow men. This is heavily established by having Draba strung up for refusing to kill Spartacus in combat, the very gladiator who resisted friendship with Spartacus for fear of confronting him in the arena. Nor is it to suggest that sexual repression is not a legitimate cause for revolt. After all, the 1968 upheavals in France were precipitated by student complaints about hostel sleeping restrictions. But in *Spartacus* the personalised sexual triangle is used as the fundamental emotional premise of the story.

There is no suggestion of serious internal strife in the slave army. In reality Spartacus had a hard, mainly unsuccessful time trying to curb Crixus's disorderly elements, but in the film he and Crixus remain buddies to the end. As well as being unified, the slave army is depicted as being pretty consistently humane. We witness no looting, no sacking of Roman villas, nor do we see soldiers being killed in a battle which has only one Roman survivor, the consul Glabrus (has the sequence perhaps been cut?). True, Spartacus has to stop his men from setting two elderly Roman senators to fight each other like gladiators. But the reality was less edifying: Spartacus himself is said to have set 300 prisoners to fight against each other in expiation of Crixus's defeat and death. Such human failings have no place in the film. Nor is there room for the idea, as there is at least in the novel, that the soldiers are as much slaves in their condition as the rebels they are ordered to fight.

The rhetoric in the film – hackneyed phrases posturing as deep sentiment – occurs, for instance, when Spartacus addresses his slave army: "We've travelled a long ways together. We've fought many battles and won great victories... Maybe there's no peace in this world for us or for anyone else. But I do know that as long as we live we must stay true to ourselves. I do know that we're brothers, and I know that we're free." Staged to suggest the Sermon on the Mount, the shots of all those smiling peasant faces gazing trustfully up at Kirk Douglas are unsavoury as well as sentimental.

Spartacus is Kirk Douglas's film. In a star vehicle the star must survive as long as possible. So instead of expiring in battle, Spartacus is not only preserved but actually identified personally by Crassus, who makes him fight against his former slave, Antoninus, now Spartacus's loyal friend. And Varinia, who daffily gives birth to her child on the very night of the final big battle (another neat equation of the personal with the political) is permitted not only to see Spartacus on the cross but hold out to him her new-born baby and utter the lines, "Goodbye, my love, my life, goodbye, goodbye," before driving off into the future accompanied by, of all people, Batiatus, master of the gladiators' training school! In what sense, one wonders, is her baby "born free"?

This final uplifting note is one of Hollywood's identikit sets of liberal, inspirational endings. It can be seen, for instance, at the end of *Viva Zapata!*, in the image of Zapata's white horse stalking the hills – the spirit of revolt symbolically living on. (We are rarely allowed to see the spirit of oppression living on too – that would be too depressing.) *Spartacus* and *Viva Zapata!* can be instructively compared in other ways. Zapata, the peasant rebel leader, stays awake on his wedding night brooding unhappily over his inability to read. Spartacus, lingering in a moonlit glade with Varinia, similarly laments his ignorance: "I want to know where the wind comes from, where the sun goes at night, why the Moon changes shape." In *Viva Zapata!*, the scene ends with Zapata's bride beginning to teach him how to read. Spartacus's hunger for knowledge ends in a good old-fashioned clinch on the grass.

Of course, the film has its welcome reticences and restraints. No public gladiatorial displays, no tame upper-class orgies à la *Quo Vadis*, no verbal archaism (although some of the lines, on the other hand, sound as American as apple pie). While the underdogs utter the usual lugubriously earnest lines about freedom and love, the villains have some refreshingly literate shafts of irony and wit. We are spared the most Hollywood-inspired image in the novel: Spartacus striding off at the head of his army with his arm around Varinia's waist; and the long sentimental rapprochement between the elderly Gracchus and Varinia is mercifully reduced in the film to a brief kiss on his forehead. The first part of the screenplay, no doubt aided by Kubrick's cuts, manages very well to convey the terrible indignity of men treated as so much meat: Batiatus showing off his stable of studs to the lascivious Roman ladies, Spartacus crying, "I'm not an animal" to Batiatus as he and Varinia are watched in their cell, and Varinia's response: "Neither am I." There is restraint also in Alex North's martial musical score which, although lapsing into cinemuzak when Varinia is around, is less banal than usual.

Spartacus is, of course, partly a cash-in on the profitable gory barbarisms of Bryna's *The Vikings*, but it also suggests at times an anachronistic version of the War of Independence, with the suave British heavies in their togas lined up against the more rustically garbed American underdogs – an impression reinforced by the fact that only a year earlier Douglas and Olivier were pitted against each other in *The Devil's Disciple*.

Olivier, Laughton, and, in a certain sense, Ustinov, all give splendid performances, and one of the pleasures of the movie is seeing any two of these actors playing in conjunction. Olivier as Crassus is at his most silkily poised and authoritative, a sharp saturnine senator with a profile lifted straight off a Roman coin. It's reported that he and Ustinov, dissatisfied with their lines, rewrote some of them themselves. Olivier commented: "I play it head on. I have to, because the script keeps changing, and you can't know what the whole is going to be until the picture is finally edited together. And so you attack each scene as best you can, with the knowledge of your role as worked out between you and the director, and simply hope for the best."[12] Laughton, donning the toga for the first time since the thirties (*The Sign of the Cross* and *I, Claudius*), and Peter Ustinov have a fine meal scene together, the two beefy actors conveying relish in their preposterous roles. Ustinov's Batiatus, said to be based on a theatrical agent of his acquaintance, owes surely as much to his previous Roman incarnation as Nero in *Quo Vadis*: unfinished ingratiating gestures, shifty glances, hands fluttering nervously, voice cautious and vacillating. There is a refreshing whiff of improvisation when in the opening Libyan mines sequence, after testily complaining to his sunshade-bearer that "The sun's over *here*," he mutters: "What do you pay these people for?" The trouble with the performance, though, is that he makes Batiatus such a loveably laughable rogue that we scarcely have time to consider his vicious social role, an unscrupulous dealer in human flesh who runs the biggest gladiators' training school in Italy. Thus an Academy award-winning performance serves to distract us from grim social reality.

The remaining performers are there strictly for decoration. Kirk Douglas, with a slick butch haircut and haggard face that sometimes makes him look uncannily like Karloff as Frankenstein's monster, turns in his usual inexpressive portrait of stubborn integrity under stress. I will settle for Brendan Gill's comment in *The New Yorker*: "There is something about the desperately conscientious way he throws himself into a role without embodying it that I begin to consider endearing."[13]

Jean Simmons, veteran of several Ancient Roman movies (*Caesar and Cleopatra*, *The Robe*, *Androcles and the Lion*) looks lovely – lovely enough not to be rendered in romantic soft-focus, as she is in her post-natal scenes with Olivier – but, handicapped by the script and her high, ingenue's voice, she is never much more than just cute or sorrowful. Douglas's old *Vikings* buddy, Tony Curtis, turned down a role in the abortive Brynner-Ritt *Gladiators* to make a guest appearance as Antoninus, poet, singer and magician. When this unlikely Brooklyn bard replies to Crassus's question, "Whom do you sing for?" with the words "For d'children of my master for whom I also taught d'classics," one's suspensions of disbelief groan under the strain. After his final, fatal combat with Douglas, the sight of these two wealthy, plainly indestructible Hollywood film stars, declaring their father-son love for each other is an embarrassing one indeed.

*

While it's possible to detect stylistic qualities in *Spartacus* which are recognisably Kubrick's, I think it true that on the whole his individuality, pressed into the service of the genre, is submerged and rendered anonymous. The style of the film, in fact, varies from the finely executed action sequences to the artificiality of the love scenes, over which hovers the saccharine spirit of Cecil B. DeMille.

It is in the action sequences that Kubrick, displaying his fine compositional flair, is at his best: the branding of the slaves; the training of the gladiators and later of the slave army, a body daubed with paint to illustrate its vulnerable points, targets of fruit sliced in two by charging armed horsemen; above all, the exhilarating uprising sequence, in which superb use is made of the tall spiked railings surrounding the gladiators' compound. First it is scaled, then one section falls forward towards the camera with men clinging to it, crushing others beneath it; finally, it is picked up and used as a deadly ram against the guards. The whole sequence is staged and edited with thrilling forcefulness. Kubrick is as successful with his epic images: hordes of slaves sweeping down one side of a valley while those in the van climb diagonally across the other side of the valley towards the camera; the beautiful shot, opening the second part of the film, of the rebel army encamped by the sea at dusk; and the final battle preliminaries, the Roman army advancing in spaced-out cohorts across the length of the wide screen towards the still line of the slave army in the foreground, stopping, running, regrouping, a mobile glinting quilt stretching back endlessly to the horizon. The calm symmetrical deliberation of these authentic manoeuvres have something of the beauty and tension of *Henry V* and *Alexander Nevsky*. And when the rebels release flaming logs on the advancing Romans, the flames really do seem to engulf the soldiers. The spirit of Olivier's *Henry V* is present elsewhere in the movie: Spartacus is seen to patrol his camp the night before the battle, affectionately greeting his people who gaze up at him with looks of respect, love and admiration. This is rather less stirring than the fine post-battle scene in which the survivors all claim to be their leader, crying "I am Spartacus."

While the action sequences are brilliantly achieved, the Roman sequences are disappointing. The Senate, though it may be a historically accurate reconstruction, is unimpressively set and the scenes are staged with a stiff theatricality which increases the air of phoniness. One brief scene outside the senate allows us virtually our only glimpse of the teeming streets of Rome and its plebs – a few aimless extras wandering across an otherwise deserted street. The domestic interiors are equally as unconvincing, recalling at times the garish vulgarity of *Quo Vadis*. One interior scene does have atmosphere: Crassus's suggestive conversation with Antoninus, as he is bathed, the whole warmly lit scene shot in one take through a gauze curtain. It's a pity, however, that the psychological basis of the scene is so implausible, as if in Ancient Rome a senator would have to make a pass at a slave by means of coy hints concerning his taste for both oysters and snails!

But all this will pass. What is appalling are the two or three scenes set in woodland glades at dusk, involving romantic encounters between Spartacus and Varinia. In the first he meets her on the road after the breakout, in the second the slaves are encamped listening to Antoninus, the "magician," perform and sing, and in the third Varinia is discovered bathing in the nude before announcing her pregnancy. These chocolate-box pastorals are shot in ridiculously obvious studio set-ups complete with lurid Technicolor skies. The film reaches its apogee of corniness in a shot of Spartacus sweeping Varinia across a sunset horizon like something out of *Duel in the Sun*. The love scenes are so blatantly bad as to make one seriously suspect that when he shot them Kubrick not only had his tongue in his cheek but his boot unlovingly up Kirk Douglas's arse.

One must also record one or two bits of carelessness in continuity: some mid-scene colour continuity botches, and some remarkable transformations undergone by Varinia's baby at the end. One moment it's a dummy prop wrapped in a shawl, next a real screaming baby being held up to Spartacus on the cross, next – with no transition – fast asleep in mum's arms.

Despite such embarrassments, something of the Kubrick of *Paths of Glory* is present. One notices the careful use of low-key lighting contrasts in the cell scenes in the gladiators' school, shot in warm dark browns, figures isolated in darkness, in contrast to the spacious yet sterile-looking Roman scenes. Also, again, his fondness for symmetrical set-ups, like that of the four gladiators waiting for their entry in the hut, the doors of which are opened to reveal the aristocratic spectators dead centre of the screen; the tracking shots in the opening mining scenes (if indeed shot by Kubrick); Spartacus reviewing his slave army encampment; the vistas of dead slave bodies. There are some striking compositions: Batiatus inviting his wealthy female patrons to select gladiators for the combat, speaking to them off left of the screen before they come into view; the first combat shot through the slates of the hut. There is also a scene strongly reminiscent of *Paths of Glory*: Spartacus and Antoninus, the only survivors of the final battle, ask each other in hushed tones whether they are afraid to die. And the shots of the faces of women, children and old folk in the rebel army remind one of the faces of the emotionally overcome soldiers at the end of *Paths of Glory*. Some of these images in their context are dangerously close to cuteness and sentimentality, but there is a genuine tenderness in the photography. One feels at times that these are not just any old extras but a real community on the march.

How then does *Spartacus* stand as an expression of Kubrick's art? Skilfully, even thrillingly executed as many of the scenes are, I'm not sure that, embedded as they are in the mere routine Hollywood footage, they are much more than one might expect of any expert Hollywood craftsman. Could one, in short, confidently identify Kubrick as the director if one had not seen his name on the credits?

Kubrick himself, constraints notwithstanding, is on record as saying: "It's just as good as *Paths of Glory* and certainly there's as much of myself in it."[14] The statement, made close upon the film's release, is perhaps best interpreted as discreet public relations talk, but it is true that the subject is one that he might well have chosen himself. The theme, he has stated, has direct parallels with his other film work, for "it concerns the outsider, who is passionately committed to action against the social order. I mean the outsider in the Colin Wilson sense – the criminal, maniac, poet, lover, revolutionary."[15]

The theme of *Spartacus*, as it happens, does fall within the mainstream of Kubrick's work, relating in particular to *Paths of Glory*. Here again the concepts of totalitarian order and underdog decency are personified in two determined protagonists. But what must also be noted is that this is the standard melodramatic formula for countless dramas, especially Hollywood dramas, especially Hollywood Westerns and Spectaculars, which largely depend on such broad simplistic confrontations for their narrative drive. *Paths of Glory* and *Spartacus* both suffer from simplification and polarisation, but *Paths of Glory*, though it may have been compromised in some ways by certain commercial pressures, excites and ravishes in a way that *Spartacus* does not, because it bears the stamp of its director's intelligence and taste, while in *Spartacus* his individuality is sunk not without trace, but well into the depths.

Kubrick has said: "The important thing in film is not so much to make successes as not to make failures, because each failure limits your opportunities to make the films you want to make."[16] *Spartacus*, in this respect, was clearly not a failure. It is superior to most Hollywood Spectaculars, but that isn't saying very much. One would be indeed naive to expect a film of real revolutionary impact to be made within the Hollywood studio system. Clancy Sigal, in a perceptive review, has the measure of *Spartacus* when he describes it as "a model of high-minded commercialism, a deafening example of what Mr. Dwight MacDonald calls 'mid-cult' and what I call discerning mediocrity."[17] So, too, from their somewhat different standpoints, have the *Motion Picture Herald* – "a great human story" – and the *Hollywood Reporter*, with whose definitive summary of the picture[18] I can't resist closing this chapter:

"Said to have cost more money than any other motion picture ever made in Hollywood, Spartacus is a credit to Hollywood and a credit to money... It is a magnificent picture, spectacle to dazzle the eye, political conflict to tease the mind, intimacy to hug the heart... It is a cruel and bloody narrative, but its central story line is one that will be particularly appreciated by women, and they will best respond to its bittersweet ending, an anguished note of hope and faith." Reserving a discreet neutrality on the question of Trumbo's employment on the picture, it reassuringly concludes: "At any rate, there is nothing more subversive in *Spartacus* than contained in the Bill of Rights and the Fourteenth Amendment."

Spartacus loses again.

1. Walter, Renaud. "Entretien avec Stanley Kubrick," *Positif,* December 1968-January 1969.
2. Gelmis, Joseph. *The Film Director As Superstar* (Doubleday, 1970).
3. Mann, Anthony. "A Lesson in Cinema," *Cahiers du Cinéma* in English, December 1967.
4. Renaud. "Entretien avec Stanley Kubrick."
5. Kohler, Charlie. "Stanley Kubrick Raps," *Eye,* August 1968.
6. Uncredited. "*Spartacus,*" *New York Times,* 2 October 1960.
7. Château, René. "Entretiens avec Michael Wilson et Dalton Trumbo," *Positif,* August/September 1964.
8. Uncredited. "Credit to Trumbo Disputed by Fast," *New York Times,* 23 February 1960.
9. Château, "Entretiens avec Michael Wilson et Dalton Trumbo."
10. Mann, "A Lesson in Cinema."
11. Laing, Nora. "£3,500,000 Film Is Wrapped Up After 115 Days' Shooting." *Evening News,* 11 September 1959.
12. Knight, Arthur. "The Many Faces of Sir Laurence," *Saturday Review,* 11 October 1960.
13. Gill, Brendan. "*Spartacus,*" *The New Yorker,* 15 October 1960.
14. Uncredited. "*Spartacus,*" *New York Times,* 2 October 1960.
15. ibid.
16. Schumach, Murray. "Trumbo Will Get Credit for Script," *New York Times,* 8 August 1960.
17. Sigal, Clancy. "Slaughter Sugar-Coated," *Time and Tide,* 17 December 1960.
18. Uncredited. "*Spartacus,*" *The Hollywood Reporter,* 7 October 1960.

7. How Did They Ever Make a Film of...?
Lolita (1961)

> ...pity no film had recorded the curious
> pattern, the monogrammatic linkage of our
> simultaneous or overlapping moves.
>
> If you want to make a movie out of my book, have
> one of these faces gently melt into my own, while
> I look.
>
> Vladimir Nabokov, Lolita (1955)

While *Paths of Glory* was being edited, Kubrick and Harris outbid four other companies for the film rights of *Lolita*, very shortly after its first publication in the U.S.A and hired the author, Vladimir Nabokov, to write the screenplay. It cost them $150,000. Initially they approached Warner Bros. for backing but Warners' lucrative offer of $1 million plus 50% of the profits entailed having the script vetted by the company. Kubrick and Harris were not prepared to relinquish artistic control and the project was eventually set up with Ray Stark-Seven Arts Productions. Other companies meanwhile tried unsuccessfully to buy the film rights from them for as much as $650,000.

It was decided to make the film in England for several reasons. Firstly, Peter Sellers, one of the stars, was in the process of getting a divorce and couldn't leave the country for extended periods; secondly, there was some danger in the U.S.A. of interference from various moralistic and patriotic organisations which had put on pressure to have the project aborted; and thirdly – perhaps relatedly – the necessary funds for making the film were not available in the U.S.A. Making the film in England, according to Kubrick, was supposed "to mitigate censorship problems."[1]

Kubrick's and Harris's statements to the British press on arrival in England seemed calculated to allay fears that the film might deprave and corrupt: "We regard it as a masterpiece and we intend to handle it with delicacy and dignity."[2] "We will keep all of Nabokov's drama in, but will eliminate anything that might be considered offensive."[3] "The relationship between Humbert and the girl is more psychological than erotic."[4] And in an interview in *Film Quarterly*, Kubrick declared that his primary interest was to explore the development of Humbert Humbert's character. He didn't plan to change the ages of the principles or their relationship, but, he stated, he and Harris had a "way" of handling the subject which allowed them to consider making the film at all.[5] This "way" presumably answered the question which blared from the posters: "How did they ever make a film of *Lolita*?"

This cautious approach was, of course, due to the fact that *Lolita*, Nabokov's thirteenth and favourite novel, written at the age of 55, was scandalously concerned with a sexual liaison between a middle-aged man and a 12-year-old girl. Published initially in 1955 by the notorious Olympia Press of Paris, its eventual publication in Britain and the U.S.A. stirred up one of those fatuous literary controversies as to whether it was a masterpiece, a work of obscenity, or both.

So hot was the subject that a number of actors are said to have shied away from the role of Humbert in the film version. "We want a top rank male actor like Olivier or Niven or Ustinov," Harris had said.[6] Olivier was definitely offered the role but other commitments intervened. It's not known how many actors were unable to accept the role before it finally settled upon James Mason.

Some three or four hundred girls between the ages of 13 and 20 were seen before the crucial role of Lolita was awarded to Sue Lyon, who had been acting professionally for only a few months, mainly playing television bit parts. Kubrick and Harris were sufficiently impressed by her screen-test with Mason to offer her a seven-year contract – the only performer to be so contracted by the partnership, although she was to make no more films for them. Her favourite activities were swimming, dancing, listening to pop music and going to the movies, and – a deliciously Nabokovian touch – she had actually won a Smile of the Year contest organised by Los Angeles dentists.[7] (Quilty's Uncle Ivor, it may be remembered, was a dentist.)

The film was shot at Elstree Studios from November 1960 to March 1961 under conditions of great secrecy, Sue Lyon being kept completely protected from publicity. This served only to increase the air of sensationalism with which the film was surrounded and which was, of course, totally beyond Kubrick's control. Two different versions of the film's total cost are in circulation: $2,250,000 (£750,000) and about $1,500,000 (£500,000).

In February 1962, M-G-M outbid several other major companies for the world distribution rights. The deal was only clinched after the film obtained the approval of the Production Code of the Motion Picture Association of America and the seal of the Catholic-based Legion of Decency. On condition that about thirty seconds of cuts were made, the Legion withheld its "Condemned" rating, placing the film in a "separate classification," which banned under-18s from seeing it in the States. A further condition was that no reference be made to the book for promotional purposes.

Despite this qualified official blessing the film was banned outright in Ireland. In England, it received an "X" certificate, although Kubrick had hoped for an "A." Middle-aged men, the category of person most likely to fall about in lust and depravity on seeing the picture, were not excluded. According to Kubrick, "even after it was finished, it laid around for six months."[8] A hot property indeed.

Despite its restricted audience, *Lolita* was a big box-office success. Opening in the U.S.A. in June 1962, it played to record-breaking business there and (in a cruelly dubbed version) in Germany, before coming to Britain in September 1962. Sue Lyon, having reached the age of 16 years and 2 months, was legally entitled to see the picture.

Even before the film was submitted to the British Board of Film Censors, unsuccessful attempts were made, notably by Canon John Collins' Council for Christian Action, to pressure the Board into refusing the film a certificate. In his correspondence with Collins, Kubrick stated: "I regret that you and your council have found it necessary to devote time to something which you will find completely unobjectionable."

From the point of view of Canon Collins, Kubrick was, unfortunately, right. The film of *Lolita* is, however, objectionable on other grounds.

*

Of Kubrick's independently made films (*Spartacus* must be excepted), *Lolita* seems to me to be his only failure; and a very puzzling failure at that, insofar as it largely lacks the very stylistic qualities which distinguish his other work in the cinema, qualities that would have admirably suited this particular subject. It is often argued that source material should not be taken into account when evaluating film adaptations. But even if the novel, *Lolita*, were not so well known as to make it impossible not to have it in mind while viewing the film, I would contend that some understanding of the film's stylistic peculiarities – peculiar, that is, in the context of Kubrick's work as a whole – can be found by considering the film's nature as an adaptation.

Before shooting, Kubrick consulted John Trevelyan, the Secretary of the British Board of Film Censors, as every director must who considers filming a controversial subject. Precisely what advice was given by Trevelyan may be deduced not only from the film itself but from Kubrick's frank admission that he could not introduce any eroticism into the film or it would never have been released.[9]

The absence of eroticism, rather than the casting of Sue Lyon, is the one feature of the film which Kubrick really regrets. "I believe many viewers were disappointed because they'd heard about the troubles over distributing the film and found that there was nothing shocking in the picture. The film was true to their characters, their psychology in the novel, but it didn't have all the violent sexual element it should have had."[10]

While shooting *Paths of Glory*, Kubrick stated that he was resolutely against the adaptation of great novels to the screen, but later he qualified this in justifying a film version of *Lolita*.[11] "I believed it was possible to make a great film of *Lolita*. If it's like a game of chess that's only because of the absence of eroticism. I believe there are great novels, particularly in the nineteenth-century tradition, of such complex structure, in which memories intermingle, the comments of the author, etc., that they can't be adapted to the cinema. Whereas *Lolita* is in fact the simple moving account of certain events, and not only the thoughts, impressions, philosophy, etc. of the author. I believed *Lolita* was feasible."[12]

"The simple moving account of certain events." It is not just the absence of eroticism, then, that makes the film so disappointingly flat and theatrical, but also, it seems, Kubrick's puzzling disregard for the novel's thematic and structural complexity. His principal objective, he has stated, was to "render something of the characters and situation," to "stay faithful to the spirit of the novel." But does the desexualising of the relationships and a simplistic conception of the novel make such fidelity possible? The question would not matter so much if stylistic atrophy had not resulted.

The completed film does not follow very closely the screenplay actually written by Nabokov. As Kubrick states in his revealing *Positif* interview: "There was very little in the scenario that wasn't already in the book. Nabokov had in certain instances selected different passages from the book and put them into a different dramatic form."[13] While, for instance, parts of the dialogue of the opening murder sequence were retained from Nabokov's screenplay, the after-the-party debris and the ping-pong match were created on the set. And the bathroom scene in which the apparently grief-stricken Humbert is consoled by Charlotte's friends appears neither in the novel nor in Nabokov's screenplay; the idea arose during rehearsals. There is also a good deal of improvised dialogue in the film, notably from Peter Sellers.

Familiar Nabokovian alliterations are present: "Oh, excuse the soiled sock," "It's a tragic treasure," "Must you pamper your pimples," "Queer, how I misinterpreted the designation of doom." There are a few felicitous additions – Charlotte remarks "Humbert Humbert – what a thrillingly different name," and Lolita's husband, Richard, calls Humbert "Dad" and "Professor Haze." But for the most part the dialogue is surprisingly banal and the novel's dazzling incongruity of detail is absent. To take a small example: when Humbert re-encounters the married Lolita, a friend of her husband is present who cuts his hand opening a bottle. In the novel, because the friend is one-armed, it becomes a piercingly vivid detail. In the film, because for some reason he is not one-armed, the cut hand becomes pointless. But then the whole scene at Richard Schiller's, with its long theatrical exposition of what we already know about Quilty goes on endlessly, diluted by the absence of odd physical detail that makes the scene glitter in the novel.

Let us consider the main characters: Humbert Humbert, Lolita, Clare Quilty and Charlotte Haze, as they are conceived and acted in the film.

Save for a very fleeting use of the word "nymphet" in a brief narrated diary extract, we learn nothing and see nothing of Humbert's taste for pre-pubescent girls in general, nor do we hear anything of his unconsummated childhood affair with the 13-year-old Annabel Leigh, the affair that may have traumatically created his fixation. He is thus deprived both of his past and his nympholepsy.

James Mason is less an actor than a screen personality, deploying his urbanity within fairly narrow limits of silky poised sophistication. Once before, in *The Seventh Veil*, he suffered from a secret passion for a young girl – his ward, Ann Todd. His performance in *Lolita*, one of two or three of which he is proud in a long career, is not bad as far as it goes, which is certainly beyond his usual range, but is still not far enough.

He manages very well the "tender-hearted," morbidly sensitive, infinitely circumspect hero, the melancholia and the old-world politeness, but conveys next to nothing of the secret predator behind the mask. The ape is absent in Mason's Humbert, the beast who in the novel so brilliantly insults his neighbours on his return to Ramsdale. Passively playing off the other actors, initiating nothing, he becomes a wilting nervous fellow, lacking the vein of fierce self-deprecating irony that dispels all suspicion of sentimentality in the novel. Mason is at his best on the veranda of the Enchanted Hunters hotel, politely evading Quilty's intrusive questions, and in his bathroom scene after Charlotte's death, and he maintains a fine sickly smile as he hears from Charlotte that Lolita is to be sent away. But one is tempted to speculate what an actor with a stronger comic edge might have imparted to the role. Olivier (involved with immature young girls in *Rebecca* and *Term of Trial*), Ustinov or Peter Sellers could have been devastating.

Humbert's first sight – and our own – of Lolita, craftily defines her for the rest of the movie. She is discovered sunbathing in the garden, wearing a bikini, sunhat and sunglasses, reading a book (a book! Lolita?) and listening to a transistor radio. Lingeringly framed in a pose not unlike publicity shots for *Baby Doll* and *Et Dieu... créa la femme*, she is firmly and deliberately established as a shapely, seductive teenager. She looks like a Hollywood starlet rather than a pre-pubescent girl trying to look like a Hollywood starlet. Her appraising stare at Humbert over her sunglasses is insolently self-assured, poised and knowing.

No red-blooded male in the audience, white, widowed or otherwise, has any difficulty in identifying with Humbert in finding this blonde and evidently available young chick desirable. What attracts Humbert to Lolita in the novel is her "indefiniteness," the fact that she is balanced between childhood and puberty. But this knowing teenage doll is very definitely with it, we are with Humbert all the way for fancying it, and it comes as no surprise to hear that Charley of Camp Climax has already had it.

In the novel, Humbert ages from 39 to 44. Lolita was 12 years and 8 months old when Humbert met her, and 17 at the conclusion. The ages of Humbert and Lolita are never actually mentioned in the film, but as a matter of interest Mason was 51, and Sue Lyon was 14 years and 4 months when shooting began and 14 years and 8 months when it ended. Many critics complained that she looked too old for the part, but Kubrick has consistently defended his casting on the grounds that many 13-year-old American girls in America today do in fact look as well-developed as Sue Lyon.

But the point is not whether Lyon looks as physically precocious as many 13-year-old American girls but whether she embodies the characteristics of nymphets in general, and Lolita in particular, as carefully defined by Humbert in the novel. There is a crucial difference, and one, which, if not observed, fundamentally changes the nature of Humbert's desire, and hence the social implications of the story. Since a matter of only a few months of physical development can put a prototypical Humbertian nymphet beyond the pale of desirability, Kubrick's justification does not really hold water and one cannot help concluding that censorship considerations determined the way Lyon was presented.

Humbert defines nymphets as being between the ages of 9 and 14 (which puts Lyon at the outermost limits). They have a fey grace, an elusive shifty charm, a feline slender elfin quality. They are "thin-armed... girl-children," "awkward and fey and dimly depraved." Lolita herself is "a mixture of tender dreamy childishness and of eerie vulgarity, stemming from the snub-nosed cuteness of ads and magazine pictures." "She it was to whom ads were dedicated: the ideal consumer, the subject and object of every foul poster," "this beautiful hardly formed girl whom modern co-education, juvenile mores, the campfire racket and so forth had utterly and hopelessly depraved."*

Now the pretty and baby-faced Lyon manages Lolita's "heartless, vaporous eyes," the "slouching, bored way she cultivated," the "combination of naïveté and deception, of charm and vulgarity, of blue sulks and rosy mirth," but she is hardly awkward, elfin or fey. And a vital dimension of Lolita's character is so utterly absent from the film portrayal as to rob her of any claim to nymphetry: her childishness. The Lolita of the novel likes comics, plays with a ballerina doll, wears short white socks, has a plaster on her toe, a

---

* *Lolita* can be viewed as one of a whole cycle of contemporary films, mostly adapted from novels and plays, which broadly depart from the traditional representation of children as cute, comical or sentimental in dramatic function, to represent them as destructive forces threatening adult security. The cycle includes Buñuel's *Los Olvidados, The Bad Seed, The Miracle Worker, Village of the Damned, Zazie dans le Metro, The Loudest Whisper, Lord of the Flies, A High Wind in Jamaica,* and – Buñuel again – *The Young One.* The trend is partly expressive of adult anxiety about the growing power and attraction of youth as an economic, social and cultural force. In *Wild in the Streets* the anxiety becomes overt.

"thin knobby wrist," "a sticky hot neck," an "inky, chalky, red-knuckled hand" and she doesn't wash her hair enough. Lyon, always flawlessly clear-complexioned, well-groomed and coiffured, has left such things behind her long ago. The novel's Humbert preserves a clear eye for off-putting child-like physical details. The film's Lolita has none for him to notice.

Within the limits of the film's conception, Lyon nevertheless makes an impressive debut, playing with a likeable mocking poise that shows resources of genuine acting ability. The coolness, gum-chewing, verbal hesitation, secretiveness and harsh abusive slang suggest the influence of Marlon Brando, her favourite actor at the time. Witness the way she responds to Humbert's recitation of a Poe poem: "Well, I think it's a li'l corny, to tell ya the truth."

What, then, of Quilty? In the novel we see a gradual disintegration into the grotesque and bizarre. As Humbert loses his hold on Lolita so he drinks more and more, talks of hallucination, and Quilty, glimpsed only fleetingly at first, becomes a more and more substantial presence. For Quilty is an embodiment of Humbert's increasing fear and self-loathing and paranoia, a projection of Humbert himself. By the time Humbert is in pursuit of Quilty, he has entered a world of almost Gothic madness and disorder exactly reflecting his own inner disintegration. By placing the murder scene at the beginning of the film and making Quilty so prominent early in the story, this hallucinatory progression is not possible.

The idea was originally James Harris's, and it was agreed with Nabokov early on to structure the film so that Humbert tells his story to Quilty. Kubrick has justified the placing of Quilty's murder at the beginning on two – surely contradictory – grounds. Firstly, "if one began with the murder of Quilty, without really knowing why Humbert killed him, each time Quilty intrudes in the story, people would be more interested in him and there would be more suspense."[14] Secondly, it is supposed to emphasise from the beginning what the murder signifies in the novel – how much Humbert really loved Lolita. But the second justification is invalidated by the absence in the film of the development from mere sensuality to love, which Kubrick sees as the main dramatic line of the novel.

And one has only to view Truffaut's handling of the pursuing stranger in *Baisers volés* to see that the repeated unexplained appearances of a mystery man *increases* our curiosity and interest in him. The opening scene of *Lolita*, on the other hand, explicitly reveals Quilty as the man who stole the girl Humbert loved, and stole her less as a function of his own nympholepsy as of his prankish sense of humour.

Peter Sellers has been criticised for hogging the picture with a series of turns, but it is not his fault that Quilty's role has been expanded, and it should be noted that since Quilty is a compulsive impersonator, all his turns are done perfectly within character and situation, retaining throughout a basic Quilty lisp. Quilty's voice was in fact based on that of Norman Granz, the jazz impresario, who read sections of the script into a tape recorder for Sellers to study.[15] Sellers's soft-voiced plump intruder has a pleasingly slick, wide-boy quality. His impersonation of the detective at the overflow Policeman's Convention, all coyly lowered lids, small smiles and stumbling hurried speech, is extremely droll but goes on perhaps a little longer than is structurally necessary.

His next appearance as a very Nabokovian Beardsley High School psychiatrist, Dr. Zempf, quite legitimately serves the same dramatic function as Miss Pratt's pep talk in the novel: he threatens to have Humbert's home invaded by one Dr. Cuddler and his four psychologists, unless over-protective Humbert lets Lolita appear in Quilty's play. With German accent, back-brushed hair, and densely lensed spectacles, which he has to raise in order to light his cigarette, the performance goonishly anticipates his later Germanic American, Dr. Strangelove. The particularly close and profitable relationship between Sellers and Kubrick resulted in this superb comic actor giving one of his finest performances as Quilty.

As Charlotte Haze, Shelley Winters is cast and plays perfectly. True, the sexually available dumb blonde spurned by the man she adores is a familiar role, but she's never done it better than in *Lolita*. Daintily holding her cigarette holder, laughing archly as she pulls the chain of the fabric-covered lavatory while showing Humbert around the house, or tinkling the dinner bell with fake refinement, she is both funny and touching. And she is moving, too, when she weeps at the disruption of her big evening with Humbert, or when she miserably assaults Humbert with the pages of the abusive diary she has secretly read.

The characters thus transformed – Humbert normalised, Lolita thrust well into puberty – the relationship is conventionalised into the familiar story of the older man hopelessly in love with a frivolous faithless young girl, a situation seen countless times on the screen from *The Blue Angel** to *Baby Doll*, and, of course, of venerable literary genealogy. If *Lolita* is fetching for us in the audience, then Humbert's hankering counts for little more than we have seen often enough before. The novel's central emotional tension, based on our inability to find Lolita as sexually desirable as Humbert does, our ambivalent desire for him to succeed and yet not succeed, is thus removed. Never do we get the feeling that, in the words of the novel, "a North American girl-child named Dolores Haze had been deprived of her childhood by a maniac." In short, Lolita without its nymphetry is like *Hamlet* without the Prince.

The normalisation of relationships is complemented in the screenplay by a greater emphasis on the concept of "normality" than occurs in the novel. Quilty's nervously loquacious policeman keeps reiterating the word "normal"; when Humbert tells Lolita of her mother's death she says, "Everything was so... I don't know... normal."; and in the long confrontation scene near the end Lolita praises Quilty: "He wasn't like you and me. He wasn't a normal person. He was a genius." So Lolita has redeeming standards, odd ones admittedly, of normality, and the audience is implicitly invited to reassess its own standards. But this hinted moral element in

---

* Lola-Lola in Joseph von Sternberg's *The Blue Angel* (1929) must surely be one of Lolita's forebears, although Nabokov, who was living in Berlin at the time the film opened, says he cannot recall whether he saw it or not. Von Sternberg, whose public utterances have an uncannily Nabokovian ring of ironic arrogance, mentions in the 1968 Lorrimer Edition of the screenplay: "The workmen assigned to me were competent. One of them brought his eleven-year-old-daughter to watch the scenes and when I objected, saying that she would be corrupted, he remarked 'Ach, die is ja so verdorben! [But she is already so corrupt!]'"

the film doesn't quite work since the characters are portrayed so "normally" in the first place.

Humbert, in the film, naturally does not deceive Charlotte with Lolita's bracelet, nor does he masturbate against an all-unknowing Lolita as she plays on his lap. Apart from Lolita's quick pre-departure embrace, they are never seen to kiss. At no time does Humbert even make advances to her, let alone force himself on her. When Lolita unhappily hears of the death of her mother, in the film she cries, "Promise you'll never leave me. I don't ever want to be in one of those horrible places for juvenile delinquents." In the novel, it is nasty Humbert who *threatens* her with just this fate unless she complies with his sexual demands. For Humbert's first night in bed with the sleeping Lolita, a night tense with sexual expectation, Kubrick substitutes a silly diversion with a collapsing cot.

The relationship is not only normalised and sanitised – it is also sentimentalised. In the worst scene in the film, Lolita rushes upstairs into the arms of Humbert before leaving for summer camp. "I guess this is goodbye," she says. And as Nelson Riddle's over-lush music surges up romantically, she adds sincerely "Don't forget me" and flees downstairs as the camera moves in on the stricken Humbert. This and other moments in the film tends to invest their relationship with the quality of a conventionally doomed movie romance.

However, the film is not without a certain sexual audacity in places. The dialogue is sometimes quite suggestive, and there are two scenes which get near the necessary knuckle: Lolita proffers Humbert a dangling fried egg ("Just one bite," she invites), and he suddenly pounces, grabbing her wrist to bite the egg. And in a bedroom scene with Charlotte, Humbert first primes himself with booze. As he gazes over Charlotte's shoulder at a photo of Lolita, she remarks with satisfaction (but without animation), "Oh, you man you," but Humbert is stricken to hear Charlotte tell him Lolita is to be sent away. Charlotte in turn is disappointed: "Darling, you've gone away." This is possibly the first explicit verbal reference to a male erection ever made in a commercial movie. Perhaps Kubrick would have gone further elsewhere in the film if he'd realised that Lolita was to get an "X" certificate after all.

✻

The orthodoxy of the screenplay and of the relationships is reflected in the mostly anonymous camera style.

The film opens with the bravura sequence of the murder of Quilty – the best, cinematically most fluent scene in *Lolita*; the rest of *Lolita* is an extended flashback (cf. *Killer's Kiss*), culminating in repeated shots (cf. *The Killing*) of Humbert's approach to and entry into Quilty's mansion. Proceeding mainly by a succession of conversations in rooms, *Lolita* looks more like the adaptation of a stage play than of a picaresque novel.

There is a very perfunctory smattering of exteriors, mainly establishing shots framing the interior scenes which, for a Kubrick film, are remarkably clogged with dialogue. Their static theatricality is emphasised by the way they are shot, mostly in long takes and contained within slow fade-ins and fade-outs, a ponderous editing technique utterly different from the dynamically abrupt cutting Kubrick generally employs. He makes use of back-projection for all the car interior scenes, and such background exteriors as the Haze garden and the garage where Lolita telephones Quilty are too obviously studio staged. Equally as phony-looking are the Ramsdale High School Summer Dance and the Camp Climax scenes – a desultory matter of silent girls operating a duplicating machine, attending to laundry or wandering around looking like extras.

Compared to *Paths of Glory* and *Dr. Strangelove*, to take the two black-and-white films which precede and follow *Lolita*, Ossie Morris's photography is disappointingly flat, lacking for the most part depth, perspective or contrast – a factor which contributes to the general air of theatricality. The night scene at Charlotte's, for instance, after the Ramsdale High School Summer Dance, is surely overlit. There is little of the baroque camera angling and compositional flair that were so effective in Kubrick's treatment of the Peatty-Sherry scenes in *The Killing*. Here he is mainly content to set up his characters in medium two-shot, with few close-ups and only the occasional high-angle shot, as if such flatly conventional compositions were designed to make the Humbert-Lolita relationship look as irreproachably neutral as possible. This may account for the oddly impersonal style, a miscalculation that betrays the spirit of the novel and paralyses the film for much of the time.

The year-long car journey through a strange landscape of hotels, roadside restaurants and assorted tourist traps, before Humbert and Lolita end up in Beardsley, is reduced in the film to a few minutes of footage. And there is nothing of Humbert's desperate search for Quilty. In the film, Humbert turns up at the pregnant 17-year-old Lolita's home immediately after her disappearance – the novel's transition of three years effected by a single typewritten letter. It's very hard to believe that the entire action of the film is supposed to cover five years. Moreover, shooting the film in England makes the environment look decidedly synthetic and un-American, and the presence of familiar British faces in the cast and a Penguin book or two in the hospital scene further undermines that sense of authenticity which so distinguished Kubrick's earlier films set in America.

The best of the scenes are those involving physical action: the camera pursuing Humbert's car as it drives eerily through the mist towards its destination with Quilty; Humbert in a rare low-angle shot feverishly hunting for the ringing telephone as he miserably huddles in his eiderdown; the droll sequence of overlapping hands at a drive-in Frankenstein movie – one of the few attempts at an allusive motif in the film.

But the two outstanding sequences in the film occur in the hospital and in Quilty's home. At the hospital, on hearing of Lolita's disappearance, Humbert is shot in low-angle bursting through the swing doors (a symmetrical shot) into the weirdly lit corridor. Pinned to the floor by the doctors, lights are shone into his eyes as if he were a madman. He gets up, totters unsteadily, and is assisted out by attendants who soothingly stroke his hair into place. The camera pursues him down the corridor, lights shining in the background.

The opening scene is best of all. As Humbert wanders through the debris of glasses, bottles, statues, tapestries and paintings of Quilty's mansion, bottles and harp tinkling magically at his touch, he calls for Quilty who emerges like a ghost from beneath a sheet-covered chair. He wears the sheet like a shroud or a toga. "Are you Quilty?" Humbert demands, and with a brilliant in-joke, referring back wryly to Kubrick's previous film, Quilty replies, "No, I'm Spartacus. Have you come to free the slaves or sump'n?"

The scene proceeds grotesquely, Quilty challenging Humbert to "a game of Roman ping-pong like two civilised Roman senators" and, conjuror-like, produces ball after ball from the folds of his toga-sheet. "Say, I'm really winning, I'm really winning. I hope I don't become overcome with power," Quilty burbles and when Humbert produces a gun he observes, "Hey, you're a sorta bad loser, captain… it's not really who wins, it's how you play."

The camera retreats before Quilty and Humbert's entry into another room. Quilty dons boxing gloves ("why don't you and I settle this like two civilised people?"), suggests a song-writing partnership, assumes a Western old-timer accent to read Humbert's poetic death-sentence ("Listen, Mac, you're drunk and I'm a sick man"), and finally offers Humbert book-ends and a private seat at an execution as he flees up the stairs and crawls behind a Gainsborough painting to be riddled with bullets. The whole scene, with its bric-a-brac cultural wreckage, strongly reminiscent of *Citizen Kane*, beautifully evokes the wreckage of Humbert's mind. After this, the rest of the film is largely anti-climax.

These few scenes excepted, Kubrick on the whole makes little attempt to find cinematic equivalents for Nabokov's jokey glittering style. The film largely lacks the pellucid clarity, lightning wit, audacity and unexpectedness of physical detail that keeps the reader constantly delighted and alert, and virtually no visual motifs are introduced that might function as do the verbal motifs in the novel. For instance, while there is a certain claustrophobia in the succession of interior scenes, only in a brief shot or two in the hotel room is lighting exploited to remind us that *Lolita* is a story of prisons, and that Kubrick in his two gangster films – also stories of pursuit and retribution – is master of prison imagery. And one would have thought that he might have made more of the novel's chess motifs than the passing moment of Humbert taking Charlotte's queen in a briefly seen chess game.

Nabokov himself has expressed a liking for the film. In a reply to an *Observer* dispatch headed "Lolita Fiasco," Kubrick, defending his film, quotes Nabokov's remarks to him after the premiere: "This is a great film. Sue Lyon is marvellous, she is Lolita. There are even some things in it I wish were in the book."[16] Nabokov's wife, in a letter to me, quotes him as saying that he thought all the players were excellent, and that "some bits thought up by Kubrick or Sellers (such as the ping-pong sequence) reached the level of a novelist's art." He was "appalled by a number of details" but "surely you and Stanley [sic] must realise that one tends to remain on the sunny side of one's opinion in complimenting the director of a picture which was very good in as much as it represented Mr. Kubrick's vision of the book."

Speaking as an admirer of Nabokov's novels, I find this verdict generous to the point of extravagance, as well as double-edged in its implication that the cinema is some poor relation of the novel. Perhaps Nabokov's enthusiasm is due to the fact that his original screenplay was so much more theatrical even than the finished film (Nabokov has written some plays in his time) that he was pleasantly surprised by the cinematic ideas in the picture.

But this hypothesis doesn't quite square with Nabokov's adept use of cinematic imagery in his novels. The conservatism of the film's style is all the more baffling when one considers how highly film-conscious a writer Nabokov is. That none of the cinematic syntax of his novel, such as dissolves and jump-cuts, is used by Kubrick means paradoxically that *Lolita*, the book, remains a richer visual experience than *Lolita*, the film.

The film opens dynamically and amusingly but as it goes on it becomes more and more ponderous and lachrymose. Every frame confides a deadening respectability and "tastefulness," as if Kubrick and Harris, anxious to avoid accusations of frivolity of treatment, were determined to get that "A" certificate. One sympathises with the censorship problem and the difficulties of shooting American location scenes in England, but one wonders in the end whether the enterprise was worthwhile in view of the obstacles.

There are good things in *Lolita*, but in too many respects it squanders, impoverishes and conventionalises its source material, draining it of its complexity, nymphetry and eroticism, its doppelganger and hallucinatory elements, and its uproarious vision of motel America. The orthodoxy of this stolid, well-intentioned but ultimately castrated movie is reflected in its stylistic anaemia. Significantly, Kubrick's only failure happens to be his only attempt to deal with character in depth, with a man and a girl in the depths of a complex sexual relationship. His best work lies in quite different areas of experience – to which, happily, he was to return at last with his next film.

1. Walter, Renaud. "Entretien avec Stanley Kubrick," *Positif*, December 1968-January 1969.
2. Uncredited. "Lolita and Friends," *Daily Mail*, 5 November 1960.
3. Burch, Stanley. "Lolita's Saucy Sue will stick to script," *Daily Mail*, 29 September 1960.
4. Nathan, David. "*Lolita* film men to meet censor," *Daily Herald*, 5 November 1960.
5. Burgess, Jackson. "The 'Anti-Militarism' of Stanley Kubrick," *Film Quarterly*, Fall 1964.
6. Hopkirk, Peter. "*Lolita*: Now It's Going on Celluloid," *Daily Express*, 6 July 1960.
7. Zec, Donald. "Lolita and the Lollipop," *Daily Mirror*, 17 May 1962.
8. Kohler, Charlie. "Stanley Kubrick Raps," *Eye*, August 1968.
9. Renaud. "Entretien avec Stanley Kubrick."
10. ibid.
11. Haine, Raymond. "Bonjour Monsieur Kubrick," *Cahiers du Cinéma*, July 1957.
12. Renaud. "Entretien avec Stanley Kubrick."
13. ibid.
14. ibid.
15. Evans, Peter. *Peter Sellers: The Mask Behind the Mask* (Prentice-Hall, 1968).
16. Kubrick, Stanley. "*Lolita* Fiasco," *The Observer*, 24 June 1962.

8. Bloc-Heads, or The Ultimate Pratfall
Dr. Strangelove (1964)

> The world is living under a nuclear Sword of
> Damocles which can be cut by accident,
> miscalculation or madness.
>
> > President Kennedy's speech to the United
> > Nations during the Cuban Missile Crisis,
> > October 1962
>
> He has taken The Bomb and used it as a banana
> skin, with a nuclear pratfall as the ultimate pay-off
> gag.
>
> > Bryan Forbes
> > *Films and Filming*, February 1964

Kubrick's highly profitable partnership with James B. Harris dissolved after *Lolita*, not because of any serious disagreement but because Kubrick wanted to produce as well as direct, and Harris wanted to direct as well as produce. Harris thought Kubrick could do everything they had done so far without him, while Kubrick thought Harris perfectly capable of directing. Kubrick went on to make *Dr. Strangelove or: How I Learned to Stop Worrying and Love the Bomb*, while Harris made *The Bedford Incident*, both for Columbia. Together with *Fail Safe*, they form a kind of Columbia Studios trilogy on the theme of nuclear crisis.

Dr. Strangelove, Kubrick says, "came from my great desire to do something about the nuclear nightmare. I was very interested in what was going to happen and started reading a lot of books about four years ago. I have a library of about 70 or 80 books written by various technical people on the subject and I began to subscribe to the military magazines, the Air Force magazine, and to follow the U.S. Naval proceedings. I was struck by the paradoxes of every variation of the problem from one extreme to the other – from the paradoxes of unilateral disarmament to the first strike."[1]

"When you start reading the analyses of nuclear strategy, they seem so thoughtful that you're lulled into a temporary sense of reassurance. But as you go deeper into it, and become more involved, you begin to realise that every one of these lines of thought leads to a paradox."[2]

The more he read on the subject, and the more experts he talked to – they included Herman Kahn and Thomas Schelling – the more paradoxical and terrifying seemed the solutions offered. Most of the nuclear strategists did agree, however, that the chance of annihilation through accident, miscalculation or madness was far greater than the possibility of nuclear war being started deliberately by either side. Kahn, for instance, stated: "If the system was safe for 99.99 per cent of the days in the year, given average luck it would fail in 30 years."

With this in mind, in October 1961, shortly after finishing *Lolita*, Kubrick talked to Alastair Buchan of the International Institute of Strategic Studies, a non-governmental London research group. Buchan gave him a copy of a novel, *Red Alert*, as one instance of how the subject had been treated as fiction. Buchan, says Kubrick, recommended it to him "as the only feasible, factually accurate fictionalisation of the way in which an H-bomb war could start without any sane cause or prompting."[3] Buchan later claimed in a letter to the London *Times* that he warned Kubrick "that parts of it were quite implausible. I also told him that I thought his project was unwise because he would not be able to describe precisely what precautions the United States or other powers take to guard against the danger of accident or false command, and the film might therefore easily mislead anxious people all over the world, however amusing* or skilful the treatment."[4]

Fortunately, Kubrick ignored this advice to spare people anxiety about the bomb. Captivated by *Red Alert*, he bought the film rights for $3,000 and hired the author to co-write the screenplay with him.

Written in 1958 by former Flight-Lieutenant Peter George under the pseudonym of Peter Bryant, the novel was first published in England as *Two Hours to Doom*,

---

* This strikes an implausible note, since at this time Kubrick had not yet thought of treating the subject humorously.

then under the title of *Red Alert* in the U.S.A., where it sold over 200,000 copies. It is not to be confused with George's commissioned novelisation of the film, *Dr. Strangelove*, nor with a hack *Saturday Evening Post* "novelette," "Red Alert," by one William Chamberlain, published in May 1955, a piece of cold-war fodder concerned with the successful efforts of an officer to tighten up discipline at a slack USAF base.*

In *Red Alert* (the American title is better known), the nuclear Sword of Damocles is cut by madness. It is a completely serious suspense novel describing with meticulously thorough circumstantial detail what happens when a psychotic general in charge of a Red Alert base unleashes a fleet of H-bombers on Russia. Kahn and Schelling were among those who wrote to congratulate George for the originality of his thought, the accuracy of his background detail, and the feasibility of his central hypothesis. They informed him that the book was widely circulated and highly thought of among professional nuclear strategists.

Kubrick and George worked on the screenplay for several months before Kubrick suddenly hit on the idea of making the film as a comedy: "I found that in trying to put meat on the bones and to image the scenes fully one had to keep leaving things out of it which were either absurd or paradoxical, in order to keep it from being funny, and these things seemed to be very real. Then I decided that the perfect tone to adopt for the film would be what I now call nightmare comedy, because it most truthfully presents the picture."[5]

"The film keeps the same suspense frame. But the more I worked on it, the more I was intrigued by the comic aspects – the facade of conventional reality being pierced."[6] "It's a situation created by a mistake, the impossibility of communicating, the bungling of bureaucracy, etc… all things which, in reality, belong without doubt to the world of comedy."[7] "The story, in addition to making the possibilities seem real, shows the sub-theme of mutual interest in avoiding nuclear war, certainly avoiding the possibility of causing one inadvertently. You may want to be fatalistic about nuclear war, but not about accidental nuclear war."[8]

---

* This story, a veritable red herring, includes unironic references to "Russkies" and, as in *Fail Safe*, a false alarm incident involving an un-identified aircraft which turns out to be a lost civilian plane.

Kubrick, a chess player, was more interested in the strategy associated with having the bomb than what happens after it goes off. "It is often difficult not to have a cynical view of human relationships," he says. "But I think that in a subject like this the cynicism should at least try to serve some constructive purpose. It seemed to me that, since this is a tragedy which has not yet occurred, any insight which could be provided, any sense of reality which could be given to it so that it didn't seem just an abstraction (which the nuclear problem is in most people's minds) was really useful. The paradoxes of deterrence have become so abstract, and so many euphemistic expressions have been thrown into it, that I seriously doubt that the problem is at all real to anyone."[9]

Kubrick was ready to go into production when he decided that the screenplay needed a humorous brush-up. Terry Southern, author of *The Magic Christian* and co-author of *Candy*, had been assigned by *Esquire* to do an article on the filming of the picture, and Kubrick hired him for $2,000 "to see if some more decoration might be added to the icing on the cake." (It may be remembered that at the end of *The Magic Christian*, Guy Grand, the millionaire practical joker, goes off to investigate the new space programme – Peter Sellers again starred in the film version!) Kubrick was later upset that critics, in attributing the film's brilliance to Southern, tended to ignore his own and George's contribution. When producer Martin Ransohoff took a full-page ad in *The New York Times* to announce that the writer of *Dr. Strangelove* was going to meet with the director of *Tom Jones* on *The Loved One*, Kubrick threatened legal action and released a statement to the press, part of which read: "Mr. Southern was employed from the period of November 16 to December 20, 1962, during which time I wrote in close collaboration with him. During shooting, which began on January 28, 1963, many substantial changes were made in the script by myself and/or Peter George, and sometimes together with the cast during improvisations. Some of the best dialogue was created by Mr. Sellers himself. Mr. Southern took no part in these activities, nor did he receive any further employment, nor did he serve in any consulting role."

The incident led to bad feeling between Kubrick and Southern, although Hollis Alpert has said that the idea for a projected Southern novel, *Blue Movie*, concerning a director so rich and powerful that he employs two big box-office stars to copulate on screen, was given to him by Kubrick.[10]

It took Kubrick about one month to find the backing for *Dr. Strangelove*. It was made on a budget of $2 million (£710,000), which included such costs as insuring Peter Sellers for $2 million and an IBM computer 7090 for $2 million (the same data processor that calculated when John Glenn would drop into the ocean after Earth orbit). The film was made without military permission or the blessing of anyone in authority, and in fact an opening caption disclaimer firmly tells us, "It is the stated position of the USAF that the events depicted in this film could not happen."

Like *Lolita*, *Dr. Strangelove* was made at Shepperton Studios, again ostensibly to accommodate Peter Sellers. Principal photography began on 28 January and ended in May, 1963. The War Room was one of the largest interior sets ever devised and took up a whole sound stage. It was 130 feet long, 100 feet wide and 35 feet high. More than 150 carpenters, electricians, riggers, painters and plasterers worked on the project for three months under the supervision of the designer Ken Adam. Intricate electronic maps completely covered one raked wall and reflected weirdly off a high-gloss ebony floor kept so highly polished that shoes were not allowed on its surface except for actual takes. The circular conference table in the centre was 380 square feet in surface area. Unlike normal indoor shooting practice, a proper ceiling was built into the set to get the effect of real as distinct from studio light sources.

Since the appearance of the actual Pentagon war room is not known to outsiders, the set had to be designed from imagination. Ken Adam provides some revealing insights into Kubrick's working methods:

"He wanted to know just as much about me as I wanted to know about him, and though we had arguments we always seemed to work on parallel lines. Stanley is an extremely difficult and talented person. We developed an extremely close relationship and as a result I had to live almost completely on tranquillisers...

"Kubrick has the mind of a chess player, and though he might instinctively know that my design was right he would say, 'Think of something else,' or 'But can you think of a different way of doing it?' We went through all the possible permutations until we settled on the original design. Kubrick has to be sure that he has the very best and he likes to justify intellectually everything he is doing, to find the intellectual reason. Very often as an art director you work on instinct. You digest all the problems and overall aims but the actual designs come mainly instinctively. To justify intellectually every line you've drawn isn't easy. Take the War Room set. I did my design sketches and he said, 'Why a triangular shape?' I said, 'Why not? And anyway the triangle is the strongest geometrical shape there is.' He said that wouldn't do. I said, 'If we built it in reinforced concrete it would look like a bomb shelter,' and that gave him his intellectual justification. In the end he cut out the only shot that showed the whole set. With Kubrick everything must have a realistic possibility, a potential for use. He doesn't believe in stylisation for its own sake."[11]

The aerial and aeroplane interior scenes were designed with similar thoroughness. "I've seen a lot of aeroplane films," said Kubrick, "but I've never seen one where I get the feeling of really being inside a plane." So $150,000 were spent authenticating the interior of a B52 bomber and on sending an airborne crew to shoot exteriors in the frozen north. In November 1963, Gil Taylor, the Director of Photography, went off with a 12-man location unit in a specially equipped B17 bomber to shoot air sequences over the Arctic, Greenland, Iceland and the Canadian Rockies. The hazards of this operation included flying as low as ten feet off the ground, and keeping four cameras, the film and crew unfrozen in 40 below zero. The unit returned home at Christmas Eve having logged 103 flying hours, with 40,000 feet of film shot. This footage provided the rear projection against which a ten-inch model plane was photographed in the bomber scenes. The opening credit sequence of a plane refuelling consisted of stock shots. The air base combat exteriors were shot at London Airport (or in a London suburb, according to a differing report), while the opening sequence with Mandrake was shot in the IBM Computer Room.

The screenplay of *Dr. Strangelove* follows the structure of *Red Alert* rather closely. The novel dwells on the detailed strategy of the crisis and hops regularly, with one or two minor time overlaps not unlike *The Killing*, among its three basic settings of Airport Base, B52 Bomber and Pentagon War Room. The Doomsday device, the General's suicide, the Russian ambassador, the hot-line and the O.P.E. code are all there in the novel. But there is no counterpart of Dr. Strangelove, and the psychotic general justifies his action entirely in terms of political self-protection, without any mention of water fluoridation or any sexual implications. The underling who tries to reason with him is an American major and not the RAF type depicted in the film. And in the original novel, a city-for-city swap is arranged as in *Fail Safe*, but disaster is averted at the last moment by the nuclear device not exploding properly on target. The novel at times lends itself to parody: the bomber crew are represented as ordinary joes who don't pretend to understand the score. "There's some things right, some wrong, hell I don't know," one of them ponders in a plain statement lacking only the exclamation "Shucks!"

Peter George's commissioned novelisation of the film, published in 1963, is a completely revised work, its mood and characterisation reflecting the film rather than the original novel. It does include some interesting details not present in the completed film, some of which may have been planned or even shot at some stage.

President Muffley's first entry surely parodies the President's entry in *Fail Safe*: Muffley comes through an elevator escorted by ten Secret Service men, travels along the corridors by a small electric car, is refused admission to the National Security Room because he has left his Pass Card at home, and eventually ascends into the War Room by another elevator. He utters some sober words of wisdom, fortunately cut from the film, if indeed they were ever filmed, which give him an unfair moral advantage over his opposite number, Premier Kissof: "There are too many fingers on the buttons. There are too many reasons both mechanical and human for the system to fail… The great nations have always acted like gangsters, and the small nations like prostitutes." The code letters in the novelisation are supposed to be based on the phrase "Joe (Stalin) for King" – JFK! The bomber is damaged by a malfunctioning decoy rather than by Russian missiles. In the novelisation and in production stills, but not in the completed film, President Muffley uses a menthol inhaler for his sinuses. Perhaps some of these absent or excised details were thought to over-balance the absurdist elements in the treatment.

The climax of the film was to have been a custard-pie melee in the War Room, for which at least 2,000 shaving-cream pies were ordered every day. Peter Bull, who played the Russian ambassador, describes it: "Towards the end of the script, as shot, all the personnel went berserk and started hurling them from one end of the studio to the other. The film ended with P. Sellers as the U.S. President and me sitting on the floor, waist-deep in custard pies, making custard castles out of them and singing 'For He's a Jolly Good Fellow.' The 'he' we were referring to in this case was that macabre Dr. Strangelove (Mr. Sellers again, of course). This section of the film took nearly a fortnight to complete and must have cost thousands and thousands of pounds but Stanley decided, when he came to cut the film[*], that it was completely at variance with the rest of it and, though apparently sensationally funny and effective, it just didn't fit in. So it was scrapped. It must have been agony for him but his integrity is such that I bet he was right."[12]

*

The film proceeds, like the original novel, through a series of cross-cut sequences from Strategic Air Command (SAC) headquarters at Burpelson Air Force Base to the Pentagon War Room to a B52 bomber, until the final nuclear holocaust. Between the opening caption disclaimer, already mentioned,

[*] The sequence was, in fact, cut after the first public preview.

and the credit titles sequence, a narrator informs us against a slow pursuit shot across high cloud formations that American scientists have located the site of a terrible weapon – a Doomsday device on which the Russians have been working for over a year (this doesn't quite gel with everyone's surprise towards the end). After the credits, we see Group Captain Lionel Mandrake receiving orders from General Jack D. Ripper to come to his office, while in the background whirling spools of tape suggest unfathomable mechanical computations. Mandrake is ordered to put the base on Condition Red – it must be completely sealed off from all outside contact.

After a second and final intervention by the commentator, who gives us a short documentary rundown on the SAC defence system, we cut to the interior of the main B52 bomber (in the novelisation but not in the film, we learn its nickname – "Leper Colony"). The camera retreats to reveal that one of the crew members is reading *Playboy* and we are treated to a sight of Playmate of the Month, Miss Foreign Affairs, whose naked posterior is discreetly covered by an open book which looks like a Top Secret government document.

Other crew members are eating, card-playing and dozing. They move into action as they receive the crucial code signal from SAC base to advance past their "Fail-Safe" points. As the camera zooms in on the code letters, the pilot, Major "King" Kong, dons a cowboy hat, and we hear stirring drums and a male chorus ominously humming "When Johnny Comes Marching Home" on the sound-track. This effective theme is used only in the bomber sequences, and is in fact the only music in the film apart from the opening and closing popular songs. "Well, boys," drawls the lugubrious Major Kong to his crew, "I ain't much of a hand at making speeches. The folks back home is counting on you and, by golly, we ain't gonna let 'em down. You're all in line for decorations, regardless of race, creed and colour once the bomb is dropped."

We cut to the flat of General "Buck" Turgidson, Chief of the Joint Chief of Staff. Miss Foreign Affairs in the flesh is sunbathing in *Playboy* pose under a sun-lamp. She answers the telephone and mediates between the caller and the off-screen Turgidson who is occupied in what she daintily refers to as "the powder-room." The contrast between her efficient secretarial voice and the intimate tone she adopts for "Freddie" at the other end of the line suggests vistas of high-level vice. Turgidson presently comes to the phone, absurd in long shorts and tropical shirt, slapping his hairy belly and chewing gum as he does compulsively throughout the movie. "What's cooking on the threat board?" he enquires, and when he hears of General Ripper's action, still not unduly perturbed, he decides to "nosey over to the War Room for a few minutes, see what's doing there."

Back at Burpelson, Ripper instructs his troops over the loudspeaker system: "Trust no-one unless known to you personally," "If in doubt shoot first and ask questions afterwards" (but not as also in the novelisation: "defend the constitution of the United States whatever may be the outcome of this defence"). After Mandrake's arrival, Ripper moves away from the camera to the door to lock it, and Mandrake follows him; the shot is similar to that in the library scene of *Paths of Glory* in which an important revelation is strikingly made at the farthest point from the camera. Here Ripper reveals to Mandrake his paranoid fear of fluoridated rainwater, and, in lines taken verbatim from George's original novel, quotes Clemenceau's dictum that war is too important to be left to the generals, transposing the word "politicians" for "generals."

This provides a neat link with *Paths of Glory*, for Georges Clemenceau was the patriotic politician who railed against the mutineering French soldiers and anti-war factions in 1917. Since Ripper can no longer abide "Commie infiltration, indoctrination and subversion to sap and impurify our precious bodily fluids," he has put into operation Plan R, originally devised to appease a Senator who complained that the American deterrent lacked credibility. Plan R is a safeguard measure by which a lower echelon commander can order nuclear retaliation in the event of higher echelons getting knocked out of action. Ripper is sure that total commitment is the only course of action the government can now take.

In the plane, the crew unlock the combination safe, a piece of equipment that seems both archaic and ironic inside a SAC bomber. Pin-ups are taped on the inside of the safe (a forties touch). They remove the code books and open their sealed envelopes. Despite the complexity of the electronic gear involved, the mechanics of their operation are made very clear. The routine procedures in the bomber are observed with care and concentration, the camera zooming into and away from the instrument panel, registering and, as it were, clinching each stage of the inexorable process. Later the men check over their survival kits, a bizarre package including chewing gum, nylons, lipstick and a miniature combined Russian phrase book and Bible.

The first scene in the vast War Room is shot from three basic camera positions: a slightly overhead shot of the huge circular table, a close medium shot of Turgidson in right frame, and a medium shot of President Merkin Muffley framed between other figures in the foreground, which gives the sequence a feeling of live T.V. newsreel presentation. All except the principals sit as motionless as dummies, and Dr. Strangelove can be unobtrusively glimpsed among them.

Turgidson explains the situation and reads a message from Ripper which ends with a reference to preserving the purity and essence of our natural fluids. Muffley is shocked that Ripper could ever have passed the Human Reliability Test, and take over in this way. Turgidson replies: "I don't think it's fair to condemn a whole programme for a single slip-up, sir." But he later concedes in a key line, "Well, Sir, I will admit that the human element seems to have failed us here."

Turgidson proposes an all-out strike against the U.S.S.R. "It is now necessary to make a choice, to choose between two admittedly regrettable but nevertheless distinguishable post-war environments – one where we've got ten to twenty million people killed and the other where we've got 150 million people killed." The lines recall the Generals bargaining over the number of sacrificial victims in *Paths of Glory*. Turgidson again concedes with admirable understatement, "I'm not saying we wouldn't get our hair mussed." Muffley resists this suggestion and calls for the Russian ambassador, de Sadesky. He and Turgidson are soon scuffling when the ambassador is discovered secretly taking photographs of the War Room. The appalled Muffley admonishes them with the memorable line, "Gentlemen, you can't fight in here – this is the War Room!"

Under instructions from the War Room, the SAC base is attacked in order that the recall code known only to Ripper can be obtained. In the background of these combat scenes we see billboarded, as elsewhere in the movie, the authentic motto of Strategic Air Command: "Peace is our Profession."

In the War Room, the Russian Premier Kissof is located on the Hot Line. He is evidently drunk and is asked to turn down the music at his end. The conversation between Muffley and Kissof observes all the guarded trivialities of polite social discourse: "Hello?... Hello, Dimitri... Yes, this is Merkin. How are you?... Oh, fine. Just fine. Look, Dimitri, you know how we've always talked about the possibility of something going wrong with the Bomb?... The bomb? THE HYDROGEN BOMB!... That's right. Well, I'll tell you what happened. One of our base commanders... well, he went a little funny in the head, and... you know, funny... he ordered his planes... to attack... your country... well, look, let me finish... *Let me finish*, Dimitri! Uh-huh... Thirty-four planes. They won't reach their target for at least another hour... I'm positive... Uh-huh... Well, how do you think I feel about it?" This Hot Line scene was in the can just one week before the Geneva announcement that Russia had accepted the U.S. proposal for a direct telephone link between Washington and Moscow.

Back at Burpelson, Ripper expands on his theme with his arm around a nervous Mandrake's shoulders who now calls him "Jack" with a wary humouring intimacy. "Water is the source of all life. We need fresh pure water to replenish our precious bodily fluids... Fluoridation is the most monstrously conceived and dangerous Communist plot we have ever had to face." As the firing reaches Ripper's office, he takes a machine gun out of his golf bag (war equated with sport) and returns fire.

In the War Room the camera moves in on Ambassador de Sadesky revealing the existence of the Russian Doomsday Machine, a device which will encircle the world with a radioactive shroud for 93 years if Russia is attacked. Turgidson in his excitement at stating the problem of a "Doomsday gap" falls over. For the first time, the crippled Dr. Strangelove, Director of Weapons Research and Development, appears, vigorously wheeling himself out of the shadows of the main conference table. He explains that such a device is indeed possible and reminds the President that he commissioned the Bland Corporation to investigate the possibilities. With his weird entry and demonic words "All it requires is the will," the film enters its final accelerated phase of progressive lunacy.

Ripper explains to Mandrake that he first became aware of the plot after the physical act of love. "A profound sense of fatigue and physical emptiness followed – loss of essence… Women sense my power, they seek my life essence. I do not avoid women, Mandrake. I do deny them my essence." In identifying paranoid right-wing political attitudes with sexual inadequacy, *Dr. Strangelove* goes further than any previous American film. When the Burpelson troops are forced to surrender, the stricken Ripper goes off to the bathroom, obviously to kill himself, and Sellers as Mandrake utters the great line, "Going for a wash and brush-up are you, what a good idea." The sequence is interrupted by a grippingly filmed explosion in the B52 bomber as it suffers attack from Russian missiles alerted to its position. A wavering hand-held camera invests the scene with a documentary flavour of real danger.

Mandrake is left puzzling over Ripper's schizoid doodles. Just as he hits on the recall code initials P.O.E., embedded in the recurrent phrases "Purity of Essence" and "Peace on Earth," he is captured by the cold-eyed Colonel "Bat" Guano who suspects him of being "some kind of deviated prevert" – another character with sexual obsessions. Mandrake desperately persuades Guano to let him telephone the President. "If you try any preversions in there," Guano warns, "I'll blow your head off." (This malapropism appeared first in Southern and Hoffenberg's *Candy*.) Mandrake doesn't have the correct change – so much for modern communications – and has to persuade the outraged Guano to blow open the Coca-Cola machine. "If you don't get hold of the President of the United States," Guano threatens, "you know what's gonna happen – you're gonna have to answer to the Coca-Cola company."

There is general relief in the War Room once Mandrake has communicated the recall code, and Turgidson, adopting an evangelical pose, calls upon the assembled personnel to get down on their knees and pray. His line, "We have heard the angel of death fluttering above us," is spoken against a shot of Strangelove sitting in the shadows. They then discover that the radio of Leper Colony is unable to receive the recall code and is still careering on towards its target, the Russian missile base "Laputa" (a name with an aptly Swiftian ring).

As the bomber approaches its target, further suspense is generated when it's realised that the bomb bay doors have jammed. Kong goes down to try a last-minute repair job mounted on one of the warheads. The missiles are labelled "NUCLEAR WARHEADS. HANDLE WITH CARE" and nicknamed in chalk "Hi there" and "Dear John" (in the novelisation, "Lolita"). Just as the doors open the missiles are released and, in a very weird shot, the warheads fall at first slowly and then very quickly, straddled by Kong, who swings his hat and whoops like a rodeo rider, which Slim Pickens (who plays Kong) happened to be before he became a film actor. The shot eerily fuses the Western, sexual and destructive motifs in an image at once ludicrous, obscene and nightmarish. A comparable effect is achieved in the film *Fail Safe*, with nuclear anxiety expressed through a colonel's recurring dream of a bloodily stricken bull.

Dr. Strangelove now holds the floor in the War Room, with a plan for survival involving the selection by computer of superior samples of manhood and womanhood to be hidden in the deepest mineshafts in the country. In his enthusiasm for the idea he loses control of his artificial arm. Turgidson speaks of the danger of a Mineshaft gap. Meanwhile, the Russian Ambassador is busily at work again taking secret photographs. Over Muffley's shoulder we see Strangelove dementedly pushing himself out of his chair screaming "Mein Fuhrer – I can walk!" On this crazed climactic note the screen explodes into a succession of blossoming H-bomb mushroom clouds and Vera Lynn is heard on the sound-track singing "We'll Meet Again." The song evokes at once a profound nostalgia and sense of loss for the relative simplicities of the last war while expressing a wicked and piercing irony. This ending must be among the most audacious ever devised for a movie backed by a big American company and intended for general release.

*

The main credit titles appear over shots of a bomber re-fuelling in mid-flight to the strains of "Try a Little Tenderness." The camera serenely floats up and down in drowsy, balloon-like contentment, the connected planes suggesting a ludicrous form of mechanical copulation, while Pablo Ferro's credit titles, spidery and spindly as a child's first uncertain attempts at lettering, reinforces the feeling of infantilism. The images and sound-track beautifully define and establish the key conjunctive motifs of the film: childishness, machinery, feeding, sex and dreams.

Dr. Strangelove is replete with feeding images, somehow managing to suggest that all Americans are fixated at the oral stage of infant development. The bomber crew are first seen munching hamburgers or chewing gum. Turgidson is a compulsive gum-chewer. Ripper's concern about water contamination extends to such foodstuffs as fruit juice and ice cream, while Mandrake cannily recognises that Ripper gets a kick out of being "fed" machine gun ammunition. And, of course, there is the rich buffet set out in the War Room, totally destroyed in the culminating "custard pie" sequence that was edited out of the final print.

If General Jack D. Ripper's cigar and gun carry both oral and phallic significance, the very names of the characters scurrilously blare their sexual hang-ups. The President's name, Merkin Muffley, connotes not only one who muffs things but also the female pudenda. "Bat" Guano means literally "bat-shit." General "Buck" Turgidson's name incorporates the idea of "swollen" which, in his case, has the dual significance of bluster and rampant lechery. His farewell to Miss Foreign Affairs (a lady of dubious moral standing) is revealing: "Look, you start your countdown right now and old Buckie will be back before you can say blast-off" (or "re-entry," as the novelisation has it). For Turgidson, sex and ballistic missile warfare have become totally identified.

Perhaps Group Captain Lionel Mandrake's name is the most expressive. The mandrake plant was thought to have certain magically emetic, purgative and narcotic properties. When pulled from the ground it utters a shriek that can kill or madden those who do not block their ears, but once freed from the Earth its properties become beneficent and healing. The sexual motifs are there for a purpose. As F. Anthony Macklin has persuasively argued, *Dr. Strangelove* wickedly celebrates a process of foreplay to mechanical orgasm in a dehumanised world.

When men are still ruled by primitive hunger and sex drives, then how expect them to cope any better with the machines they are leaning to live with, and love? When so much reliance is placed on machines, mechanical malfunctioning becomes equated with human impotence. Radios, telephones, cameras, aircraft, Coca-Cola machines, H-bombs and prosthetic arms (Strangelove is more cyborg than human being) are liable to go horribly wrong, to block communication and create frustration rather than facilitate human relations. The theme is to reappear with a vengeance in *2001: A Space Odyssey*.

Dr. Strangelove's basic satirical device is to set up a discrepancy between the enormity of the situation and the casualness of human response to it. When Miss Foreign Affairs phones Turgidson at the War Room, for instance, his reaction might be that of any businessman irritably trying to put off a too attentive mistress. Muffley's very decency and orderliness render him almost impotent to deal with the grandiose proposals of his advisers.

It is not just the characters' casualness, incompetence and ego-defensiveness that gives the film its comic drive. They also behave as though they are acting out a Hollywood Western. The prospect of total nuclear annihilation is treated as a simple frontier town dispute. One of the film's most trenchant points is that the New Frontier is not much different from the Old Frontier; American foreign policy is still founded and still foundering on simplistic pioneering myths. The film even goes so far in its satire as to show political policies buttressed by religious platitudes. Anyone familiar with the usual respectful attitude towards religion in the American cinema must marvel that the references to prayer and the Bible were not censored.

The film's use of incongruity is expressed stylistically by the tension between the "real" surface detail and the ridiculous way in which the characters behave. Actually, the camera style is mostly such as to render things with just the necessary degree of distortion to evoke the unease of nightmare, without plunging into outright expressionism. Holding to the original novel's construction, the film is edited to a tight suspense pattern based on repeated shifts from setting to setting as in *The Killing* and *Paths of Glory*.

Its sombre lighting and extreme camera angles belong more to the world of Welles's *The Trial* than to a comedy film. Figures are seen in silhouette or emerge abruptly from the shadows. Ripper's face, shot from below against a dark background, is as harshly illuminated as that of a suspect undergoing the third degree. Lights glare with an almost neon shrillness into the camera. The element of distortion is most apparent in the gigantic War Room set with its vast intricate electronic maps and suspended ring of lights shining down eerily on each man's place at the conference table. Its gleaming black polished floor and chilling echo is reminiscent of that other setting of high-level death-dealing, the chateau of *Paths of Glory*. It is like the underground shelter proposed by Strangelove, tomb-like and comfortless – unlike the almost cosily intimate War Room of *Fail Safe*.

In its efforts to balance laughter and horror, reality and dream, to create black satirical comedy in a context of unyielding photographic realism, the whole film treads a stylistic tightrope. While on the whole it succeeds in balancing its deliberate incongruities, it is not without occasional stylistic miscalculations which momentarily send it a little askew – a slight error of stress here, a touch too much realism there, a shade too much caricature there. To be specific, I find the Air Base combat sequence too efficient a pastiche of newsreel reportage for stylistic comfort. The hand-held camera shoots from behind bushes, and hastily picks up images in the confusion of battle. Leaves wave in front of a camera masked by binoculars. The sequence disturbs the film's stylistic unity by demanding a straight response out of key with the mordant satire of the rest of the film – and the same might be said of the (excellently directed) explosion sequence inside the B52 aircraft.

The performances of George C. Scott and Peter Bull strike one as too strident in their comic caricature. Was it necessary for Turgidson to fall over while backing away from the Ambassador in the War Room? His frenetic mugging seems out of key, as does Peter Bull's Russian Ambassador, an unfunny glowering stubborn-lipped performance which Bull himself has regretfully described as "amateur, heavy-handed and plain ham."[13] One feels a similar unease with Slim Pickens as "King" Kong. Playing with a lugubrious nasal drawl, his Stetson and cracker-barrel persona don't quite fit in with the conventional anonymous playing of the other bomb-crew members – or possibly more might have been made of their stereotyped roles as token Negro, Irishman and Jew.

There is a pleasing irony in having the virulently anti-Communist General Ripper played by Sterling Hayden. A victim of the McCarthyite purges of the late forties, Hayden later recanted and was reinstated in Hollywood as, in his own self-disgusted words "a sanitary culture-hero"(!), before giving up acting to sail around the world. Only Huston's *The Asphalt Jungle* and Kubrick's *The Killing* had given him satisfaction in an otherwise mediocre film career. He came out of retirement to make *Dr. Strangelove*, and although one would like to have seen what an older, flabbier actor might have made of the role, Hayden plays Ripper competently, aided by his natural ruggedness and the camera's harsh, searching close-ups.

Peter Sellers continued in *Dr. Strangelove* the very fruitful working relationship with Kubrick begun in *Lolita*. This was partly based on a mutual respect for each other's rigorous professionalism. Both men are obsessively perfectionist in their work. Sellers, who habitually stays in character off the set, undergoes less a transference of identity in his roles as acquiring a series of temporary identities. "I have no personality of my own, you see," he says. "I could never be a star because of this. I'm a character actor… It's a funny thing, but when I'm doing a role I kind of feel it's the role doing the role, if you know what I mean."[14] A coincidental point of interest: Sellers is a former professional drummer and amateur photographer, and Kubrick is a former professional photographer and amateur drummer.

Kubrick has often expressed his admiration for Sellers and justifies his multiple-role casting in *Dr. Strangelove* as follows: "Peter Sellers is the only actor living who has the necessary degree of that unique skill: not that of a comic heavy or a comedian actor. But a brilliant actor who has that intangible sense of balance which in the midst of seriousness can suggest the ludicrous without stepping over the line into unreality... Each of the parts requires just the same sort of actor, the same kind of talent, the same kind of performance."[15]

"When you are inspired and professionally accomplished as Peter, the only limit to the importance of your work is your willingness to take chances. I believe Peter will take the most incredible chances with a characterisation, and he is receptive to comic ideas most of his contemporaries would think unfunny and meaningless. This has, in my view, made his best work absolutely unique and important."[16]

There was improvisation in many of the scenes. "Peter Sellers is perhaps the actor who responds most when one begins to improvise. His greatest talent resides in investing all he touches with the grotesque: he has a more powerfully grotesque sense of humour than most of the people I've met. If one asked the others to do the same thing in the film they would look at you as if you were mad. Peter Sellers, on the contrary, gets very excited by an idea of this kind and finds it very funny."[17]

Sellers was to have played four roles in the film: Dr. Strangelove, the President, Mandrake and – "King" Kong. But when he broke his ankle just after completing his wheelchair-bound Dr. Strangelove scenes, he was unable to go ahead with the part of Kong, which, in any case, was affording him some difficulty[18] and Slim Pickens was hastily summoned from California to play the part. At no time, by the way, has Kubrick suggested that this multiple casting was intended to convey an identity of mutual responsibility for the nuclear disaster.

In all three of his quite differentiated roles Sellers is superb. His Dr. Strangelove is a brilliantly bizarre creation, compounded of Wernher von Braun, Edward Teller, Dr. Mabuse, Robert S. McNamara (the then Secretary of Defence's middle name is "Strange"), Adolf Hitler, and a host of horror-film deviants. His blondish hair combed sideways in a wavy quiff, a fag-end thrust between his lips, a fixed almost paralytic grin on his face, he pushes himself about in a wheelchair, expounding his views on the Doomsday machine and enforced breeding in a strained constipated voice, his eyes glinting with expectant relish behind smoked glasses. The final sequence in which he tries to gain control of his unruly artificial arm is a great piece of comic acting. The mutinous limb unexpectedly presents him with the radioactivity calculator his normal hand is seeking. Twice it jumps into a stiff Hitlerian salute. When it strikes him on the jaw Strangelove bites it and forces it down but it rises again to attempt strangulation. Apparently this arm business was not discovered until the day of shooting.

In Southern's *The Magic Christian*, the eccentric Guy Grand tampers with the film *The Best Years of Our Lives* by inserting shots of the handless sailor groping with his hooks beneath the skirts of his ingenue sweetheart. But there are more obvious antecedents: Professor Rotwang in Fritz Lang's *Metropolis*, a demented scientist-inventor-magician in the service of capitalist society, has a black-gloved artificial limb.* So too has Lionel Atwill's Inspector Krogh in *Son of Frankenstein*, who manipulates it into a military salute, inserts his monocle between the fingers when it needs a polish, and, best of all, uses it as a pin-cushion for his darts in a deadpan match with Frankenstein Jnr. Bela Lugosi's Ygor, of the same film, is somewhere in Sellers' characterisation too, as well as the crawling beast with five fingers which does away with Peter Lorre in *The Hands of Orlac*. Dr. Strangelove is in short the definitive mad scientist of horror-film mythology, an essential personification of aberration, inhumanity and death. †

Sellers' portrayals of Muffley and Mandrake, though less bizarre, are equally as brilliant. In perfect command of an American accent, he plays Muffley as a bald bespectacled Stevensonian diplomat in a permanent state of dignified alarm.

---

* Eric Rhode (119) has pointed out the association between *Strangelove* and *Metropolis*: "A scientist with an iron hand, a doom-laden situation in which doom is equated with the inexorable power of machines, an office with flashing bulbs and huge maps."

† Dr. Strangelove has had his progeny. In Mario Bava's *Dr. Goldfoot and the Girl Bombs*, Vincent Price plays an evil genius with a black patch over his eye who is conspiring to ruin and rule the world; he plans to steal a USAF jet during a military exercise, bomb Moscow, start a war and then pick up the pieces after it's over with the help of Red China.

He is quietly authoritative at first, but as he gets involved with Kissof on the hot line, his speech begins to hesitate, hurry and stumble. His mounting panic, conveyed by the subtlest gradations of vocal and facial disintegration, demonstrates absolute mastery of realistic acting technique.

No less effective is his Group Captain Mandrake. According to a recent biography of Sellers, he habitually impersonated RAF officers such as Mandrake when he was an Airman Second Class during the war. Conceived very much as a pukka but decent Englishman, Sellers' Mandrake stays within a hairbreadth of his Major Bloodnok of *Goon Show* fame, preserving a dignity and restraint which is funny and at times even touching. Initially at ease, he adopts a more military manner as he realises Ripper is up to no good. "Do I take it, sir, that you're threatening a brother officer with a gun?" he demands with pained formality. Spruce and melancholy, he plays a superb scene with Ripper on the sofa, his voice cautiously reasonable, his whole body tensely apprehensive of some violent assault at the hands of the mad general he is trying to humour.

*

Before assessing the critical reaction to *Dr. Strangelove*, a short digression on the relationship between *Dr. Strangelove* and *Fail Safe* is in order. Just as Kubrick was finishing *Lolita* and being recommended *Red Alert* by Alastair Buchan, the publication of *Fail-Safe* (book title hyphenated, film not) by Eugene Burdick and Harvey Wheeler threatened to grab the limelight, especially when a film version by Max Youngstein's newly formed Entertainment Corporation of America was announced.

Some people assumed that Kubrick's film was a plagiarisation of the new novel, whereas *Fail-Safe* reads, if anything, like a plagiarisation of *Red Alert*. Believing that the marketing of *Fail Safe* would be prejudicial to the public desire to see *Dr. Strangelove*, Peter George and Columbia Pictures filed suit against Youngstein's Company which counter-claimed that as *Fail Safe* was not a comedy there was no resemblance between the two pictures. The case was settled out of court in George's favour, and *Fail Safe* was finally filmed one year after *Dr. Strangelove* by Sidney Lumet – for Columbia Pictures!

Youngstein's counter-claim was a trifle disingenuous, since *Fail-Safe* is based on a nuclear confrontation very similar to that of *Red Alert*. It cross-cuts from War Room to Bomber Base to SAC in the same way, and ends in nuclear catastrophe. In *Fail-Safe*, however, the crisis is caused not by madness but by an unexplained malfunction in a computer which sends out an irrevocable attack order to in-flight SAC bomber aircraft.

The two stories are interesting to compare in detail. *Fail Safe*'s highly idealised President is plainly modelled upon Jack Kennedy and is played in the film by rangy, short-sleeved, unflappable Henry Fonda, in striking contrast to Peter Sellers' dumpy distraught Muffley, who has virtually no control over anything. Muffley's opposite number, Premier Kissof, is equally as incompetent. In the novel version of *Fail-Safe* the Russian leader is explicitly named as Khrushchev; he moralises and pontificates but eventually comes round to expressing admiration for the Americans' conduct in the crisis, a detail which effectively puts the Americans one up.

In both novels the American President offers the Russians the information they need to jointly destroy the deadly bomber fleet. In *Fail Safe* the co-operating American General suppresses his pleasure at one crew getting through; in *Dr. Strangelove*, General Turgidson gleefully expresses it. In *Fail Safe*, hawk-line and dove-line are safely (and incredibly) polarised between a civilian spokesman and a military spokesman. Groteschele, the hawk, whose father fled from Nazi Germany, is embittered about Jewish passivity. He can be compared both to the ex-Nazi Dr. Strangelove and with General Ripper, whose sexual problems Groteschele would have understood: "She would, without mercy and as if it were her due, draw the energy and juices and fluids and substance from his body through the inexhaustible demands of pure sex." (*Fail-Safe*) It looks as if a neat bit of counter-plagiarisation may have been going on here, not to mention counter-counter-plagiarisation, for in the film version only of *Fail Safe*, the Secretary of State for War,

Swinson by name, is played as a cripple. Who has been lifting what from whom?

The point of *Fail Safe* is that the probability of accidental war "increases with the increasing complexity of the man-machine components which make up our defence system." Like *Dr. Strangelove*, it effectively creates a sense of nightmare in dwelling on the imperfections of the system – but the crucial difference between the two films is that *Fail Safe* blames things on the machines, whereas *Dr. Strangelove* flays the men who run them. Too much reliance on the machine is bad, *Fail Safe* seems to say, while leaving you with unvarnished respect for the wise and dutiful authorities – especially the American authorities – who control the bomb. *Dr. Strangelove* indulges in no maudlin exchanges of regret and noble assertions of mutual responsibility because it does not consider those who maintain the system worthy of respect. *Fail Safe*'s fatalism ends in an ineffectual plea for multilateral disarmament. *Dr. Strangelove*, viewing the whole thing as a crazy game, ruthlessly eschews the easy liberal gestures.

However, it's worth saying that the message of Peter George's original novel, *Red Alert*, is rather different from *Dr. Strangelove*, the movie. The novel seems to conclude that war is, after all, important enough to be left in the hands of the politicians and that if peace is to be maintained the balance of terror must be restored; when both sides have automatically retaliating missiles, war becomes profitless. Thus the averted catastrophe in *Red Alert* does in effect secure Peace on Earth since no-one, it is presumed, will now take the crucial action leading to war. The conclusion is as dubious in its way as the hushed respectful tones of *Fail Safe*.

※

The opening of *Dr. Strangelove* was delayed for six weeks by the assassination of President Kennedy, and no doubt the delay would have been longer if the President of the movie had been modelled upon Kennedy. It was premiered simultaneously in January 1964 in London, New York and Toronto, and became an overwhelming critical and box-office success. At the Columbia Cinema in London, attendance receipts were up 25% on all previous films and a special late-night showing had to be added. But, disgracefully, it was only given a partial release on the Rank circuit and therefore did not receive in Britain the widespread distribution it deserved. The New York film critics voted Kubrick the best director of 1964. In Europe, the film was well received on the whole as an example of the American ability to criticise itself, and was particularly popular in Scandinavia, Italy and France. Only in Germany, according to Kubrick, was the film unfavourably received.[19]

It was not only in film circles that the film generated widespread discussion. The political implications of the film, the argument over whether fail-safe procedures had been misrepresented or not, occupied political and military commentators in the press, TV and radio. Alastair Buchan and Leonard Beaton of the International Institute of Strategic Studies insisted that the plot strained belief by ignoring the elaborate procedures whereby one base commander cannot give the order for war.

Buchan felt he had been right in advising Kubrick against making the film: "Although Mr. Kubrick has attempted to take the sting out of the subject by turning horror into black comedy, only a limited number of people in the many lands in which it will be shown will be aware that the basis of the plot is a series of distortions even of the known facts about American control and safety procedures."[20] His colleague, Leonard Beaton, wrote that "if the film depicted a plot which nuclear safety designers have already made impossible on a dozen counts, most of the blame must rest with the British and American governments," which have been tardy in reassuring the public by spelling out precautions. A Gaullist commentator, André Frossard, writing – rather fancifully, I'd say – in *Le Figaro*, thought that France's stand-offish attitude to NATO could be partly attributed to the film.

Firstly, it should be noted that accidents do in fact happen. The USAF has had a dozen or more publicised incidents or crashes in Bomber Command with nuclear weapons on board. While Kubrick was filming *Dr. Strangelove*, for instance, two incidents took place: a USAF bomber dropped its nuclear bomb which luckily did not explode – luckily, since six of its seven safety devices failed to work. Secondly, a berserk airman at a station in Britain was allowed near nuclear warheads and tried to explode one with a revolver. The psychiatrist knew he was disturbed, but didn't know the airman's job as it was so classified.[21]

And, as I write, *The Guardian* reports that a USAF major has been suspended after allowing three men with dangerous psychiatric problems to guard a secret nuclear weapons base in the San Francisco area. A sergeant, who was accused of going berserk with a loaded carbine, "had pleaded not to be assigned to a job in which he would handle explosives and weapons, saying he was afraid of them and afraid he might hurt someone, yet on several occasions, he had been the sentry N.C.O. of a two-man guard for nuclear-tipped missiles stored at the base." The major had received unfavourable psychiatric reports on the sergeant and other guards, but had not replaced them due to understaffing![22] In 1962, the Human Reliability Programme was incepted, but only some colonels and generals come under its purviews. One SAC colonel was discovered to be alcoholic purely by chance.

As for the Doomsday machine, its feasibility has been maintained by more than one commentator, including, as long ago as 1961, Herman Kahn. (By 1964, however, Kahn, who regards *Dr. Strangelove* as "a brilliant joke," no longer believed a nuclear holocaust could be unleashed accidentally.)

The issue of accidental disaster is, of course, important in reality. But one can't help feeling that those who are worried about the way it is represented in the film have been fooled by its deceptively documentary style into misunderstanding the basic comic strategy of the movie, to misunderstand, in short, its purgative Swiftian function. The crisis situation is used for a slashing satirical attack on certain attitudes common in American strategic circles. After all, Jack D. Ripper's views on fluoridation are actually held by bedrock American conservatives, and are representative of what Richard D. Hofstadter aptly calls "The Paranoid Style in American Politics." And all Strangelove's ideas, however bizarrely expressed, are genuinely held by certain "authorities." Louis Mumford's letter to *The New York Times*, though perhaps overgenerous to our leaders, must be quoted here as a corrective:

> *Dr. Strangelove* would be a silly, ineffective picture if its purpose were to ridicule the characters of our military and political leaders by showing them as clownish monsters – stupid, psychotic, obsessed. For we know that most of them are in fact intelligent, devoted men, with only a normal proneness to suspicion, pride and error. What has masked the hideous error of our demoralized strategy of total extermination is just the fact that it has been the work of otherwise well-balanced, responsible men, beginning with Henry L. Stimson.
>
> By representing the individual components of this strategic system as colossal paranoids and criminal incompetents, Mr. Kubrick has happily found the only way possible to characterise the policy itself. Since in our case the "final solution" of the Communist problem would call for our own country's dreadful mutilation, as well as Soviet Russia's, and might even, if carried on beyond the first day, destroy the human race, there is hardly any method short of the wildest kind of farce, to describe overt madness on this catastrophic scale. Unless the spectator was purged by laughter he would be paralysed by the unendurable anxiety this policy, once it were honestly appraised, would produce.
>
> [...]
>
> What the wacky characters in *Dr. Strangelove* are saying is precisely what needs to be said: this nightmare eventuality that we are concocting for our children is nothing but crazy fantasy, by nature as horribly crippled and dehumanised as Dr. Strangelove himself...
>
> This film is the first break in the catatonic cold war trance that has so long held our country in its rigid grip.[23]

Kubrick himself has said that he doesn't think *Dr. Strangelove* has made any difference to anything, for we are today as much "living with" the bomb as ever we were before. I disagree with Mumford that spectators are purged by laughter of their otherwise paralysing anxiety; the social value of the film lies rather in contributing to a general undercurrent of healthy scepticism, an undercurrent which surfaces on the political plane in various forms of active dissent.

Pushing unreason to its ultimate, offering no saving graces, *Dr. Strangelove* belongs to the Swiftian tradition of black bilious satire, together with the novels of Terry Southern, and Joseph Heller's *Catch-22*, numerous off-off-Broadway plays, and underground films such as *12-12-42* and *Oh Dem Watermelons*. It has been criticised for unfair exaggeration. But are the rigid stereotyped postures and grotesque conduct of present-day international affairs any less horrifyingly absurd than what is depicted in the film? One does not criticise a Vicky or a Scarfe cartoon, or Brecht's *Arturo Ui*, or Barbara Garson's *MacBird* for distorting the issues and taking too pessimistic a view of things.

Dr. Strangelove, a live-action lampoon, eschewing messages and moralising, is unique among commercial movies in its sweeping radical humour. It is not an anti-American film, or rather it is as healthily anti-American as it is anti-Russian and anti-Thanatos. It ridicules human beings as the bunglers and madmen they are for creating and enduring the nuclear situation, and it raises again the ever-vital question of whether the "authorities" who control our destiny are to be trusted.

Alastair Buchan is regretful that the film "might easily mislead anxious people all over the world," whereas he should be relieved that the film's bitter pill is so liberally coated with humour that it is not more disturbing than it is. Any work of art which helps generate public concern rather than complacency about the nuclear impasse is to be applauded. It is against the political background of the Bay of Pigs fiasco, the Berlin Wall crisis, and the Cuban Missile crisis that this film must be assessed. One of the great things about *Dr. Strangelove* is that Kubrick proved such a film of dissent could be made and exhibited at the time. One remains astonished and grateful that he got away with it. It still looks good – and relevant – today.

1. Kubrick, Stanley. "How I Learned to Stop Worrying and Love the Cinema," *Films and Filming*, June 1963.
2. Bernstein, Jeremy. "How About a Little Game?" *The New Yorker*, 12 November 1966.
3. Piler, Jack. "Dr. Strangelove or how Stanley Kubrick and Peter Sellers are making a nightmare comedy about The Bomb," *Scene*, 23 March 1962.
4. Buchan, Alastair. "Basis of a Film," *The Times*, 31 January 1964.
5. Walter, Renaud. "Entretien avec Stanley Kubrick," *Positif*, December 1968-January 1969.
6. Piler, "Dr. Strangelove."
7. Renaud. "Entretien avec Stanley Kubrick."
8. Kubrick, Stanley. "How I Learned to Stop Worrying."
9. ibid.
10. Alpert, Hollis. "Offbeat Director in Outer Space," *New York Times Magazine*, 16 January 1966.
11. Hudson, Roger. "Three Designers," *Sight and Sound*, Spring 1964.
12. Bull, Peter. *I Say, Look Here!* Peter Davies (London: 1965).
13. ibid.
14. Evans, Peter. *Peter Sellers: The Mask Behind the Mask* (Prentice-Hall, 1968).
15. Renaud. "Entretien avec Stanley Kubrick."
16. Evans, *Peter Sellers*.
17. Renaud. "Entretien avec Stanley Kubrick."
18. Evans, *Peter Sellers*.
19. Agel, Jerome (editor). *The Making of Kubrick's 2001* (Signet, 1970).
20. Buchan, Alastair. "Basis of a Film," *The Times*, 31 January 1964.
21. Mallone, Ronald S. "Message of Dr. Strangelove." *Sunday Telegraph*, 9 February 1964.
22. Uncredited. "Missile Guards had Mental Trouble," *The Guardian*, 18 August 1968.
23. Mumford, Lewis. "*Dr. Strangelove*," *New York Times*, 1 March 1964.

9. The Space-Suited Ape
2001: A Space Odyssey (1968)

Behold! I shall show you the Ultimate Man.

Friedrich Nietzsche
Thus Spake Zarathustra (1883-5)

In six days God created heaven and earth. And
on the seventh Stanley Kubrick sent it back for
modifications.

M-G-M studio mythology

Stanley Kubrick conceived the idea of a space film, typically, through reading, in this case some Rand Corporation statistics on the probability of life in outer space. As a reader of science-fiction and popular science for many years, he decided to approach Arthur C. Clarke. "I'd been an admirer of Arthur Clarke's work, and it seemed to me that he was not only the most talented of all the science-fiction writers, but that his knowledge and his general scientific background made him an even more appropriate person to work with, to try to develop a story that would revolve around my central interest in advanced extra-terrestrial civilisation."[1]

Kubrick and Clarke agreed to work on a story set in the year 2001. "We didn't want to go too far out into space," Kubrick stated, "because the thing that seemed most interesting was man's first awareness of extra-terrestrial life and the first contact with extra-terrestrial intelligence. Beyond that stage the mind tends to boggle."[2]

Clarke has written over forty scientific books and novels, published in thirty languages. Qualified in physics, maths and applied astronomy, he contributed to studies for a Moon rocket as long ago as 1938 and in 1945 originated in a technical paper the idea of communications satellites, describing, twelve years before Sputnik, exactly how they would function. He has won several awards and prizes, is a past Chairman of the British Interplanetary Society, and has lived in Ceylon since 1956, where he pursues his hobby of underwater exploration.

The idea of a redeeming intelligent force from outer space intervening in man's evolution first appeared in Clarke's novel, *Childhood's End* (1954). The Earth is kept in forcible quarantine to forestall man from nuclear suicide and infection of extra-terrestrial civilisations. As in *2001*, the strange beauty of an alien planet is revealed to a single awe-struck man before mankind evolves into a new transcendent species. Abraham Polonsky is said to be planning a $7 million film version of *Childhood's End.*

From its beginnings, the science-fiction genre has been used as a medium for theological and mystical speculation. The most notable example is C.S. Lewis's *Ransom Trilogy*, beginning with *Out of the Silent Planet* (1938). Mel Mckee has cogently argued[3] that many of the ideas in *2001* derive from the *Ransom Trilogy*, although Lewis – a friend of Clarke's – was more theologically than scientifically orientated.

Kubrick and Clarke's jumping-off point for *2001* was not *Childhood's End* but an eleven-page story, "The Sentinel," first published by Clarke in 1950. During an expedition to the Moon in 1996, a geologist discovers on a mountain face a rough glittering pyramidical structure. Its mechanism is beyond the understanding of man, and the story simply raises the tantalising possibility of a race from another galaxy leaving behind millions of signals all over space in order to make contact with other intelligences. The story ends with: "we have broken the glass of the fire alarm and have nothing to do but wait."

Kubrick and Clarke decided to write *2001* in prose form before turning it into a screenplay. What they were attempting was artistically quite unprecedented: a mutually evolving film and novel, a cross-fertilisation at the creative stage in two different media. How did this work? "We spent the better part of a year on the novel," Kubrick says. "We'd each do chapters and kick them back and forth. It seemed to me a better kind of attack. If you do a screenplay from an original story idea you tend to leave out the ideas you can't find a ready way of dramatising. But by doing it as a novel first you have a chance to really think everything out, after which you can figure out ways of dramatising what you know are valuable points of the story."[4]

They worked on the novel, or, as Kubrick describes it, the "fifty-thousand-word prose 'thing' looking more like a novel than anything else,"[5] working four hours a day, six days a week. Then Kubrick "prepared the film for approximately six months, spent about four and a half months shooting the portion of the film in which the actors appear, and then spent a year and a half shooting the two hundred and five special effects."[6] Clarke in his turn took all the existing pre-filming material plus an impression of some of the rushes and wrote the novel. It was, again in Kubrick's words, "an essentially original literary work based on glimpses and segments of a film he had not yet seen in its entirety."[7]

The first draft of the screenplay, together with a meticulously detailed budget breakdown, was submitted to Robert H. O'Brien, President of M-G-M, who gave approval to the project. This quick assent was rather unusual practice. Science-fiction films are generally costly and their previously limited appeal makes major companies reluctant to invest heavily in them. In any case, few productions receive large-scale budgets without the pre-selling advantages of a best-selling novel or stage hit, or the presence of top box-office stars That O'Brien accepted Kubrick's project so readily says much for his confidence in Kubrick's money-making potential. *Spartacus*, *Lolita* (distributed by M-G-M) and *Dr. Strangelove* had, of course, all been commercially successful. So too was M-G-M's own *Forbidden Planet*, made ten years earlier.

For nearly four years, therefore, in conditions of utmost secrecy, hundreds of craftsmen and technicians laboured under Kubrick's direction to produce what was to be the most expensive, realistic and awe-inspiring science-fiction film ever made.

*

The film was first announced by M-G-M in February 1965 as *Journey Beyond the Stars* with locations in Britain, Switzerland, Africa, Germany and the U.S.A.

Shooting began at Boreham Wood, M-G-M's British studios, on 29 December 1965. The production spread to nine out of the ten sound stages, effectively halving the studio's normal feature output, and it overflowed into Shepperton Studios for the prehistoric sequences. The lunar set, in fact, occupied 29,750 square feet of Shepperton's Stage H, which had been built for Korda's *Things to Come* thirty years earlier.

2001 was originally scheduled for release in December 1966 but so painstaking was the production that it overstepped its deadline by fifteen months. It also overstepped its budget by a matter of £1,600,000. The film cost £4,500,000 ($10,500,000 dollars), and a further £2 million was spent on prints, publicity, promotion and use of Boreham Wood Studios.

During this very protracted shooting period, M-G-M ran into internal difficulties and Robert H. O'Brien had to fight for his position against dissident personnel. Carrying on work on *2001* so far beyond the agreed deadline depended on O'Brien's personal co-operation. If O'Brien had not retained his position, it's possible that Kubrick would have been compelled to abandon his film in mid-production.

Kubrick has acknowledged his debt: "It was necessary to conceive, design and engineer completely new techniques to produce the special effects. This took 18 months and $6,500,000 out of a $10,500,000 budget. I think an extraordinary amount of credit must go to Robert H. O'Brien... who had sufficient faith to allow me to persevere at what must have at times appeared to be a task without end. But I felt it was necessary to make this film in such a way that every special-effects shot in it would be completely convincing – something that had never before been accomplished in a motion picture."[8]

Still the production dragged on. Eventually O'Brien was obliged to fix the premiere date in order to hurry the film towards completion. He may well have been anxious. With a stake of over £6 million, M-G-M's own financial health is said to have hinged on the success of this single picture. But Kubrick's confidence in it was such that he bought $20,500 worth of M-G-M shares.[9] He cut the film on a moviola installed on the Queen Elizabeth on his way to New York and cut the final shot into the negative at M-G-M's Hollywood studios. The film was eventually given its first preview – eight days after Kubrick viewed the final edited print, two years after completing the main shooting work with the actors – on 31 March 1968 in Washington before an invited audience. A few days later it opened in New York.

The first New York reviews were mixed but generally hostile. The film was castigated as dull, pretentious and overlong. Andrew Sarris described it in *The Village Voice* as "a thoroughly uninteresting failure and the most damning demonstration yet of Stanley Kubrick's inability to tell a story coherently and with a consistent point of view."[10] A few championed it with enthusiasm. Gene Youngblood's review in the *Los Angeles Free Press* described *2001* as a masterpiece[11] and was reprinted as an ad in *The Village Voice*. Other opinions ranged the entire critical spectrum between these two views.

Between its third and fourth public showing in New York, Kubrick (on his own initiative) tightened the film from 160 to 141 minutes, and two explanatory titles (to parts three and four of the film) were added. This is not uncommon practice. Kubrick had trimmed *Paths of Glory* after its first showing, and completely cut the final pie-throwing sequence from *Dr. Strangelove* after a preview. Nearly thirty short cuts were made in *2001*. No scene was entirely removed but several individual shots were trimmed in length and deleted. These included: (a) shots from the sequence in which Bowman replaces the "faulty" unit in the Discovery's antenna, (b) HAL, the computer, asking for permission to repeat the message from mission control which first reports the possibility of his own malfunctioning, and (c) shots from Poole's repair excursion, including the moment when HAL switches off the radio in the pod immediately before it attacks Poole (making it now difficult to understand why Bowman asks HAL in the following scene whether the radio is still dead).

In the following weeks, *2001* opened in several major cities. Its London premiere was on 1 May 1968. Subsequent reviews were milder; everyone praised the special effects, and tentative ideas were put forward about the last sequence. Then assessments in the monthly and quarterly journals began to appear. These reviews were far more enthusiastic. Underground and college newspapers singled out the film for special attention. There were even re-reviews. No film since *L'Année dernière à Marienbad* has provoked such a mixed and vehement critical response nor perhaps such eagerness to supply a definitive interpretation. Something of the tremendous impact made by the film is conveyed by Jerome Agel's book, *The Making of Kubrick's 2001: A Space Odyssey.*

Within a year of its publication, over one million copies of the novel's paperback edition had been sold, and in 1969 *Childhood's End* was reprinted three times. Arthur C. Clarke went on a 15-city tour to promote the film (as did Keir Dullea and Gary Lockwood, the stars of the film). It soon became clear that the film was attracting a young, quasi-hippie audience who, of course, had no difficulties with the film's mystical ending. It has become quite common for people to sit deliberately near the front of the cinema and watch the film stoned. Mick Jagger stated: "For me, *2001* is the most fantastic film I've seen," and John Lennon said: "I see it every week."

Among the directors who admired it were Richard Lester (who disliked *Paths of Glory*), Zeffirelli ("YOU MADE ME DREAM EYES WIDE OPEN STOP YOURS IS MUCH MORE THAN AN EXTRAORDINARY FILM THANK YOU"), Fellini ("I SAW YESTERDAY YOUR FILM AND I NEED TO TELL YOU MY EMOTION MY ENTHUSIASM STOP I WISH YOU THE BEST LUCK IN YOUR PATH"), Schlesinger, Boorman, Donen and Polanski. Charles Chaplin is said to have been so overwhelmed that he wept. Antonioni was puzzled. And so, too, though he admired the film's beauty, was Ray Bradbury. "Ray also claimed," says Clarke, "that I had been raped by Kubrick. I assure you it was mutual."[12]

Here, too, is Marshall McLuhan on the film: "A movie like *2001* belongs to 1901, or even the world of Jules Verne. It is filled with nineteenth-century hardware and Newtonian imagery. It has few, if any, twentieth-century qualities. This is natural. The public is not capable of being entertained by awareness of its own condition. Fish do not love to think about water, or men about air pollution."[13]

The first box-office returns were not good, but by the end of a five-week run in eight engagements it had broken box-office records for comparable runs of *Gone with the Wind* and *Doctor Zhivago*. Shown initially in 70mm Cinerama, a 35mm wide-screen version is frequently revived. *2001* has turned into M-G-M's biggest box-office success, and is predicted to earn $25 million dollars in the U.S.A. and Canada alone. It also won an Oscar for the best Visual Effects of 1968 and numerous other awards in the U.S.A. and abroad.

The remainder of this chapter falls into four sections: production techniques; comparison of the film with the novel and earlier draft screenplays; an exposition of the film with notes; and a more general analysis. Readers who prefer not to know how a magician does his tricks should skip the next section.

Production techniques

Kubrick's objective was to make a film that would be exciting, beautiful, scientifically accurate and impeccably realistic. "What I'm after," he said, "is a majestic visual experience." He had seen practically every science-fiction film ever made, but "no one had the time or money to create visually interesting effects or try to present sci-fi subjects realistically."[14]

Determined that everything on the screen would be in accord with what the scientific community believed likely, he convened in the spring of 1965 a meeting of three dozen technical advisors from 36 countries. To ensure absolute authenticity he studied technical reports and scientific documents and read every science and science-fiction book he considered relevant. More than sixty leading industrial and scientific firms and organisations lent their services with technical and design consultation, including Vickers-Armstrong, Eastman Kodak, IBM and Dupont, which designed a special fabric. The space suits were made by a Lancashire firm called Frankenstein!

The care for detail extended to clothes (designed by Hardy Amies), domestic arrangements, and colour schemes. NASA (the National Aeronautics and Space Administration) plotted on their computers the Discovery's actual trajectory to Jupiter. And two former NASA experts, Fred I. Ordway III and Harry Lange, who had worked under Wernher von Braun on the American space programme, were permanently retained in the art department.[15] *2001* was to be a highly realistic projection of current space technology and something unique in the cinema – a documentary of the future. As Kubrick commented: "The trip and the magical alignments of Jupiter and its satellites are the only things in *2001* that don't conform to what is known to physicists and astronomers."[16]

Kubrick had been impressed by *Universe* (1960), a 20-minute black-and-white documentary by the National Film Board of Canada. What appealed to him in *Universe* was the integration of 3D models with 2D art works; miniature shooting at high speed into small areas to get huge cataclysmic effects; and the achievement of huge spatial relationships by using very small areas on the animation stand. He wanted the team who made the film to work with him on *2001*, but as it turned out Wally Gentleman was the only member free to join the *2001* unit as a Special Effects Supervisor.

The story-boarding was already well-advanced under Tony Masters, the Art Director, when Gentleman went to Boreham Wood to advise Kubrick on the acquiring and setting-up of equipment. He remained for nine or ten weeks into floor production until illness and/or ill-feeling caused his departure. Gentleman disliked Kubrick's working methods, which he considered wasteful. He also considered that the original screenplay, which he had liked, underwent changes for the worse and felt, on the whole, that *2001* was turned into a special effects vehicle to the neglect of the story-line.[17]

Meanwhile, two Americans, Douglas Trumbull, a young expert in space documentaries, and Con Pederson, joined the team as Special Effects Supervisors and largely influenced the design of the spacecraft. The Special Effects team was completed by Wally Weevers and Tom Howard. Weevers had begun his career as an apprentice on the 1936 Shepperton production of *Things to Come*, for the last twenty years had been Head of Special Effects at the same studio, and had worked on *Dr. Strangelove*. The very exacting equipment required for the film was built in the engineering department at Elstree Studios.

2001 is probably the most technically complex film ever made. Each scene took weeks of preparation and every shot had to be perfect in every way before Kubrick would accept it. Where old techniques were inadequate, new ones had to be invented. To keep track of the highly complex technical operations of the film and the 106-man production unit, a control room, constantly manned by four people, was set up. Since there were 205 special effects, each of which required ten stages to reach completion, each stage needing to be repeated eight or nine times until it was right, something like 16,000 separate steps had to be carried out. Every scene was named. For instance, each of the effects in the culminating "trip" sequence was named after a football play: "deep pass," "kickoff" and "punt return."

The locations for the Dawn of Man sequence were found in a desert region of South West Africa. However, it was impossible to take a full crew and cast there, since their dependence on weather conditions and light quality would have made cost and time factors prohibitive. Instead, it was decided to shoot the sequence in the studio.

A painted backcloth or rear-projection was not considered convincing enough, so a new method of front-projection was invented. Three still camera units worked for several months taking thousands of 8"x10" Ektachrome transparencies of the desert locations. The chosen stills were then projected across a 90-foot-deep stretch of barren rocky ground constructed on the studio floor and onto a vast screen 110 feet wide by 40 feet high. This Stereoptican Front Projection Process, the largest and most sophisticated ever constructed, is likely to be used extensively for visual effects in the future.

The ape suits and masks were evolved out of painstaking experiment. Originally the apes were to have been more man-like, and Dublin acting agencies were scoured in search of short actors with long upper lips. When later it was decided to use suits and masks, the make-up department presented Kubrick with no fewer than 75 samples for his inspection. Eventually Stuart Freeborn devised an intricate head-piece within which the facial muscles could be manipulated by tongue movements. An ingenious arrangement of magnets and elastic corresponding to facial muscles enabled the actors to snarl, lick their lips and gnaw red meat. Dancers and mimes were the only performers whose bodies were of a suitably slight build to wear and move in the ape-suits (all the actors cast in the future sequences were over six feet tall).

The now famous monolith was originally to have been a tetrahedron (a four-sided solid triangular pyramid) but, according to Con Pederson, it "didn't look monumental or simple or fundamental. It tended to express diminution more than impressive scale. And there would be people who would think of pyramids."[18] Five monoliths were actually used in the production, some three feet long, and one twelve feet long.

The fleet of spaceships were probably the most precisely detailed models ever constructed for a film. Each vehicle was built to the scale which best suited the filming of it, and not to relative scale with the other models. The Orion spaceship which commutes between Earth and the Hilton Space Station Five was approximately three feet long. The Hilton Space Station, a rotating spoked centrifuge supposedly 1,000 feet in diameter, was actually eight feet in diameter. The Moon Research Bus, which zooms between lunar base headquarters and the Tycho crater, was about two feet long. And the mammoth Discovery spaceship, supposedly 600 feet in length, in fact measured 60 feet. For the long shots, a 15-foot model of the Discovery was built. Its basic framework was covered with metal foil and moulded plastic, and finished off in meticulous detail with parts taken from thousands of plastic model kits. In fact, many of the models designed were not shown in the completed film.

For the central living area of the Discovery, the pressure hull, a "real" centrifuge, was built by Vickers-Armstrong, 36 feet high, 38 feet in diameter, it took three months to build and cost nearly £250,000. The spinning action of a centrifuge forces objects outwards to the rim, and the centrifugal force with which they are pushed to the rim takes the place of the force of gravity, which pushes objects to the ground. Thus people are given the sensation of normal weight.

Everything – lighting, rear projection units, even the camera – had to be designed or modified so that they could function properly within the wheel while its circumference slowly rotated at three miles an hour. The camera was on a remote-control head, and it was all controlled from the outside. In its original conception the centrifuge was to have been equipped, in addition to what we see in the film, with an electronically-operated medical dispensary, a shower, and a recreation area complete with ping-pong table and electronic piano.[19]

To support this massive piece of equipment, the studio floor had to be reinforced, and technicians were required to wear crash helmets inside it. Kubrick directed the actors from the studio floor by means of a closed-circuit TV system; when clad in their spacesuits and helmets a two-way radio transmitter was used. Music was relayed into the centrifuge by an electrophone to help create atmosphere for certain scenes.

In this revolving chamber, normal perspectives of "up" and "down" lose meaning. In the opening shot Poole (Gary Lockwood) appears to be running 360° around the interior rim of the centrifuge, holding to the floor by centrifugal force. In fact, as the centrifuge moved at its steady 3 mph, Lockwood ran in the opposite direction to maintain his position on the spot, while the camera also moved to keep position a little ahead of him, shooting on its side. Similarly, we see Bowman enter the chamber close to the camera on the right while at the opposite end, seemingly above our heads, Poole sits eating a meal. The camera appears to remain stationary as Bowman walks slowly around the chamber to join Poole. In fact, they both remained, as always, at the bottom of the revolving centrifuge, but cleverly thought-out camera movements make it seem as if they are standing upright at any angle.

Poole was in fact strapped upside down to his seat and the meal-tray was fixed to the table. The centrifuge then rotated and Bowman walked on the spot. It was the camera, locked in position, which rotated through 180°, thus creating the effect that the two actors were defying gravity. The same technique, with camera and set revolving, made it look as if the "space-hostess" could walk upside down in the Orion, whereas she remained upright all the time, walking a treadmill in the rear portion of the set.

Incidents involving action in a weightless condition, such as Poole whirling away into space and Bowman blasting himself back into the spaceship through the emergency airlock were filmed with the players supported on wires. Since the actors' weight pulling against the supporting harness tends to stretch the costume material into stress lines, and in order also to hide the wires themselves, the actors were suspended from the ceiling with the camera positioned directly beneath them. As for Dr. Floyd's floating pencil, it was simply hung from a nylon string.

The computer read-outs, ever-shifting relays of colour-coded linear projections appearing on the banks of monitor screens at the various spaceship controls, were all scientifically authentic and to scale. It took one unit, using a stop-motion 35mm Mitchell camera, nearly a year to film them. A year was spent unsuccessfully trying to build a model of the Moon, and in the end back-lit Ektachrome transparencies were used, as for shots of the Earth, Jupiter, and Jupiter's satellites. Live-action shots were inserted into the models by miniature projection.

The dazzling journey through the Stargate was created by Douglas Trumbull on a Split-Scan machine, a completely automated image-scanning device involving a bank of photo-electric controls. The succeeding images of exploding galaxies and cosmic energy patterns were counterfeited by the *Universe* technique of shooting various chemical reactions with powerful lenses on a camera field no bigger than a cigarette packet. Wally Weevers regards as the most difficult shot in the film, "daddy of them all, the mindbender," a diamond shape rotating with eight triangular facets, on each of which three separate moving pictures were projected while it was rotating.

All these effects were achieved by directly mechanical contrivance. Some of the most complicated work was in the laboratory processing. To obtain the unusually crisp and grain-free images, Kubrick dispensed with most of the conventional methods of optical printing such as travelling mattes. He used instead multiple exposure, i.e. photographing different parts of the scene separately and then combining them on a single print. For instance, model Moon terrain was blended into the live action of a scene, the Earth was another exposure, and so were the stars. Since normal matting techniques were difficult or impossible, mattes had to be hand-drawn laboriously for the entire length of a scene. Because of the difficulties, few of the multiple exposure shots involve overlapping objects.

Frank Cordell was hired to work on an original musical score for the film. Cordell wanted to write a memorable score after the manner of Arthur Bliss or William Walton, but Kubrick wasn't satisfied and brought Alex North, composer for *Spartacus*, over from Hollywood. This did not work out either. In the end, it is said, Kubrick listened to almost every modern composition available on record, including electronic music, to find something suitable for the film. He chose music by Richard Strauss,* Johann Strauss, Aram Khachaturian (who in 1956 composed music for a ballet version of the Spartacus story) and György Ligeti. None of this music was electronic, although Ligeti's sometimes sounded like it. Ligeti, in fact, successfully sued for having had his music distorted.[20]

Such were some of the exhaustive measures by which Kubrick achieved his technical tour de force. Only one technical error has been detected in the film: when Dr. Floyd sips his Liquipak, the food slips back into the container instead of staying in the straw as it would in real gravity zero.

Novel, screenplays and life itself
The novel of *2001*, published in 1968, is credited to Arthur C. Clarke, "based on the screenplay by Stanley Kubrick and Arthur C. Clarke," and includes a foreword initialled by Clarke and Kubrick. There are some significant differences between the novel and the film. Kubrick and Clarke regard the film and novel as variations on a central theme, each artist remaining pre-eminent, as it were, in his own medium.

Thus, although Clarke, who was around during the preparatory stages of the production but ceased to appear once shooting was underway, is critical of details, he has declared himself "more than delighted" with the film. "The book and the film are *each* definitive *in their respective fields*, and give my interpretation as well as Stanley Kubrick's. Nor is his necessarily the 'right' one – whatever that means."[21]

---

* The Zarathustra theme was used in the BBC TV documentary *The Epic That Never Was*, about Von Sternberg's *I, Claudius*.

"Stanley might make a great scientist with his insatiable curiosity. When it comes to film-making, he's the best."[22] However, Clarke did feel that a more explicit explanation of HAL's behaviour should have been given in the film, and he also objected to the detail of the breaking glass in the final sequence.

The screenplay underwent many changes during preparations and shooting, and indeed many scenes that were shot were later dropped. (Keir Dullea: "There is no similarity between the script and the final picture, because it is all visual, and even the director couldn't know from reading it how it would evolve in terms of modern technology."[23]) An early screenplay, dated 6 July 1965, is very significantly different from both the novel and the film. An intermediate screenplay (I.S.), representing the period October 1965 to February 1966, bears a much closer resemblance to the novel than the finished film.

The differences between the I.S. and the film mainly concern the use of a narration. The I.S. makes much use of an intermittent but at times quite lengthy commentary which supplies a good deal of background information. It places the action in a brief political context, provides detailed explanations of the cause of HAL's disorder, and the true nature of the black obelisk, and also explains how the Discovery's instruments work. The lunar sequence is preceded by a brief narrated montage establishing the social life of the Clavius research colony; there are to be shots of children engaged in unusual gymnastics and a geography lesson on the planet Earth.

As in the novel, a very long narration precedes Bowman's arrival in what was originally conceived to look like a conventional hotel bedroom: the narration explains exactly what is happening and exactly the motives of the extra-terrestrial beings who brought Bowman there. Much of this narration is identical to passages in the novel, and in this form the scenario has much more of the quality of a dramatised documentary. While one regrets the loss of political context, the cutting of the narration was absolutely the right decision. Less explicit, more enigmatic, the completed film exercises a far greater grip on the imagination by forcing the viewer into speculations and interpretations of his own.

Other changes are briefly as follows. In the I.S. there is much more banal conversation about the rumoured Moon "epidemic." The African sequence is longer and differs in detail: the apes are seen to wander across country foraging, to kill a lion and plant its head on a stick to frighten a rival tribe. The obelisk is a transparent crystal cube which makes drumming noises and programmes discontent and envy into the apes (in the film we never learn the obelisk's explicit function). The audacious jump cut from hurled bone to spaceship has not yet been conceived. Floyd not only telephones his daughter (a scene absent from the novel) but also orders from Macy's of New York a bush-baby for her birthday – this part of the scene was shot but not included.

The Discovery is bound for Saturn, not Jupiter. In fact, many months were spent trying to design Saturn until it was decided that Jupiter might be visually more interesting and possibly easier to produce. There is a split-screen montage sequence showing a typical day's schedule for the two astronauts. The plotting of the two astronauts and HAL's lip-reading occur neither in the I.S. nor in the novel. Bowman does not go out to rescue Poole but plans instead to revive the hibernating crew members. HAL opens the pod-bay doors to drain the ship of air instead of locking Bowman out. And in the I.S., part four of the film has yet to be set out in detail.

If we go back to the earlier screenplay (E.S.) of July 1965, the differences are more striking still. If anything, the screen-play in this form is even more of a dramatised documentary, the film dominated by the voice of the narrator. In the E.S., Floyd is greeted at the Moon base – Tycho not Clavius – by one Dr. Mary Boland of the Medical Reception Area, with whom he is having a furtive affair.

Instead of the discussion with the Russian team he is interviewed by a *Times* reporter, who is also enjoying a secretive liaison with his female "assistant." There is no telephone call to Earth. The black slab, a "crystallisation of night," is shaped like a cube in the Dawn of Man sequence, but later appears as a tetrahedron. Between parts two and three we see Floyd addressing a press conference in New York recommending the reconnaissance trip to Jupiter, and we also see the take-off of the Discovery spaceship.

In the E.S., HAL does not yet exist as a character in his own right. The ship is indeed controlled by a talking computer but it utters only one line, a warning to Bowman not to leave the spaceship without observing regulations. The mission is upset by an accident while Poole is carrying out a routine repair job outside the ship, but if it is caused by computer malfunctioning the point is not emphasised in any way. The outcome of the accident is that Poole does a Captain Oates, stepping out into space when he realises a rescue operation might jeopardise the mission further, and Bowman actually revives three of the four hibernating crew. On reaching Jupiter they carry out their exploratory survey as planned. While one astronaut hovers above in his space-pod, Bowman descends into the fathomless Stargate.

Led by a fluttering phosphorescent guide, Bowman witnesses many strange and beautiful sights. In view of Kubrick's predilection for symmetrical shots, one is intrigued to find in the E.S. that the entire extra-terrestrial scenic view, "which must cover twenty or so miles, *is completely symmetrical!* [italics and exclamation mark in screenplay] It is landscaped as an emperor might order his garden. It would seem that the inhabitants have such vast energy sources at their disposal they can landscape the entire surface of their planet." The E.S. adds a note: "He will see other Stargates, other sights. The number will depend on the imaginativeness of the design concepts, of their being achievable without any sense of fakery. In all cases, the guideline is that what we see, we must be able to believe, or to put it differently, we must not disbelieve because of obvious trick effects."[24]

As in the I.S. and novel, Bowman ends up in an anonymous Earth-style hotel room and is finally returned to Earth. But instead of being turned into a Star-Child he is led by the hand through a door into infinite space by one of an extra-terrestrial species of "unbelievably graceful and beautiful humanoid creatures who appear to be about twenty feet tall… Towering above Bowman in splendid blue phosphorescence, it carefully takes the Earth-man's hand and leads him forward into the void, looking not unlike a parent leading its child."

The original idea was to make the extra-terrestrials resemble Giacometti sculpture. Near the end of the production, a television video feedback technique produced lifelike pulsating light images for the trip sequence, and some footage was actually made – too late to incorporate into the film. And for the trip sequence, the astronauts were to travel through a City of Light, a fully three-dimensional generation of geometric shapes developed on the split-screen. As for Bowman's reception in the room, Kubrick comments: "The ending was altered shortly before shooting it. In the original, there was no transformation of Bowman. He just wandered around the room and finally saw the artifact. But this didn't seem like it was satisfying enough, or interesting enough, and we constantly searched for ideas until we finally came up with the ending as you see it."[25]

Finally, from Jerome Agel's book on the making of the film, we learn: "Kubrick's original plan was to open 2001 with a ten-minute prologue (35mm film, black-and-white) – edited interviews on extraterrestrial possibilities with experts on Space, theology, chemistry, biology, astronomy… Kubrick says that he decided after the first screening of 2001 for M-G-M executives in Culver City, California, that it wasn't a good idea to open 2001 with a prologue, and it was eliminated immediately."[26]

Thus the chief developments in the evolving screenplay can be summarised as: (a) the gradual elimination of the narrator and specific documentary material, (b) the increasing prominence of HAL as an active agent in the plot, (c) a visually less ambitious but conceptually richer ending, partly on account of technical limitations, and (d) the removal of the political context.

The film of 2001 takes place in a political vacuum, that is, we learn virtually nothing of the political situation on Earth other than what is implied from American and Russian pre-eminence on the Moon. Clarke's novel postulates co-operation between the U.S.A., Britain and the U.S.S.R., with China at one point suspected as being behind the appearance of the mysterious slab. It's illuminating, therefore, to see how the narrator introduces part two of the film in the I.S:

> By the year 2001, overpopulation had replaced the problem of starvation but this was ominously offset by the absolute and utter perfection of the weapon... Hundreds of giant bombs had been placed in perpetual orbit above the Earth. They were capable of incinerating the entire Earth's surface from an altitude of 100 miles... Matters were further complicated by the presence of twenty-seven nations in the nuclear club. There had been no deliberate or accidental use of nuclear weapons since World War II and some people felt secure in this knowledge. But to others, the situation seemed comparable to an airline with a perfect safety record; it showed admirable skill and care but no one could expect it to last forever.[27]

In the novel, when Bowman returns to Earth as a Star-Child his first act is to wipe clean Earth's slate, as it were, by detonating the megaton bombs encircling the Earth, in preparation for exerting his god-like powers. This ending exactly parallels the ending of the Dawn of Man section in the novel which also culminates in an act of destruction marking a new stage in evolutionary progress. "For though he was master of the world, he was not quite sure what to do next... But he would think of something."[28] Shots of orbiting satellites carrying nuclear weapons were cut from the film, and no nuclear bomb motifs are present. Evidently, Kubrick did not want an ending so similar to that of *Dr. Strangelove.*

"What an irony," Kubrick says in his *New Yorker* interview, "that the discovery of nuclear power, with its potential for annihilation, also constitutes the first tottering step into the universe that must be taken by all intelligent worlds."[29]

It is a grim irony indeed, and one that Wernher von Braun, for one, can appreciate, that any civilisation capable of space travel must have developed simultaneously the technological means of its own destruction. The development of rocketry and electronic computers was given a strong impetus by missile research during the Second World War. The Germans invested in rocket research for specific military purposes, and von Braun developed for the Nazis the V-2 rockets which bombed London and Norwich towards the end of the war. In fact, Hitler slowed down the production of V-2s because of a prophetic nightmare about rockets.

When von Braun surrendered to the Americans, he was simply made director of the U.S. space programme and became an American citizen. A hundred German scientists went with him to the U.S.A., of whom fifty still remain with him. A hundred German scientists were captured by the Russians and doubtless continue their research there. Sputnik II, for instance, was launched with a military rocket, and the central engine of the first Soviet I.C.B.M. was an improved V-2 engine. Von Braun, whose accent, blond quiff and smoked glasses may be detected in Peter Sellers's Dr. Strangelove, is the backroom hero of the Apollo Space Programme. BBC Television's coverage of the Apollo Moon landings used the music from *2001*, Strauss's Zarathustra theme, as its signature tune. The irony is neatly clinched.

✳

2001 – an exposition

2001: A Space Odyssey is divided into four parts: "The Dawn of Man" (16 minutes); an untitled section dealing with the discovery of the Moon monolith (34 minutes); "Jupiter Mission: Eighteen Months Later" (61 minutes); and "Jupiter and Beyond the Infinite" (20 minutes). An intermission occurs during part three.

The Dawn of Man
This section takes us back three million years to the Pleistocene Age. A tribe of a vegetation-eating species of ape-man, Australopithecus Africanus, spends its time foraging and grooming. Below five feet tall, in very scruffy condition, the apes look just about due for extinction. The prologue is divided by fades into four sub-sections:

(a) A sequence of deathly still, finely composed desert landscapes evoke an arid inhospitable world. An ape is attacked and killed by a leopard.

(b) The ape tribe defends its territorial right to a small murky water-hole against a neighbouring tribe by a threatening display of snarling and ground-thumping.

(c) The apes lie or scuffle restlessly in their cave at night, eyes fearful and alert. There is a brief glimpse of a crescent Moon high in a red glowing sky.

(d) The apes emerge from their cave to find a ten-foot-high jet-black rectangular slab embedded in a crater in the ground. They approach it agitatedly. The monolith evokes at once the idea of a totem, phallus, tombstone, Stonehenge monument and Tablet of the Law, an image of Freudian and Biblical resonance. As the Moon, sun and slab fall into alignment, Moonwatcher, the leading ape, prompted by the sight of the obelisk, picks up and handles a bone for the first time. He beats at other bones on the ground, causing them to bounce upwards. Shots of the flying bones are intercut with images of felled animals in slow motion, a vivid mental association. Next, we see the tribe eating meat – one in grisly close-up – and after a further brief night-shot, a second water-hole battle occurs, culminating in the killing of an enemy ape with a bone "club."

This fascinating prologue, owing much to such recent ethological and anthropological studies as those of L.S.B. Leakey, Robert Ardrey and Konrad Lorenz, explicitly illustrates how the survival of man's primitive ancestors depended on his discovery of weapons. The amount of time elapsing between the images is deliberately made uncertain, but the opening progression from landscape, bone of beast, and bone of ape to real animal suggests a condensed prehistory of evolution, each stage of evolution occurring in the duration of an eyeblink. As indeed occurs the evolution at the end of the film.

The condensing of images suggests that the first tool was a weapon, and that the principles of propulsion (the bounced and pitched bones) and of bipedry (the ape rises triumphantly to his feet after his Cain-like murder) are contingent upon the discovery of the bone as an instrument of destructive power. The step forward towards humanity lies across the body of a slaughtered ape.

And since Moonwatcher *envisions*, by association, the killing of an animal, he also experiences "thought," "the future," "time." It is surely no accident that the first action he performs before striking one bone with another is to make a pendulum-like banging motion.

The Dawn of Man scenes are shot with a feeling of stillness, calm and objectivity, mostly at eye-level with a barely moving camera. The action is played out within strictly delimited areas in front of huge front-projected transparencies of the African Veldt, which gives the section a somewhat theatrical flavour, almost like a series of tableaux. But it is superbly staged.

The discovery of the obelisk is rendered particularly stirring by György Ligeti's elegiac yet ominous Choral "Requiem." "The idea of a magical alignment of the Sun, the Earth and the Moon, or of Jupiter and its moons," says Kubrick, "was used throughout the film to represent something magical and important about to happen. I suppose the idea had something to do with the strange sensation one has when the alignment of the sun takes place at Stonehenge."[30]

In striking contrast to the eye-level objectivity which predominates, the two moments of revelation – the discovery of the bone as an instrument, then of its power to kill – are shot in slow motion in low angle shots which invest the killer ape with eerily exultant strength. These images convey the terrible elation and fulfilment of power as something almost orgasmic in intensity.

Many of the shots have an effectively faded flat look, as of telephoto shots in wildlife documentaries. The screeches of the apes, and the sounds of the blows are amplified; and the apeskins and masks are disturbingly life-like, the more so because the ape children are played by real chimpanzees.

However, this part of the film looks much better in 70mm than in the less engulfing 35mm processing. On the smaller screen the backgrounds look more obviously like projection work, and some of the colour toning seems to lose in subtlety.

The discovery of the Moon monolith
Part two of the film falls into five main divisions:

(a) *Orion*
The bone launched into the air by Moonwatcher turns and falls, and the image abruptly changes to a bone-white spacecraft in mid-flight. A leap of three million years, audaciously equating a complex technological feat with a primitive projectile, is traversed by a single stunning jump-cut. Attention focusses on Pan-American's Orion, a sleek delta-winged spacecraft, carrying a single passenger, Dr. Heywood Floyd (William Sylvester) of the National Council of Astronautics. It is heading for its rendezvous with the orbiting Space Station Five, stopping-off point on the journey to the Moon (space is big business!).

Accompanying this first breathtaking view of outer space is Johann Strauss's "The Blue Danube" waltz, a choice of background music both unexpected and reassuring. It establishes a mood at once buoyant, lyrical, rich and majestic. Its familiarity induces us to sit back and enjoy what we see not as something strange and exotic, but so familiar to the space-traveller of 2001 that Floyd hardly spares a glance for the immense panoramas visible to him.

This music, Kubrick comments, "underlines the graceful aspect of human achievements of this epoch; it doesn't have to sound futuristic, because when Hilton Hotels are installed in Space Stations, their music will appear neither strange nor futuristic but timeless. The intention was not satirical. I just chose music I found beautiful."[31] And again, "It's hard to find anything much better than 'The Blue Danube' for depicting grace and beauty in turning. It also gets about as far away as you can get from the cliche of space music."[32] It's strange that anyone could have mistaken Kubrick's self-evidently lyrical paeon to space technology as anything but a homage of love. Can anyone who has seen *2001* now hear "The Blue Danube" without thinking of the film?

The first interior shot is of a dislodged pencil floating in mid-air beside the sleeping Dr. Floyd, one capsule afloat within another floating capsule. The image also suggests desexualisation. There is a feeling of solitude, but also of solicitude, warmth and comfort.

(b) *Hilton Space Station Five*
Spoken dialogue is heard for the first time during this sequence, 24 minutes after the beginning of the film. After checking in with Voiceprint Identification, Floyd video-telephones his small daughter at home on Earth. Their conversation is conducted in engaging daddy-will-be-late-home-from-the-office style. Amidst the dazzling space technology of *2001*, a world of birthdays and schools and shopping still goes on. Significantly, the first thing she asks for her birthday is a machine (a telephone) and the second is an animal (a bush-baby). The little girl is played by Kubrick's own daughter, Vivian, aged six, with a charming naturalness that makes one suspect she was filmed talking to her real dad (Sylvester, in fact, played to pre-shot footage of Vivian). As if to emphasise the timelessness of the scene, she wears a rather old-fashioned-looking velvet dress.

Floyd proceeds to Howard Johnson's Earthlight Room, a vast, curved space-lounge, 150 feet long, dotted with squat cerise chairs. Its spaciousness, bright illumination and echoey acoustics recall again the chateau of *Paths of Glory*. Here Floyd meets Dr. Smyslov and some colleagues from a Russian research group on their way back to Earth. Smyslov (whose name happens to be that of a Russian Chess Grand Master) discreetly enquires about rumours of an epidemic and quarantine on Clavius, the American Moon base, but Floyd cagily reveals nothing about his mission. Evidently the rival American and Russian research teams work in uneasy cold-war rapprochement.

On first viewing it is not too clear to people unfamiliar with astronomy that Clavius, where Floyd is bound, is not another planet, but an American research colony based in the Moon's second largest crater (the point is clearer in the I.S.). In the I.S. but not in the film, a Russian woman offers pills to the group as one might offer cigarettes. In the ultra-hygienic world of *2001*, no-one is seen to smoke. After Floyd is gone there is a brief exchange in Russian: "It's going to be difficult." "Yes, I think so." Edited out of this sequence was a shot of a souvenir counter selling chunks of Moon-rock, space-dolls and postcards of the Moon.

(c) *Aries*
Floyd sets off on the second stage of his trip, this time in the globular, insect-like Aries spacecraft. The prevailing mood of this sequence is entertaining and droll as various domestic features of space-travel in 2001 are paraded. The space-hostesses watch on colour television a judo or karate contest (Kubrick's combat preoccupation emerging in mellower form); they move about slowly by means of Velcro-padded shoes, turning 180° to get from one part of the ship to the pilot's cockpit. Floyd is supplied with a Liquipak container from which he sucks food through a plastic tube, like an infant; and he ponders over the detailed ten commandments of the Zero Gravity Toilet which, though illegible to the audience, were printed authentically.[33]

The landing at Clavius Astrodome has a powerfully apocalyptic splendour. The lunar module descends gently onto a light-delineated landing area and is then lowered on an immense hydraulic column into a redly glowing docking chamber, like some enormous brain cavity; gradually we become aware of tiny figures moving behind the windows of six separate observation points in the chamber, the most impressive use of back projection in the film.

It is the last time that we hear the Strauss waltz until the final credits.

(d) *Clavius base*
Dr. Floyd addresses a closed meeting of Clavius personnel. We learn that the epidemic rumour was a cover story

designed to protect people from an immense cultural shock: the discovery forty feet below the surface of the Tycho crater of a mysterious object buried there four million years ago. Floyd's mission is to examine this excavated object. The scene is again superbly composed, with three of the room's artificially-lit walls rendered simultaneously visible. As Dr. Halverson, of Clavius base, moves back from the speaker's rostrum towards his place near the camera, Floyd moves forward to the rostrum and the camera slightly pans first to the left and then to the right to take both men in without a cut. Tycho was not an arbitrary choice for the location of the object: this giant crater does apparently emit anomalous rays of unknown origin.

Scenes shot but not put into the finished film included shots of youngsters playing on the Moon, swans floating and men painting.

(e) *The Moon bus travels to Tycho*
The land-going and low-flying Moon bus transports Floyd and his colleagues to the Tycho site – the extreme contrasts of black and white on the Moon must have appealed to Kubrick. For the first time, in the cramped conditions of the bus, a hand-held camera is used and the dialogue becomes very informal – a banal conversation about their simulated sandwiches as, in their restricting spacesuits, the men look over the pictures and radiographs of the mysterious object. The wavering hand-held camera introduces an element of human uncertainty and fragility into the scene, reminiscent of the hand-held camera shots in *Dr. Strangelove*'s B-52 bomber sequences.

The slick ultra-sanitised look of everything in these spacecraft episodes bears evidence of an impeccable advanced technology within which men carry on the same trivial conversations, dominated, in a sense, by their own super-efficient creations. Once again they do not spare a glance for the Moon-scape outside.

The arrival of the party at the Tycho site and their descent towards the slab is one of the most thrillingly executed scenes in the film. Cordoned off within an excavated area shored up by golden walls, lit by arc lamps which shine into the camera, and visible against the background of a lunar landscape, is a black slab like the one seen in the Dawn of Man section. As the troubled, murmuring chorus of Ligeti's "Requiem" is heard again on the sound-track, the hand-held camera pursues and tracks the men descending the ramp, as clumsy as ape-men in their cumbrous spacesuits. Floyd stretches his hand out wonderingly towards the slab. The party's photographer urges them to pose for a picture in front of the slab like explorers of old, and, as they close in, the sun rises after the 14-day lunar night and its rays fall upon the monolith. It emits a piercing shriek which sends the men reeling.

At this point the lunar section ends, leaving us uncertain, until Floyd's reappearance in the next section, what fate has befallen Floyd's party. In the novel and I.S. we learn that the noise quickly stops and that it is a powerful blast of electro-magnetic energy signalling across the solar system towards the planet Jupiter; a "warning that man, the killer ape, is armed and on his way."[34]

Jupiter mission, eighteen months later
The great spaceship Discovery flies into the picture like some huge goods-train. It is travelling at 100,000 miles an hour, near the end of a nine-month journey to Jupiter, 50 million miles away from the sun. The slight flippancy of the earlier scenes disappears and there is a sense of real loneliness. In contrast to the fulsome "Blue Danube" music, we hear Khachaturian's wan and desolate Adagio from the "Gayaneh" ballet suite. The first interior shot is of Dr. Frank Poole exercising in track shorts by running 360° around the rim of the pressure hull sphere, which is the central living area of the spaceship. Panting, making faintly anachronistic boxing passes, he looks like a rat on a treadmill. Man has lost his pre-eminence and is back where he started, fearful of things that shriek in the night.

The sequences of the two astronauts moving about within the artificial gravity produced by centrifugal force provide Kubrick with the opportunity to create some very sophisticated visual compositions. Shots of the two astronauts occupying, at once, seemingly incompatible perspective planes suggest some of the optical illusions of the Dutch artist, Maurits C. Escher, whose work may, indeed, have influenced the film. In this sequence, camera angling takes further the visual disorientation we have already experienced, preparing us for the later complete collapse of familiar spatial relations. Frequently shot from above, to emphasise the astronauts' vulnerability and isolation, the sense of estrangement is overwhelming.

As the men eat a meal of coloured pastes, they watch a "BBC-12" relay of their pre-flight interviews. This T.V. programme, giving us the run-down on the mission, functions as a traditional exposition scene. The spaceship, we learn, is manned by Dr. David Bowman (the name has appropriate associations – David and Goliath, Star of David, archery) and Dr. Frank Poole. The two doctors, who have no knowledge of the purpose of their journey, are by way of being caretakers on the ship which, in all other respects, is controlled by a super-computer, HAL 9000 (originally to have been called Athena, after the goddess of war, wisdom and fertility). The three remaining crew members, who have been separately trained and do know the purpose of the journey, lie frozen in hibernacula, to be revived on reaching Jupiter. Their pulses and respiration slowed to almost zero, they look like entombed corpses or mummies in sarcophagi.

Critics who have objected to the superficiality or remoteness of the characters Poole and Bowman, or who assumed that they are intended to be typical representatives of the human race in 2001, have not realised that they are typical only of their peculiar profession, as anyone who has watched the Apollo astronauts in action can confirm.

Dr. Terence McGuire, Chief Psychiatrist of the Aerospace Medical School in the U.S.A., has stated the qualifications for the men he selects: "They must not be philosophical, or think about the aesthetical aspect of something, though some are interested in things like music or history. They must be cold and calculating men. They must also be extroverted, well adjusted, self-reliant, decisive, intelligent and logical."[35]

Norman Mailer speaks of the Apollo men thus:

> On the one hand to dwell in the very centre of technological reality, yet to inhabit – if only in one's dreams – that other world where death, metaphysics and the unanswerable questions of eternity must reside was to suggest they could have been the most miserable and unbalanced of men if they did not contain in their huge contradictions some of the profound and accelerating opposites of the century itself.[36]

Poole and Bowman are typical members of this new breed of pilot-technologist-scientists. They are humourless, absolutely cool types who carry out their functions efficiently, displaying neither enthusiasm nor warmth. When Poole is called by his parents on his birthday, he watches their banal celebration with bored, almost hostile, indifference. His reaction is quite different from Floyd's to his daughter. Poole has, in the words of the novel, moved into a new dimension of remoteness, his emotional links stretched beyond the yield point. Identically tall, snub-nosed, short-haired and impassive, the astronauts are as near automata as human beings can get, a feeling reinforced by the chillingly neutral drawings Bowman makes of his hibernating fellow crew-members. Each man at first seems closer to HAL than to his fellow astronaut. Bowman shows his drawings to HAL but not to Poole. Poole plays chess with HAL but not with Bowman. In fact, human beings and computer are in a sense interchangeable: automata-like humans, humanised computer.

Given the severe emotional limits of their roles, the two actors do surprisingly well at being solemn. As Bowman, Keir Dullea, in particular, has an arrestingly intelligent, sweetly reasonable yet faintly menacing look. Dullea was grateful to Kubrick for giving him the chance to do something different, having been type-cast previously as "an introverted, neuter young boy with parent problems, usually my mother."[37] I'm not so sure that Dullea wasn't cast in *2001* for those very associations. ("The Blue Danube" is played, by the way, in *The Hoodlum Priest*, which features Dullea.)

HAL's name is an acronym of two principal methods of computer programming: Heuristic (learning by experience) and Algorithmic (possibility of formation). HAL is also short for "Henry," which means "Master of the house." He is indeed master, the brain and nerve-centre of the spaceship. He controls all its systems, plotting and maintaining its course, monitoring the conditions of all the working parts, regulating and registering the life-support systems, and automatically performing a multitude of additional functions. He can hear, converse fluently and see through a system of fish-eye lenses dotted around the ship – in short, reproduce (or "mimic') most of the attributes of the human brain "with greater speed and reliability." "The sophistication of the computer," says H.A. Morris, Director of Bradley University Computer Centre, "is not beyond the probable state of the art by the year *2001*."

HAL has been programmed to act as if he has real feelings in order to make him easier to talk to – but no one knows whether he experiences real feelings in the human sense. He describes himself as "a conscious entity," foolproof and incapable of error. "I enjoy working with people," he remarks in his T.V. interview. "I have a stimulating relationship with Dr. Poole and Dr. Bowman."

HAL was originally to have been spoken by Martin Balsam but Balsam's voice was regarded as too "colloquially American"[38] or too "emotional"[39] and he was redubbed in the softer transatlantic tones of Canadian actor Douglas Rain, who had been hired originally to speak the narration. The voice is friendly, soothing, exasperatingly relaxed, with faint undertones of irony and homosexuality. (How could HAL be otherwise? one might ask – but Kubrick says that the "homosexual" tone detected by some was not intended. HAL was supposed to be straight.) In such an otherwise husky mission, HAL is certainly a queer enough fish-eye for us to suspect him from the start, especially when, on being shown Bowman's frigid-looking, comic-book style drawings he patronisingly remarks, "That's a very nice rendering, Dave."

Bowman, and later the vacant seats of the spaceship, are viewed subjectively through HAL's fish-eye lens. Bowman thus viewed, HAL is invested with identity and presence, all the more powerful because his intangibility renders him apparently inaccessible. Like God. There is a short story by Fredric Brown about a supercomputer who is asked "Is there a God?" After making sure its power supply is no longer under human control it replies in a voice of thunder, "*Now there is!*"

A sudden crisis occurs. HAL predicts 100% failure in 72 hours of a unit in the ship's radio antennae, but after the "faulty" unit has been replaced in mid-space, the astronauts can find nothing wrong with it and check with Mission Control, who in turn check with a HAL simulator at Earth base. The Mission Controller (played by a real USAF traffic controller stationed in England) confirms that HAL is in error in predicting failure of the unit. HAL thereupon insists upon his own infallibility and attributes the discrepancy between himself and his simulator to human error. He suggests to Bowman and Poole that they re-install the faulty part to prove his reliability. In the event of the predicted failure, the ship will be for a short time out of radio communication with Earth base.

A fiendishly neat paradox now exists. HAL was supposed to be infallible by the human experts who had, incidentally, programmed this conviction into him. Yet if there has been a human error, as HAL insists, it can only have manifested itself in a flaw in HAL – or his counterpart – an error which HAL is now incapable of acknowledging. This poses a pretty problem for the astronauts whose survival depends on HAL's continuing competence.

The spacemen consult together out of HAL's hearing in the privacy, as they think, of one of the Discovery's space-pods. They agree to re-install the apparently faulty part. If it doesn't fail, they will dismantle HAL and resort to ground-control of the ship. But HAL's talents, perhaps developed without his makers' knowledge, include lip-reading, by which means he learns of their strategy. On this suspenseful note the first half of the film ends.

After the intermission we see Poole going out in a space-pod to replace the original antenna unit. But while he is afloat in space, the pod turns and rushes towards him. His lifeline is cut and he hurtles through space in freefall, struggling for breath. Radio control with Earth is now cut off. Bowman mounts a hurried rescue operation. That the cool and astute Bowman should leave the mother-ship without his space helmet to retrieve the body of a dead man is one minor implausibility in the film.

While he successfully rescues the body, HAL, in a chilling scene, turns off the life-support systems of the three hibernators and then refuses to readmit Bowman. "This mission is too important for me to allow you to jeopardise it," he informs Bowman. There is a fine shot of the small space-pod impotently confronting the now menacing-looking Discovery. As Bowman argues with HAL, the lights of the control panel flicker across his face. Bowman manages, however, to explode himself back into the ship through an emergency air-lock. The breakthrough, like everything else in the film, is scientifically possible: men can survive for about ten seconds in such conditions.*

There is a fast double-exposure dissolve (the only dissolve in the film) to Bowman, now fully dressed in his spacesuit and helmet, purposefully making his way through the ship towards HAL's brain centre while HAL calmly pleads with him to sit down and take a "stress pill." For the first time in this Discovery sequence, the hand-held camera is used, imparting again a sense of urgency, fragility and danger. "I know everything hasn't been quite right with me," HAL concedes as Bowman walks implacably on, "but I can assure you now very confidently that it's going to be alright again... I feel much better now, I really do... Look, Dave, I can see you're upset about this... I know I've made some very poor decisions lately..."

Floating within HAL's brain centre, a glowing, red-lit chamber, Bowman tensely proceeds to disconnect HAL's higher memory and logic units, leaving the purely automatic regulating systems in operation. This eerie lobotomy sequence is arguably the most disturbing in the picture. As

---

* For a short story on survival in space "between spaceships," see "Take a Deep Breath" in *The Other Side of the Sky* by Arthur C. Clarke (Corgi Books).

Bowman, sweating for the first time, unscrews and releases HAL's processing grids – transparent perspex rectangles like miniature obelisks, HAL pleads as calmly and soothingly as ever for mercy: "I'm afraid... I'm afraid, Dave... Dave, my mind is going... I can feel it... I can feel it... My mind is going... There is no question about it... I can feel it... I can feel it... I can feel it... I am afraid..."

This unnerving sequence culminates in HAL's regression to babyhood and his rendering of "Daisy, Daisy," which slows down lugubriously like a record on a gramophone turntable. Nothing in *2001* is arbitrary. "Daisy, Daisy" was selected, not just for its simple-mindedness and "half-crazy" reference, but because it was in fact one of the first songs ever "taught" to a computer. It can be heard on a record called "Music from Mathematics," arranged by M.V. Mathews, sung by an IBM 7090 computer and Digital-to-Sound Transducer. And a spooky little number it is.

As HAL grinds into permanent silence, Dr. Heywood Floyd flashes onto the T.V. monitor (it is not explained how radio contact has been restored – one presumes automatically by HAL's demise) and informs Bowman of the true meaning of the mission. It is actually a reconnaissance trip to investigate the target of the monolith's sun-triggered signal – Jupiter. Jupiter is the largest of the planets, from which radio signals have, in reality, been received. Its name is also the Roman equivalent of Zeus, the most powerful of the ancient gods. So ends part three of the film.

What then was the nature of the disastrous error and at what stage did it occur? It's significant that HAL picks up the fault in the unit immediately after expressing anxiety about the mysterious circumstances of the mission (at least he does in the film – not in the novel or I.S.). Why should HAL be bothered? A strong clue to HAL's malfunctioning occurs in the lobotomy scene when HAL insists that he can "feel" it. The human error is perhaps that in programming emotional responses into HAL in order to make him more humanly responsive, he has in fact been made capable of genuine feelings – and hence as vulnerable as any human being to their incalculable influence.

My own first thought was that ignorance of the purpose of the mission had disturbed his sense of omnipotence. But after HAL is dismantled we learn from Dr. Floyd on the T.V. monitor that HAL did know the purpose of the mission. It then seemed to me that HAL had become emotionally disturbed by the prospect of an encounter with a *higher intelligence*, and began having a breakdown, making a wrong prediction, then covering up, and ultimately becoming homicidal. Other critics have conjectured that he wanted to make contact with the alien intelligences without the mediation of his passengers. And yet others that he had somehow been tampered with by these same intelligences.

In the film, explanation of this conundrum is left – happily – open, but the reader may be interested to know how HAL's mistake was explained in the novel and in a rather lengthy exposition given to Bowman by Floyd in the I.S. Floyd reveals that because HAL was ordered to conceal from Bowman and Poole the real purpose of the mission, a conflict arose between the demands of his "conscience" and his programmed instructions (I.S.), or between knowledge of the truth and the concealment of truth (the novel). This conflict so sapped his integrity that he reacted neurotically. Since he had never known unconsciousness the threat of temporary disconnection terrified him; he finally flipped, decided to remove the source of his frustrations, his human tormenters, and continue his mission alone. Kubrick has more recently explained: "In the specific case of HAL, he had an acute emotional crisis because he could not accept evidence of his own fallibility."[40]

Clarke supplies a quotable gloss in the novel version: "The fact that HAL's builders had failed fully to understand the psychology of their own creation showed how difficult it might be to establish communication with *truly* alien beings."[41]

Jupiter and beyond the infinite
The final twenty minutes of the film are equally divided between Bowman's "trip" to Jupiter, and his "reception" there. It is perhaps significant that Bowman, the artist, rather than Poole, the chess-player, should be saved for this experience.

The Discovery is plunged straight into the orbit of Jupiter, where we see a huge black obelisk turning and seemingly evaporating and reappearing in space among Jupiter's satellites. The spaceship is now so dwarfed by Jupiter that it looks no bigger than a propelling pencil floating in space. The changing scale in which objects are seen, now immense, now tiny, according to viewpoint, scale and perspective, exactly paradigms the film's unsettling psychological relativism.

Jupiter's satellites, the sun and the obelisk align themselves in perfect symmetry – proof of a controlling intelligence. (One or two critics have detected in the cross formed by the monolith and the line of planets an image of the Second Coming. Such a biblical allusion would be consistent with the film's ending: one must be reborn as a child before being allowed to enter the Kingdom of Heaven.) And now "hatched" into his space-pod, Bowman's eyes water, his head vibrates and the colours reflected from his instrument panel blur until his head is, as it were, shaken into an amorphous mass of vibrating light, a brilliant visual metaphor for the experience he is to undergo.

The I.S. simply states: "The intention here is to present a breathtakingly beautiful and comprehensive sense of different extraterrestrial worlds."

Bowman's trip, our trip, begins with a descent (or *is* it a descent? – "up" and "down" are no longer relevant) through a roaring, streaming, latticed tunnel of changing neon light patterns. We hurtle through immense star-clusters. Gaseous, organic, electronic and geometric manifestations of pure energy grow, expand, dissolve and reshape, beautiful and terrifying. There are no material elements, no Galactic Space Terminal or Cosmic Junk-Heap as there are in the novel.

We next traverse weird landscapes and seascapes, their surfaces glowing with luminous unearthly colours. (These are actually views of the Hebrides in Scotland and Monument Valley in Arizona and Utah.) Shots of this aerial journey, recalling the aerial shots in *Dr. Strangelove*, are intercut with huge close-ups of Bowman's eye, staring and quiveringly alive as HAL's never was. The eye, chameleon-like as it changes colour with every blink, is a landscape in itself, at times indistinguishable from what it sees. A fusion of the seeing and the seen is in fact taking place, a complete dissolution of the barrier between ego and non-ego, a mystical symbiosis comparable to a hallucinogenic experience. (In the novel, Bowman explicitly compares his fantastic journey to a drug experience given during training. Kubrick himself denies having taken L.S.D.) In *2001*, Meister Eckhart's words are made palpable: "The eye with which I see God is the eye with which God sees me."

As in the Dawn of Man sequence aeons of time pass in the space of an eyeblink – or rather time and space cease to be operative in this time-space warp. From one landscape to another landscape – man is an anomalous interlude in nature.

This spectacular sequence benefits enormously from the engulfing Cinerama screen, from Ligeti's stirring "Atmospheres" music, and, of course, from the carefully prepared emotional context. But spellbinding and breathtaking as it is at first viewing, it tends to lose impact on subsequent viewings. This is, I think, because it remains a succession of separate effects rather than an organically linked whole. Technically impressive as these effects are, it must be said that they are no more inventive than the best light shows and the brilliant optical experiments in such underground films as Harry Smith's *Abstractions* and Scott Bartlett's *OffOn*. (Perhaps also one can never experience abstract-fantasy imagery for a second time with the same impact of a first viewing. No one can have exactly the same dream twice.)

The giant eye resolves itself through successive colour changes into the normal spectrum. The space-pod comes to rest. Bowman looks out of the pod into, of all things, a coolly elegant room furnished in eighteenth-century style, its floors, however, underlit like those of the Hilton Space Station. Its restful green tones are those of a doctor's waiting room – or an operating theatre. In the novel, E.S. and I.S., the room is an American hotel bedroom, simulated by the extra-terrestrials to make Bowman feel at home. In the film the possibility remains that it is a random environment thrown up by the time-slips of the journey, or even a projected wish-fulfilment, mutually created by Bowman's unconscious and the alien beings, of Bowman's need for a sanctuary from the automated rigours of life in *2001*, a nostalgic return to a civilisation uncomplicated by technology. To stretch the point a little, the sequence thus becomes dramatically equivalent to Vera Lynn's "We'll Meet Again" at the end of *Dr. Strangelove*.

Bowman sees himself standing outside the pod in his spacesuit. We hear his heavy amplified breathing and also echoey intimations of voices and odd metallic clinkings on the sound-track. Bowman stares at himself in the mirror aghast: his face is ravaged by time. (The cosmonaut Gherman Titov described his stay in an experimental silence chamber as "the mirror of truth – when you come face to face with yourself.") The space-pod is seen no more. Hearing the sound of cutlery in an adjoining room, Bowman approaches the door. Inside, an elderly man in a dressing gown is eating, his back to the camera. The space-man's heavy breathing is correlated with the image of the old man. Bowman is observing his own senescence and death: each viewed image becomes his subjective viewing self, an accelerated aging process in which younger selves are sloughed off in inexplicable overlapping time and space leaps.

The elderly Bowman comes to the door, thinking he hears something, finds no one and returns to his meal, only to drop and smash his wine glass on the floor. The broken glass may symbolise man's fragility and inadequacy (some critics have invoked Nietzsche and the Judaic marriage ceremony – a marriage of past, present and future?). As he bends to pick up the pieces, he becomes aware of heavy breathing and looks around to see a senile helpless old man, himself, in bed.

The dying Bowman lifts a wavering hand (like Moonwatcher's, like Floyd's) towards the black monolith that has appeared like a tombstone at the foot of his bed. A sun rises behind the obelisk; a luminous embryonic light burns in the place of the old man in the bed; the camera zooms subjectively towards the obelisk and is swallowed into its blackness. We see a planet – Earth – turning on its axis, and from the left floats another vast planet turning in its orbit, a new kind of Space Man, a monkey-like foetus enshrined within its transparent oval placenta, glowing more brightly than the Earth, its huge eyes at once old and young, all-knowing and awe-struck, staring outwards towards the planet and, finally, towards us.

In an interview with *The New York Times*, Kubrick explains his conception: "Here is what we used for planning. In the Jupiter orbit, Keir Dullea is swept into a star-gate. Hurtled through fragmented regions of time and space, he enters into another dimension where the laws of nature as we know them no longer apply. In the unseen presence of Godlike entities, beings of pure energy who have evolved beyond matter, he finds himself in what might be described as a human zoo, created from his own dreams and memories.

"He sees himself age in a time-mirror, such as you might see yourselves in a space-mirror. His entire life passes in what appears to him as a matter of moments, He dies and is reborn – transfigured; an enhanced being, a star-child. The ascent from ape to angel is complete."[42]

In the contemporary cinema, the visionary ending of *2001* is rivalled in its multi-layered complexity only by Alain Resnais's *L'Année dernière à Marienbad*.

＊

Ideas, motifs and myths in 2001

Stanley Kubrick has described *2001: A Space Odyssey* as a space-ballet rather than a space-opera, as a romance rather than science-fiction, as a mythological history rather than a sci-fi history, and as a magical documentary in four parts. Here are various longer statements he has made about the film:

"What happens at the end of the film must tap the subconscious for its power. To do this one must bypass words and move into the world of dreams and mythology. This is why the literal clarity one has become so used to is not there. But what *is* there has visceral clarity. It is for this reason that people are responding so emotionally. The film is getting to them in a way they are not used to."[43]

"*2001* is a non-verbal experience; out of two hours and nineteen minutes, there are only a little less than forty minutes of dialog. I tried to create a *visual* experience, one that bypasses verbal pigeonholing and directly penetrates the subconscious with an emotional and philosophic content. To convolute McLuhan, in *2001* the medium is the message. I intended the film to be an intensely subjective experience that reaches the viewer at an inner level of consciousness, just as music does."[44]

"If you understand *2001* completely, we failed. We wanted to raise far more questions than we answered."[45]

To those people who rely on verbal sign-posting and neat explanations, the open-ended *2001* is bound to prove baffling and exasperating. Significantly, the most favourable response has come from the young: to a generation reared in the electronic global village and steeped in light shows, L.S.D. and the works of Alan W. Watts, *2001*, far from affording any difficulty, is exactly where it's at. I think Kubrick is right when he says, "it seems to me that there is just the right degree of ambiguity to make the film 'communicate' yet retain a fascinating allusiveness."

Stephen Koch puts it well: "*2001* is among the few great films that owe nothing at all to the assumption of the middle-class psychological novel (as Resnais's film certainly does), entirely overlooking what is supposed to be the dominant preoccupation of 'serious' modern narrative – the self and its sufferings – and substituting its own virile and deeply intelligent exploration of the human capacity for wonder... Kubrick's film is nonetheless utterly cinematic, and one of its principal departures from the sci-fi form is to abandon the peculiarly verbal play of playing off amazement against a tendency to 'scientifically explain' and rationalise events."[46]

Those familiar with Kubrick's previous films will not be bothered by the film's eschewal of conventional exposition and "establishing" narrative line; in Kubrick's best films the audience is always plunged straight into a scene without the mediation of standard linking devices. Not that *2001* is as dramatically unorthodox as some baffled critics and Kubrick himself seem to think.* It seems to me, on the contrary, that *2001* rests on very firm classical foundations: a four-act structure; concern with man's relationship with the gods;

---

*Kubrick: "The film departs about as much from the conventions of the theatre and the three-act play as possible." 125

an unfolding revelatory process rather than the naturalistic exploration of character in society; the intervention (literally) of a deus ex machina; choral elements in the music. The film harmonises its stirring subjective effects with the deliberate pace and dispassionate observation of Greek drama.

Potent visual motifs resonate within and beyond the film; motifs of feeding, fighting and reproduction. As in *Dr. Strangelove* a good deal of eating goes on; hunger lies at the dramatic centre of the Dawn of Man episode. Later, in contrast to the shots of apes gnawing raw meat, we see the citizens of *2001* almost daintily consuming their Liquipak and coloured pastes, or enthusing over hygienically wrapped sandwiches made to look like the "real thing." Bowman's Last Supper in the Jupiter reception room is the nearest thing in the film to a familiar appetising meal of the sixties.

The umbilical link between mother and child is a feeding mechanism, and *2001* is full of sexually charged maternity images (cf. the credits sequence of *Dr. Strangelove*). Space travel has, of course, a powerful sexual element. The Apollo 11 launching is described by Norman Mailer in specifically sexual terms. And the Russian journalist, Konstantin Leonidov, was moved to describe the end of Lunik 2's journey as follows: "The rocket is rushing swiftly to the Moon. In one or two minutes the Moon will take into its embrace our Soviet rocket."

Who makes it first in space has become a question of national virility. In *2001*, the Discovery space voyager is shaped like a spermatozoon, a shape that takes on immense significance as it penetrates the mysterious periphery of the vast, egg-like Jupiter planet. Moreover, the mother-ship, Discovery, hatches its extra-vehicular space-pods like eggs, and they in turn, hatch the spacemen like baby birds or insects. Their heavy breathing, amplified on the sound-track, sounds distressingly laboured, emphasising their tenuous link with life. As for the final image of the film, it leaves one as much in awe of the mysterious creative process of human birth as of super-human birth; or rather pitches human birth in visual terms onto the plane of the miraculous. The most awe-inspiring universe of all, wonderful in its complexity and its unknown potential, is the human embryo.

2001 is full of circular motifs: eggs, wheels and eyes. An opening eye may, in some symbolic contexts, be equated with birth. In Buñuel and Dalí's *Un Chien Andalou*, the slitting of a woman's eyeball, intercut with the image of a slim cloud passing across a full moon, symbolises and helps to effect an abrupt transition into a new visionary mode of seeing, a visual rebirth. A huge eye features in *Childhood's End*. In *2001*, there is HAL's all-seeing bulbous eye, compared by one lady critic to a female breast and by a male critic to a vagina! The pod-bay doors open like some reptilian eyelid. The circular Clavius Astrodome, which receives the Aries space-ship by retracting its eight-pointed segments, is another kind of opening eye. Bowman first appears in an eye-like transition corridor to the centrifuge. And his final experience, as we have noted, is literally eye-opening, a cosmic operation for the cataract of behaviourism; indeed, at one point his staring eye appears to sever and fall apart. In the novel, the Star-gate through which Bowman falls is also literally a vast cosmic eye.

Another important motif in the film is film itself. One of the most common human activities in *2001* is watching film or TV monitors, and in this respect *2001* is as much a reflection upon the dissolving distinction between "real life" and "movies" as, say, *8½*.

Arthur C. Clarke, in a useful article in *Cosmos*, states that he and Kubrick started off with the deliberate intention of creating a myth, a myth drawing upon other myths and incorporating religious elements.[47]

"The idea is that the astronaut is reborn in a superior form," says Kubrick. "He's already an angel or a super-human. He returns to Earth in the manner of the heroes of all mythologies. In fact this is the basis of all myths, or almost all: the hero descends into a magical world which represents great danger, and is involved in all kinds of terrifying adventures whereby he becomes transformed, enhanced, in one way or another. He becomes another being."[48]

"The Odyssean parallel was in our minds from the beginning," Clarke comments, "long before the film's title was chosen." *The Odyssey* is the story of a homeward journey (hence circular in design) and so is *2001*, insofar as Bowman is reborn and returns to Earth. It is about the relationship between man and the gods, as we have already observed of *2001*. It is also about a son's search for his father, and "Jupiter" is the supreme father of gods and men. In the E.S., Bowman is actually led by the hand by a huge, fatherly hominoid. The most obviously Homeric motif in the film is HAL's cyclopean eye, about which more will be said shortly.

The Odyssey is also a sea story. The experience of walking in space is comparable to undersea swimming (Clarke's hobby) and astronauts exercise underwater as part of their training. The scenes in outer space in *2001*, with their free-floating, slow-motion feeling, have a distinctly aquatic quality, while the Strauss waltz, of course, celebrates a great river. Impossible not to think of Jonah and the Whale and of *Moby-Dick*. Clarke, whose novel version of *2001* includes an explicit reference to Captain Ahab, has stated that he had Moby-Dick "constantly in mind as a prototype to construct a launch-pad for metaphysical speculation."[49] He once remarked to Kubrick that he (Kubrick) was luckier than Herman Melville, who never lived to see the world appreciate his novel.

In the same article, Clarke says: "It with quite a shock that we recently discovered there is actually a Buddhist sect that worships a large black rectangular slab! The analogy of the Kaaba has also been mentioned. Though I certainly did not have it in mind at the time, the fact that the Black Stone sacred to the Moslems is reputed to be a meteorite is more than a quaint coincidence." Not mentioned in Clarke's article is the significance of the year 2001. This is the year in which the Age of Aquarius is supposed, by some modern astrologers, to begin, an Age considered to be a time of awakening spiritual consciousness, brotherhood – and invention.

2001 is a further exploration of a theme already probed in *Dr. Strangelove*, the uneasy relationship between men and machines. But this is, of course, a contemporary variation of the Frankenstein myth, which is itself derived from the Faustian theme of man's overweening interference with "nature." *2001* is, among other things, the best film version of *Frankenstein* yet made, a version perfectly tuned into the anxieties of our own times. The dramatic tension generated by the conflict of minds in the Discovery sequence has a strong traditional element in it. But both the suspense, and the bizarre humour of the situation, work better than anything else I can remember in the vein because the conflict rests on a relatively sophisticated psychological and philosophical basis. This makes a refreshing change from the usual simple-minded spectacle of some deformed imbecile or reptilian blob blundering towards his inevitable extinction in fire, flood or mire. In *2001*, the principle is taken further by having the human "controller" himself rewrought in the crucible of some higher order Frankenstein.

Man's evolution from ape to human to super-human is the fundamental theme of *2001*, a theme of grandiose Nietzschean scale. In *Thus Spake Zarathustra*, Nietzsche attempted just that, to elevate man to a position from which he could permanently assume the place in the world occupied by God. Appropriately, Kubrick used the World-Riddle theme from Richard Strauss's "Zarathustra" to accompany the ape-man's mastery of the bone as weapon, and the appearance of the Star-Child at the end. Strauss might have conceived the music for the film. "I did not intend to write philosophical music," he said. "I meant to convey by means of music an idea of development of the human race from its origin, through the various phases of its development, religious and scientific."

"The God concept," says Kubrick, "is at the heart of *2001* – but not any traditional anthropomorphic image of God. I don't believe in any of Earth's monotheistic religions, but I do believe that one can construct an intriguing scientific definition of God."[50] This kind of definition is in line with such recent biological speculations as those of Gordon Rattray Taylor in *The Biological Time Bomb*.

Kubrick, who admits to being "really fascinated by U.F.O.s," explains: "In a final stage, one will arrive at entities which will have total knowledge and can become beings of pure energy, spirits of some kind. They will probably have quasi-divine powers: telepathic communication with all the Universe, complete mastery of all matter, capable of doing things that we only believe possible of God. That's what fascinates me in the subject. It's the basis of the film and its raison d'être." And again: "The important point is that all the standard attributes assigned to God in our history could equally well be the characteristics of biological entities who billions of years ago were at a stage of development similar to man's own and evolved into something as remote from man as man is remote from the primordial ooze from which he first emerged."[51] Kubrick, like Clarke, like Wernher von Braun, is convinced that older, technically more advanced intelligences live or have lived in our galaxy, during geological time.

"The god concept is at the heart of *2001*," Kubrick has said, but I think it would be slightly more accurate to say that the "omnipotence concept" is at its heart. Many critics have commented that in *2001*, human banality is deliberately contrasted with the marvels of technology, that the film assumes that machines will evolve more rapidly than man's moral condition. While this is fair comment, Kubrick himself denies that he is in fact hostile towards machinery, rather he finds them beautiful and sexy (see Chapter Ten). Certainly, he is fascinated by them, as witness his collection of tape-recorders, cameras and hi-fi equipment, and his preoccupation with machines in his films. It is the fascination that photographic equipment exercises on the photographer. If we substitute for Moonwatcher's hurled bone a stills camera with its accessories, the jump cut to the Orion spacecraft takes on great personal significance.

Twice in the film, HAL is invested with subjectivity when we look out from the fish-eye lens into the interior of the ship. Let us, experimentally, identify HAL with Kubrick himself. HAL, a "conscious entity" without physical substance, registers the ship he controls by means of a system of magical fish-eye lenses. He monitors the activities of the ship just as Kubrick himself monitored the production of *2001*. One recalls that Kubrick communicated with the actors in the centrifuge by means of closed-circuit T.V. HAL is proud of his ability to run the whole operation himself and grows to resent the intrusion of his fallible human collaborators. He goes so far as to dispense with them. HAL's hubris leads to his downfall; but his demise is not fatal to the whole operation, for there are other gods in control. The ultimate resolution of *2001* is the assumption by a human being of god-like powers. He becomes a pure cosmic force, ethereal and omnipotent. It may be argued that the totally omnipotent is also the most totally impotent in terms of human destiny. Tom Nairn, for instance, has questioned whether beings without human or animal functions can in any sense represent a new start.[52] When human power is so elevated and abstracted the only possible stance is perhaps one of absolute detachment, secure and invulnerable in its dissociation from human affairs – a return, in a strange way, to the simplicity of a still camera lens that snaps the face of a grief-stricken news-vendor (see Chapter One). Is *2001*, among other things, Kubrick's spiritual autobiography, a record of his own *Odyssey*? The point will be resumed in the final chapter of this book.

I hope that the amount of space I have devoted to *2001* shows that I certainly don't intend this quite tentative comment as in any way providing the vital key to a film of irreducible richness, complexity and resonance. If *2001* affects us deeply it is because Kubrick has found the means to express his private concerns and anxieties in terms which radiate psychologically and socially to encompass us all.

There are those who remain unmoved by the film. Such critics tend to dwell on the film's minor flaws – a certain slowness in the spaceship repair sequences, less than convincing make-up in the "reception room" – and to emphasise the film's "anti-humanism" and "impersonality," its rejection of the narrative conventions associated with "character development." *2001* has been criticised a good deal for its preoccupation with hardware and technical trickery. Richard Roud complains that the film fails to articulate shots and construct images as beautifully as the individual images which compose the frame.

My view, however, is that it is a tribute to the film's powerful narrative thrust and the skilfulness of the effects that as one watches effects of quite brilliant ingenuity, one is inclined to think "How did they do it?" *after* exclaiming "How marvellous!" – the essential difference between the work of a mediocre and a master magician. To make some larger claims:

2001 includes some of the most ingenious compositions ever seen on film, is the best 70mm film ever made, among the best *colour* films ever made, and is probably the best science-fiction film ever made. To be affected by it is to be very deeply affected indeed, to be, in the end, literally overwhelmed.

Kubrick and Clarke aimed to create a modern myth, and my view is that they have remarkably succeeded. The Strauss theme is used both in BBC space coverage programmes and ITV commercials. A Seattle orchestra greeted U.S. astronauts with musical selections from the film. The rebel student hero of *The Strawberry Statement* listens to a recording of the film music, and two years after the film's release, the "Blue Danube" waltz is still being played in European discotheques. The film's narrative theme has reappeared in various forms (e.g. *Space Oddity* by David Bowie, about an astronaut who goes so far out he decides not to come back). A lengthy book has been devoted to the film's origins and reception. And so on.

When a work of art so quickly and broadly permeates a culture, it may be said to have acquired something of the potency of a myth. But, more important and quite uniquely, *2001* has fused two parallel but previously antithetical contemporary yearnings: the exploration of outer space and the exploration of inner space; restoring to the former the potentiality of psychic or spiritual risk (one hesitates to say "romance" although Kubrick is not afraid to use the word) that modern technology threatens to eliminate. It also bestows upon the audience as community an artistic experience of all-encompassing grandeur of a kind that has become almost extinct in the multiplexity of fragmented modern life. In this respect, also, *2001* functions very nearly like Greek drama.

2001, a film about the future, is keenly contemporary in its utilisation of recent primate studies, its worries about man's relations with computers and its final mind-blowing catharsis. But it is also firmly plugged in both to powerfully enduring myths of Western (not to say Eastern) culture, and to the energising personal complexes of its creator. It is this, together with its visual sophistication and beauty, dignity and humour, that gives *2001* its peculiar strength. Already part of film history, it is a magisterial achievement.

*

A note on 2001 and science-fiction films
I have neither the space nor the experience to compare *2001*
to other science-fiction films in detail. In any case, *2001*
is discussed (rather unfavourably) in a new book on the
subject.[53] But I would like to draw attention to some films I
think interesting for purposes of comparison.

Godard's brilliant *Alphaville* (1965) dramatises the
struggle between human feeling and technology in a city of
the future dominated by a sinister, gravel-voiced computer.
Fahrenheit 451, *Barbarella* and *Planet of the Apes* are
relevant since they came out at about the same time as *2001*.
Rayner Banham, writing in *New Society*, finds *Barbarella*'s
soft, yielding, furry surfaces preferable to *2001*'s gleaming
hardware. *Planet of the Apes* cuts its arrogant astronauts down
to size, but has its apes posing for the group photograph;
a beautiful lady astronaut is found dead on arrival; and the
leading astronaut discovers he has ended up on Earth.

Karel Zeman's partly animated *Baron Munchausen* (1962)
includes some eerily imaginative scenes on the Moon. And
in the light of Kubrick's background as a stills photographer,
one might also mention Chris Marker's *La Jetée* (1962) a
short science-fiction film consisting of still photographs.

Of outer space films, one should mention Fritz Lang's
Frau im Mond (1929), George Pal and Irving Pichel's
Destination Moon (1950), and Byron Haskin's *Conquest of
Space* (1955). *Destination Moon* much impressed me at the
age of eleven. It depicts an inventor, a general, an industrialist
and a wireless mechanic who, against the U.S. government's
wishes, mount a rush expedition to the Moon in order to
forestall the "others" whom they fear may get there first.
Their vicissitudes include the rescue of a man adrift in space.

Perhaps the most interesting film for purposes of
comparison is William Cameron Menzies's *Things to Come*,
made at Shepperton in 1936 for Alexander Korda. It was an
attempt to make a grand statement for its time, was scripted
by a distinguished science-fiction writer, H.G. Wells, from
his own novel, and projected a future in which the little things

of life are sacrificed to an insatiable lust for knowledge. In the year 2036, "The Universe of Nothing" is man's apocalyptic slogan. The film apparently ends with the people rebelling against their scientific masters and attempting to destroy a "Space Gun" which, however, manages to take off for the Moon in the nick of time, bearing a personable young couple as passengers. Judging from the stills and extracts I have seen, *Things to Come* has not worn too well.

1. Kohler, Charlie. "Stanley Kubrick Raps," *Eye,* August 1968.
2. Alpert, Hollis. "Offbeat Director in Outer Space,"
   New York Times Magazine, 16 January 1966.
3. Mckee, Mel. "*2001*: Out of the Silent Planet," *Sight and Sound*,
   Autumn 1969.
4. Alpert, "Offbeat Director in Outer Space."
5. Kohler, "Stanley Kubrick Raps."
6. ibid.
7. Gelmis, Joseph. *The Film Director As Superstar*
   (Doubleday & Co., Inc., 1970).
8. Norden, Eric. "Stanley Kubrick," *Playboy*, September 1968.
9. Uncredited. "Stanley Kubrick," *L'avant-scène*, February 1969.
   [Note: the figure was actually $205,000. See "Kubrick's $205,000 Buy of
   Metro Shares; Ticket Orders for *2001* Perky," *Variety*, 6 March 1968.]
10. Sarris, Andrew. "*2001: A Space Odyssey*," *The Village Voice*,
    11 April 1968.
11. Youngblood, Gene. "Stanley Kubrick's *2001*: A Masterpiece,"
    Los Angeles Free Press, 19 April 1968.
12. Agel, Jerome (editor). *The Making of Kubrick's 2001* (Signet, 1970).
13. *The Dew-Line*, quoted in Agel (1970).
14. Walter, Renaud. "Entretien avec Stanley Kubrick," *Positif*,
    December 1968-January 1969.
15. Herman Oberth, the pioneer of German rocketry, gave technical
    consultation and sponsorship to U.F.A.'s and Fritz Lang's *Frau im
    Mond* (1929) in return for facilities to test one of the early petrol-
    oxygen motors. U.F.A. even planned to launch a full-scale rocket to
    coincide with the film's premiere! Thus was the development of
    rocketry linked early on with the cinema.
16. Agel, *The Making of Kubrick's 2001*.
17. Gentleman, Wally. "Inside *2001*," *Take One*, May-June 1968.
18. Agel, *The Making of Kubrick's 2001*.
19. Norden, "Stanley Kubrick."
20. Agel, *The Making of Kubrick's 2001*.
21. Private correspondence.
22. ibid.
23. ibid.
24. ibid.
25. ibid.

26. ibid.
27. Kubrick, Stanley and Clarke, Arthur C. *2001: A Space Odyssey*, Filmscripts Ltd.
28. Clarke, Arthur C. *2001: A Space Odyssey* (Hutchinson & Co., Ltd., 1968).
29. Bernstein, Jeremy. "How About a Little Game?" *The New Yorker*, 12 November 1966.
30. Agel, *The Making of Kubrick's 2001.*
31. Renaud, "Entretien avec Stanley Kubrick."
32. Agel, *The Making of Kubrick's 2001.*
33. See the reproduction in Agel's book (ref. 125).
34. Mckee, "*2001*: Out of the Silent Planet."
35. Jeffries, Michael. "A Good Astronaut Gets on With His Father," *Evening Standard*, 19 November 1968.
36. Mailer, Norman. "The Mind of an Astronaut," *The Observer*, 19 April 1970.
37. Agel, *The Making of Kubrick's 2001.*
38. Gelmis, *The Film Director As Superstar.*
39. Agel, *The Making of Kubrick's 2001.*
40. Gelmis, *The Film Director As Superstar.*
41. Kubrick, Stanley and Clarke, Arthur C. *2001: A Space Odyssey.*
42. Weavers, Wally, "Visual Special Effects from *Things to Come* to *2001*," *Film and Television Technician*, April 1969.
43. Weavers, "Visual Special Effects from *Things to Come* to *2001*."
44. Bernstein, "How About a Little Game?"
45. Agel, *The Making of Kubrick's 2001.*
46. Koch, Stephen. "Fiction and Film: A Search for New Sources," *Saturday Review*, 27 December 1969.
47. Clarke, Arthur C. "The Myth of *2001*," *Cosmos*, April 1969.
48. Renaud, "Entretien avec Stanley Kubrick."
49. Clarke, "The Myth of *2001*."
50. Bernstein, "How About a Little Game?"
51. ibid.
52. Nairn, Tom. "The Worst Trip Ever," *Oz*, No. 13, 1968.
53. Baxter. John. *Science Fiction in the Cinema* (Tantivy Pres, 1970).

10. The Magic Eye
The Cinema of Stanley Kubrick

> Cameras, and the stories they can tell have been my hobby, my life and my work.
>
> Stanley Kubrick

Career

Neither Stanley Kubrick's career as a director nor the films he has created conform to the conventionally defined patterns of the American cinema. So far his work falls into three main phases. The period of his "apprenticeship" is represented by his early work as a photo-journalist, two short documentary films, and two independently made features, *Fear and Desire* and *Killer's Kiss*.

The Killing and *Paths of Glory*, both backed on low budgets by United Artists, established him as a distinctive individual talent. His career then lapsed for a while but reached a critical turning point with *Spartacus*, his only foray into big Hollywood studio production, the only film over which he did not have complete control, and the only film he now actively dislikes. It was also the first of his films to make money.

In his third period, Kubrick left America to work in British studios. *Lolita* was, in the main, an unhappy departure in content and style from his best work, but he returned magnificently to form with *Dr. Strangelove* and *2001: A Space Odyssey*, his most recent and most ambitious films, in which he speculates on the alternatives which face mankind. He is now working on his ninth feature film, an adaptation of Anthony Burgess's novel, *A Clockwork Orange*, having shelved for the moment his Napoleon project, a subject which can fairly and precisely be called "Kubrickean" in theme and scale.

One obvious peculiarity of Kubrick's career is seldom mentioned in the context of film-making in general. He is the only director of importance to have started his career in still photography. Professional photographers – Bert Stern, David Bailey, William Klein – have made occasional films, but no former photographer has, to my knowledge, distinguished himself in the medium as Kubrick has done. Not that photographers are reluctant to make films. On the contrary, many of them are raring to make the transition from stills to movies but are simply unable to effect the break into a profession dominated by directors who have emerged from television, theatre or the technical and commercial side of film-making. Kubrick (who worked in television *after* beginning his film career) is the exception.

Kubrick once said that if he hadn't been a photographer for *Look* magazine he would probably never have got into film-making. "Since I had read Pudovkin and was a photographer, what could prevent me from making a movie? I could load the camera, shoot and I would have a movie. If I hadn't been a photographer, I would have lacked the one essential ingredient you have to have to put anything on film, which is photography. Even though the first couple of films were bad, they were well photographed, and they had a good look about them, which did impress people."[1] He speaks with favour of today's "underground" film-makers' disregard for the technical problems of making a film and for the awesome apparatus of Hollywood:

"When I made my first film, I think that the thing which probably helped me the most was that it was such an unusual thing in the early fifties for someone to actually go and make a film. People thought it was impossible. It really is terribly easy. All anybody needs is a camera, a tape recorder and some imagination."*

One thing that might have prevented Kubrick from making a movie was lack of money. He was fortunate in being able to raise money from relatives and friends to help finance his first feature film. And in two other respects he was lucky in making his breakthrough. Firstly, the beginning of his career coincided with a big decline in the popularity of the cinema; since big studio control was diminishing, more opportunities were being given in the mid-fifties to independent producers and directors. Secondly, Kubrick

---

* Kubrick on the underground film phenomenon: "It's about the healthiest thing that has ever happened in Hollywood."

was lucky to form such a fruitful partnership with James B. Harris. The two men became friends, and the administration was left completely to Harris who, while speaking often to Kubrick about direction, never tried to impose his views on him.

From the beginning of his career, with the exception of *Spartacus*, Kubrick has carefully preserved his artistic freedom. This is not easy in the film industry. The independent director of the fifties who wished to steer clear of the pressure of the big Hollywood studios was inevitably involved in financial and promotional problems. He worked on the fringes of a highly organised production-distribution-exhibition system which favoured the easily packaged commodity for the mass audience; final cutting, for instance, was more often carried out by studio executives than by the director. This situation is now much improved. Kubrick, like many other independents, benefited from his association with United Artists, the one major company which runs no studios or cinema circuits of its own but contracts with outside production companies to finance and distribute its films.

It was a long time before Kubrick derived any financial benefit from film-making. "For the first ten years of my career," he says, "I only earned money for not directing films. I was paid to make a film for M-G-M that never got made. And I was paid in full by Marlon Brando to direct *One-Eyed Jacks*, but we disagreed and I left."[2] *The Killing* and *Paths of Glory* were critical successes but only broke even at the box office.

After this Kubrick's career hit a bad patch and it is arguable that he would have remained in difficulties if he had not compromised by getting involved in the super-production of *Spartacus*. For the big box-office success of this film gained Kubrick the commercial prestige with which he was able to persuade other major distributing companies to finance his subsequent more controversial projects. And because Kubrick's artistic talent is coupled with a shrewd business sense, he has been able to capitalise on his first financial success. The films he has made since *Spartacus* have all made money, so that he is now in the enviable position of being able to gain the backing of a major company while retaining his creative independence.

His practice has been to complete a script and, if possible, get a cast selected and signed before seeking financial backing. He considers anything less to invite interference. "If they say yes, they give you all the money you want, you make the film as you like, and they distribute it. It's perfect. No one interferes anymore."[3] (Nonetheless, although Kubrick got the go-ahead from United Artists to make *Napoleon* without even having to submit a script and cast list, the project has been postponed.) To quote again his remark apropos of *Spartacus*: "The important thing in films is not so much to make successes as not to make failures, because each failure limits your opportunities to make the films you want to make."[4]

Working methods
Stanley Kubrick, who defines a director as "a kind of idea and taste machine,"[5] prepares his films carefully over long periods of a year or more. "I usually take a year to get interested in something, get it written and start working on it, and in a year, if you keep thinking about it, you can pretty well exhaust the major lines of play, if you want to put it in chess terminology. Then, as you're making the film, you can respond to the spontaneity of what's happening with the resources of all the analysis that you've done. That way, you can most fully utilise each moment while you're making the picture."[6] He puts it with a small but significant difference elsewhere: "It takes me about a year to let an idea reach an obsessive state so I know what I really want to do with it."[7]

Gary Lockwood, who experienced both being an extra in *Spartacus* and an astronaut in *2001*, says that "working with Kubrick is like working with a great military commander. He has this huge labor force working for him and he was always in control of every detail."[8]

For his first films, Kubrick financed and handled everything himself: camerawork, direction and editing. This was due partly to economic necessity and partly to his special technical interests. He soon found that he preferred controlling everything himself. This is how he defines the ideal conditions for making a picture: "You do everything you want, everybody does what you tell them, and hardly anybody ever expresses a strong, emotionally loaded, devastating criticism of what you want to do or what you're doing. Now if you're good, this is an ideal circumstance to work in, because you're not distracted by having to fend off other ideas, or even disturbed by angry criticism which may be invalid but which you can never forget."[9] This attitude may not be to everyone's taste. But since Kubrick retains personal control of every aspect of his productions, it can be said that his recent films are among the few big-budget productions today that are informed by individuality, intelligence and taste; are not, in short, compromised en route from conception to realisation.

One obvious reason for his films' individuality is that Kubrick is an "auteur." He writes or helps in writing them as well as directing them. "A writer-director," he maintains, "is really the perfect dramatic instrument; and the few examples we have where these two peculiar techniques have been properly mastered by one man have, I believe, produced the most consistently fine work."[10]

A man of immense intellectual curiosity, he steeps himself in the literature of his subject both before and during writing, absorbing information like a sponge. The first drafts of his dialogue are dictated into a tape recorder. Carefully prepared though his screenplays are, he is always ready to make changes during shooting. "One can't get the most out of a scene," he believes, "without modifying it at the shooting stage."[11] While working on *2001*, he had an extra office set up in a trailer to which he retired on set for rewriting. "I take every advantage of every delay and breakdown to go off by myself and think. Something like playing chess when your opponent takes a long time over his next move."[12]

Kubrick has described the screenplay as "the most uncommunicative form of writing ever devised."[13] In fact, he deliberately tries to avoid conceiving scenes visually at the scripting stage: "My background as a stills photographer makes it much easier for me to find an interesting way to shoot something at the last minute and not have to worry about how to shoot it. I more or less feel that if a scene rehearses well and looks interesting, then you can find an interesting way to put it on the screen. But the important thing is not to start thinking of the camera too soon, because then you stop concentrating on what's happening and start worrying about how somebody will get from one place to another and what will happen then. There's a way to shoot any scene. So you work first on the content of the scene then on how you'll shoot it.

"The one exception to this is what you might call a pure action scene, then all you are thinking of is cutting, angles, and how to make the action realistic. But in scenes which are essentially psychological and depend on dialogue, then the performance and truthful staging has to take precedence over just thinking about shots."[14]

Most of Kubrick's films have been adaptations of novels – even *2001* was written in prose and then turned into a screenplay. *Napoleon*, it appears, is to be the first exception since *Killer's Kiss*. Rather than employ professional screen-writers, Kubrick tends to hire as his collaborators the authors of his source novels (Peter George, Vladimir Nabokov) or writers he admires (Calder Willingham, Jim Thompson, Terry Southern, Arthur C. Clarke), all of whom, incidentally, are novelists rather than dramatists. Significantly, his weakest post-apprenticeship films, *Spartacus* and *Lolita*, are the only ones on which he did not share a writing credit.

As Kubrick's films have grown in scale and thematic ambition, so has he moved further and further into the studio. All the films up to and including *Paths of Glory* were shot mainly on location, on low budgets. Most of *Spartacus*, his last film to be made in America, was shot in Hollywood. And since then, Kubrick has worked mainly in English studios. He now believes in shooting on location only when it's absolutely impossible to create the right setting within the studio. Studio work enables everyone to work with maximum concentration, undistracted by onlookers and uncertain weather conditions. A "closed" set is favoured. Very few people not involved in the production are allowed to watch work in progress.

This way of working, Kubrick maintains, especially benefits the actor. Although Kubrick has recently referred to actors as "essentially emotion-producing instruments,"[15] his generous respect for the actor's contribution is one of his most appealing characteristics, and one worth bearing in mind by those who think of him as a coldly clinical director, more interested in hardware than humans. His enthusiasm for actors is all the more remarkable considering that Kubrick has no background experience in the theatre, and limited television experience. However, he admired Max Ophüls not only as a stylist but as a director of actors, and when pressed by a *Cahiers du Cinéma* interviewer to comment on American directors, he praised Elia Kazan for his ability to "work miracles with his actors."[16] It was only after his first two feature films that Kubrick began to take an interest in acting problems. He was helped, he says, "by studying Stanislavsky's books, as well as an excellent book about him, *Stanislavsky Directs*.[17]

Anthony Harvey, who edited *Lolita* and *Dr. Strangelove*, says that Kubrick always subordinates montage to acting, and Kubrick himself has said: "One must always compromise between the cinematic style one wants and the playing of the actors: it's always better to choose the actors."[18] This favouring of the actor has only once, in my view, been artistically miscalculated: in *Lolita*. None of his other films could possibly be described as "actors' movies," i.e. movies in which a subordination of montage to performance is sometimes uncomfortably apparent.

Actors accordingly tend to speak highly of Kubrick for the close attention he pays to their performances and the amount of time he spends on rehearsals. Yet as carefully as he rehearses before shooting, he always welcomes last-minute changes, especially when working with a strong improvising talent like Peter Sellers.

The care he gives to casting is as great as he gives to any other aspect of his production. "When I make a film," he says, "I consult a list of all the actors in the world. Of course, a name comes to mind immediately, but I go through all the names of all the actors in the world because you might find someone you hadn't thought of and who is just right."[19] For instance, he has this to say of Slim Pickens, who replaced the indisposed Peter Sellers as Major "King" Kong in *Dr. Strangelove*: "I had seen him ten years ago in a Western and found him formidable. In this film he did superlative things. I never forgot him. And without any preconceived ideas when I came across his name in reading through a list of possible actors, I thought 'He'd be great.'"[20]

Kubrick's approach to acting is only typical of the meticulous care he devotes to every aspect of his productions. His background as a photo-journalist makes him unusually involved in and sensitive to the technical side of film-making – photography, lighting and editing; an involvement which can be exasperating to those who prefer to do things their way. His perfectionist attitude to detail extends to every facet of the production. He will alter lighting set-ups, choose his camera angles, dictate the camera lenses and closely supervise the editing. "Nothing is cut without me. I'm in there every second, and for all practical purposes, I cut my own films; I mark every frame, select and segment, and have everything done exactly the way I want it."[21]

Since Kubrick finds it impossible to tell a cameraman exactly what he wants for hand-held camerawork, he himself operated the camera for the hand-held shots in *Dr. Strangelove* and *2001*. He will mercilessly reject anything which does not look to him absolutely authentic, and shoot a scene over and over again until he is satisfied.

David Robinson, one of the few journalists admitted to the *2001* set, describes how a scene with William Sylvester (Dr. Floyd), "already meticulously rehearsed and set up, was reshot several times because Kubrick was not happy with the way moisture in the corner of the actor's eye glistened; and then again reshot because Kubrick felt that Sylvester gave an inflection that was vaguely British to a line of very little importance."[22] For Kubrick, nothing is of little importance. He even works on the publicity and trailers of his films.

Kubrick gets his results by means of a stringent technique: exhausting all the possibilities. He acknowledges a distant relationship between chess and making a film. "With chess you have to explore different lines of play, and think of different possible outcomes. In films you're always juggling more things than you can ever think about at any one time, and trying to analyse as many moves as deeply into the consequences as you can. So there is that analogy... Films are a peculiar combination of the worst circumstances imaginable for on artist to work in and the most powerful art form ever devised."[23]

This method is more rigorously applied with each new film. In the case of *2001*, on which he is said to have worked eighteen hours a day for four years without a break, Kubrick would describe to an artist what he wanted; the artist would go away and come back with eight designs; Kubrick would then pick out the bits he liked and ask the artist to go away again and re-do them. In his quest for authentic-looking Moon-dust, he had samples of every grain and colour of sand in the British Isles sent to him for inspection, and finding nothing of a suitable colour, he had ninety tonnes of a certain grain washed, dried and dyed the correct grey. In the habit of keeping track of things in small notebooks, he requested samples of every type of notepaper made by a prominent paper-making firm – a hundred samples in all – in order to make the best choice.[24]

Obviously there are other directors who work with perfectionist thoroughness and devotion. Re-taking shots over and over again, for instance, is hardly unusual practice. But it is doubtful that any director goes to such extreme lengths as Stanley Kubrick to ensure perfection. Whether one considers such methods sometimes to verge on the eccentric perhaps depends on how highly one values the results. Certainly this exhaustive approach, this refusal to compromise, this dogged pursuit of the absolutely authentic, can be infuriating to some of Kubrick's colleagues, and his career is marked by troubled or collapsed working relationships – with Marlon Brando, Kirk Douglas, Dalton Trumbo, Terry Southern – though these rifts are probably no more frequent than those occurring in the career of any artist working in the difficult collaborative medium of film-making.

Wally Gentleman, who worked for a while as an Effects Supervisor on *2001*, commented bitterly: "No-one works with Kubrick, one only works for him – one simply becomes an extension of what he wants and this is not what I consider to be good. He has the talent for collecting really good people around him and dissipating their talents in futile chases after some ephemeral thing. But he knows where he is going and he knows what he wants, so the film stands or falls on Kubrick himself."[25]

Against this kind of response must be balanced the great respect in which Kubrick is held even by those who find him exhausting to work with. Ken Adam had to resort to tranquillisers while designing *Dr. Strangelove*, but preserved his admiration for Kubrick. Arthur C. Clarke remarked: "Every time I go out of a meeting with Stanley, I must go and lie down." But he was "more than delighted" with *2001*. And Anthony Harvey, who began in films in 1946, and went on from editing to make *Dutchman* and *The Lion in Winter*, states: "He has the most fantastic energy of any man I know. I don't believe he sleeps more than four hours a night... I was eighteen months on *Lolita* and a year [on] *Strangelove*. Looking back, I feel I learned more about films than at any other time of my life."[26]

Among others whose friendship or admiration Kubrick has earned are Peter Sellers, James Mason, John Trevelyan, Secretary of the British Board of Film Censors, and Sir Laurence Olivier, who writes: "I like him very much indeed and found him a most admirable director."[27]

For an outside view of Kubrick, here finally is David Robinson on the set of *2001*: "On the set he is quiet, severe, giving an impression of being rather forbearing than actually patient (which is his reputation) and keeping himself, for the most part to himself. It seems no accident that he has an assistant director of N.C.O. firmness. *The New York Times Magazine* made great play of the 'awe' in which his collaborators hold him; and you feel that this is the sort of relationship that he encourages. Only occasional small jokes break the intensity of his concentration and suggest that his work actually gives him pleasure. In between attending to everything else, he is forever snatching up a Polaroid camera and snapping off photographs, some apparently for immediate reference, but others, it seems, simply as stills."[28]

Controlling every aspect of his productions, knowing exactly what he wants, obsessive in his determination to achieve perfection and impeccably organised to do so, eliciting extreme reactions of admiration and resentment, Kubrick is obviously a formidable personality, the first *enfant terrible* of the American cinema since Orson Welles. Each new film of his is a major cinematic event. Let us now turn to his style and his thematic preoccupations.

Style

"Style," says Kubrick, "is what an artist uses to fascinate the beholder to convey to him his feelings and emotions and thoughts."[29] From the beginning of his career, Kubrick has sought to fascinate the audience by establishing in his films a context of verisimilitude within which the occurrence of wayward behaviour has heightened emotional impact.

Kubrick began as a photo-journalist and his first two films were short documentaries. His fictional feature films are a true continuation of this early work insofar as he has always taken pains to create a feeling of "actuality," in the documentary sense of that word, an effort based on the key principle of authenticity. This goes as much for the "nightmare comedy," *Dr. Strangelove*, as for the dossier-style thriller, *The Killing*. His films are at their weakest where, probably for reasons of insufficient control (*Spartacus*) or expediency (*Lolita*), this principle has been compromised.

Kubrick has observed that a lot depends on what is meant by "documentary": "If you really want to shoot something as a documentary you have to answer the question, 'Do the people in the film know that there's a camera?' – because there's never yet been a film in which people did not take account of the camera's presence." That becomes very complicated. If there's a scene with dialogue, should people look at the camera and speak to it? Should the cameraman appear in the scene? If one wanted to be absolutely rigorous about it, one would end up demanding that in all documentaries the actors speak to the cameraman or ask him to leave the scene, etc... This kind of reality is a clumsy formal requirement. *It's better*

---

* Except, of course "candid camera" documentaries.

that the camera be a kind of magic eye. No one knows how it got there and it doesn't matter."[30] [my italics]

Obviously, if it interested him Kubrick could make superb documentaries in the manner of, say, Pierre Schoendoerffer's *The Anderson Platoon*, to name one modern war documentary Kubrick is known to admire. For Kubrick, however, the illusion of "reality" is created the better to trap the viewer into a susceptibility to the emotionally disturbing ideas he wishes to develop, to exercise power over the audience by creating suspense. Godard, to take a contemporary director as concerned as Kubrick with the feeling vs. mechanisation problem (cf. *Alphaville* and *2001*), also uses documentary techniques in his films, but less to create a context of objective reality than to "catch" his characters in all their naked subjectivity or political essence, their fugitive responses to a fragmented inhospitable environment.

The documentary texture of Kubrick's films is achieved by standard techniques: hand-held camerawork to create the feeling of hazardous on-the-spot reportage; the camera as intruder peering into a group set-up over the shoulders of characters in the scene; the recognisable flatness of telephoto and zoom shooting; light sources shining directly into the camera. The light quality is probably the most important textural element in a Kubrick film. "We are all used to seeing things in a certain way, with the light coming from some natural source. I try to duplicate this natural light in the filming. It makes for a feeling of greater reality." In *2001*, for instance, almost all the lighting in the live-action sequences was natural, i.e. an integral part of the set itself, and additional lighting was used only for critical close-ups.

The sense of objectivity or detachment created by this documentary approach is reinforced by certain other distancing effects. A captioned or spoken commentary, present in every film except *2001* (which originally had the most extensive narration of all), implies the existence of an outside authority who already knows the outcome of events and hence imparts what we see with a certain fatality. The occasional use of flashbacks (*Killer's Kiss*, *The Killing*, *Lolita*), extensive use of long-shots, especially at climactic moments, and long tracking shots also contribute to this sense of distance.

Upon this foundation of objective realism, Kubrick deploys a variety of subjective effects to evoke a disordered emotional climate. These effects, which one also associates with the films of Fritz Lang and Orson Welles, can be loosely described as "baroque": frequent play with the contrasts created by dramatic lighting, typified by the placing of a very strongly lit figure against a dark background, and the reverse effect of silhouetting; bizarre and ironic juxtapositions; diagonal and circular compositions to create deep three-dimensional perspectives; low-angle and high-angle shooting to distort the viewpoint; and restless fluid camerawork characterised by tracking, pan and crane shots.

In the earlier films especially, the camerawork is extremely fluent, movement within a shot as dramatically striking as movement from shot to shot. After *Spartacus*, tracking shots are used very sparingly. *Lolita*, its fine opening sequence excepted, is often as flat and static as a British second-feature thriller. In *Dr. Strangelove* the relentless drive of the earlier films is restored by dynamic cutting, yet the story is told through relatively restricted camera set-ups. By *2001*, one can speak of a quality of restraint or composure in the style. Here camerawork is subtly and economically used to change the perspective of an image in mid-shot. It is a mainly contemplative approach, punctuated by rare jolts of hand-held camerawork and, of course, the big subjective effects near the end.

The decorative element in the baroque style can be noted in some of the elegant settings of Kubrick's films; in his mirrors, cages and staircases, in the chateau of *Paths of Glory*, Quilty's mansion in *Lolita*, and the eighteenth-century suite in which Bowman finds himself at the end of *2001*; environments redolent of a past culture and luxury which ironically contrast with their inhabitants' spiritual poverty. The element of nostalgia in such settings is reinforced by Kubrick's use of sentimental or romantic theme music – in the songs which end *Paths of Glory* and *Dr. Strangelove*, the gushing piano concerto theme of *Lolita* and "The Blue Danube" waltz of *2001*.

In Kubrick's best films the viewer is plunged into a scene with the minimum of preparation by way of establishing shots. This dynamic editing device serves to immerse the viewer so quickly into a scene as to disorientate him slightly and thus keep him on the alert. It also tends to invest the narrative with an urgency and drive that contributes to the feeling of fatality and doom, as if the film is driven by a powerful engine inexorably bearing its characters towards disaster.

We have mentioned elements of fatality, ironic contrast and nostalgia. It is time to consider what Kubrick's films are about.

Kubrick's vision
Broadly speaking, the central concern revealed in Kubrick's films is with the conflict between the irrational forces of man's emotional nature and his rational repressive control mechanisms. These mechanisms are manifested at the socio-political level by certain impassive social structures and on the psychological plane by the authority of the super-ego, which is also to be identified with the discipline exerted by a powerful father-figure. The tension between these two states, the rational and the emotional, is given a tragic ambiguity and irony in that the power structures, be they legal procedures, military defence systems or super-machines, are supposedly created for the greater benefaction of mankind, to protect him, each in its own way, from his innate destructive impulses and maintain a peaceful environment.

But all too often these "progressive" civilised structures become repressive systems which cut man off from his basic and most precious origins; for, to put it in crudely simplified terms, his very humanity depends as much on his capacity to feel as on his ability to control his feelings. The problem of control, then, becomes a crucial issue in Kubrick's films: the relationship between the powers invested within the individual and the powers invested outside him; how he copes with the crises of decision-making – crises which frequently entail the defining of responsibility for action where such definition is difficult or impossible.

At its simplest dramatic level, the division is expressed in the clash between man, the individual, and the System or "Machine." The System is represented in various ways. In *Killer's Kiss* it is the city itself, a depressing environment which saps and devitalises hero and villain alike; freedom is crudely represented by a return to the country with a girl in tow. In *The Killing* the city is still oppressive. Johnny Clay fashions a team of criminals into a highly complex robbery machine, which in turn is a spanner in the works of a much larger robbery machine, the racetrack. Obviously the System is present in the military hierarchy of the French Army in *Paths of Glory* and in the politico-military apparatus of the Roman state in *Spartacus*. In *Lolita*, to stretch the point a little, the System is "normality," the conventional standards of society which become internalised in the tormented machinations of Humbert Humbert's conscience.

In Kubrick's most recent films, *Dr. Strangelove* and *2001: A Space Odyssey*, the Machines literally take over. The military and political leaders, themselves cogs in a rigid system, sit around the conference table in the War Room, helpless to restrain the destructive powers they have invested in their own creations. Is Dr. Strangelove, with his wheelchair and uncontrollable metal hand, more man than machine? The borderlines have become blurred. By *2001*, a year of the utmost scientific precision, definition becomes an almost insoluble problem. Who (or is it which?) is the more human – the seemingly emotionless astronauts or the wilful, suffering computer HAL? And what is the quality of human existence when a man's very life-functions have been voluntarily handed over to a machine?

Clearly the component parts of many of these Machines are individuals. But they are men like General Mireau, Marcus Crassus or Dr. Strangelove; each sterile or impotent in personal relations, each using his power, which is derived from his dominant position in the System, to degrade or destroy others. Put another way, problems of authority in Kubrick's films are manifested in a very hostile depiction of more or less menacing father-figures: Rapallo, the middle-aged villain of *Killer's Kiss*, and a succession of

Generals from *Fear and Desire* to *Dr. Strangelove*. That the
general in *Fear and Desire*, and the young Lieutenant who
kills him in his quest for freedom, were played by the same
actor, vividly suggests that Kubrick recognised quite early
the impossibility of completely externalising the sources of
destructive power.

Fifteen years later he is still exploring the problem
of identifying the ultimate origins of authority: in *2001*, a
sinister father-figure, HAL, has to be incapacitated before
David Bowman can at last meet his cosmic father, a super-
human ethereal intelligence located on the planet Jupiter. In
the early screenplay draft, Bowman is simply taken by the
hand like a child and led out into space by a vast humanoid
creature. In the final version he himself is turned into a
cosmic force, safe and guiltless as a foetus in the womb,
cleansed, unified and omnipotent, a god no less. Innocence,
wholeness and invulnerability – such are the yearnings at
the heart of Kubrick's work.

Kubrick's heroes, or rather central characters, since they
often do not possess the conventional image of the movie
hero, are unable to function merely as cogs in the Machine,
especially when it means running against their essential
natures. As individuals who try to exercise their will in setting
or upholding their own standards, their power to influence
events is sorely tested – and usually found wanting. The
Machines, whether power blocs or doomsday contraptions,
are not capable of adapting to change. They must destroy or
render inoperative any challenge. The heroes respond with
varying degrees of resourcefulness, but their efforts mainly
end in failure.

Most of these men – criminals, soldiers, rebels,
astronauts – operate outside conventional society by virtue
of their special occupations and preoccupations. "The
protagonists of *Paths of Glory*, *The Killing*, *Spartacus*
and my next film *Lolita*," says Kubrick, "are all outsiders
fighting to do some impossible thing, whether it's pulling
a perfect robbery or saving innocent men from execution
by a militaristic state or carrying on a love affair with a 12-
year old girl."[31] Colin Wilson, although he liked *Spartacus*,

disagreed that its hero was an outsider in his sense, since it was not "society" he was fighting but only the brutality of Roman society.[32] The rebellion of Kubrick's heroes is not against social organisation as such but against the repressive and manipulative social organisation.

These individuals must face the ultimate resolution of their moral commitment, pursuing their course with a grim determination often amounting to obsession. The word "obsession" is used without the usual connotation of neurosis since in almost every case their struggles and quests are fully justified in terms of escape from unendurable situations. Because Kubrick's heroes function close to the brink of physical disaster, success is usually a matter of life and death. Most of Kubrick's films are expositions of failure, ending in disillusion, defeat or annihilation. The happy ending of *Killer's Kiss* is arbitrarily tacked on to a film of generally depressing atmosphere. In *Paths of Glory* and *Spartacus* the defeats are qualified but remain essentially defeats. Napoleon's fate speaks for itself. *2001* is unique in that the astronauts appear to be heading for disaster – one of them is, in fact, destroyed – but for the first time a major breakthrough occurs, admittedly on the plane of the super-human rather than the human: the hero is annihilated only to be reborn. Thus, in the cinema of Stanley Kubrick, paths of glory generally lead to the grave, with only the possibility of man's *future* transcendence over his fatal imperfections as a prospect of hope.

The films are politically charged to the extent that they deal with the operations and strategies of institutionalised power factions. But the basic political concern revolves around the possibility of man exercising his will without being crushed by the Infernal Machine. It is man against the gods, the stubborn implacable forces which interfere with his autonomy. An inescapable word comes to mind: hubris. And a reminiscent link: classical Greek drama. Kubrick's most recent films have a quality of catharsis – each in its own way, they purge the world of its imperfections.

Whether or not one finds Kubrick's vision pessimistic and cynical or realistic largely depends on the relative position of one's own viewpoint. To those who have detected misanthropy in his work, he replies: "In *Dr. Strangelove*, I was dealing with the inherent irrationality in man that threatens to destroy him; that irrationality is with us strongly today, and must be conquered. But a recognition of insanity doesn't imply a celebration of it – nor a sense of despair and futility about the possibility of curing it."[33]

Nevertheless he is said to be somewhat pessimistic and sceptical by nature. He is doubtful whether human beings will survive their capacity for inventing new weapons of destruction, but feels that space exploration might change our view of ourselves and the world, might be the only thing we could learn to do to keep from blowing ourselves up. His own self-description is revealingly dualistic: "Emotionally I am optimistic. Intellectually I'm not. I do things in spite of all the things I'm intellectually aware of, such as the burden of my own mortality."

In the cinema of Stanley Kubrick, the action is where the men are, the only action, that is, worth investigating: men pitted against each other or against machines of various kinds. Women either play very peripheral roles in Kubrick's films – the peasant captive in *Fear and Desire*, the German girl in *Paths of Glory*, Miss Foreign Affairs in *Dr. Strangelove*; or they are spoils the males are fighting over, the apexes of conventional sexual triangles. Davy and Rapallo fight over Gloria Price, Spartacus and Crassus over Varinia, Humbert Humbert and Quilty over Lolita. One cannot take seriously the romantic clichés of *Killer's Kiss* and *Spartacus*, while *Lolita*, the only film that attempts to explore a sexual relationship in any depth, fatally conventionalises its characters. In all three cases there are reasons which partially account for the failure – neglect of characterisation and acting, an imposed script and production concept, censorship considerations. But still a consistent tendency to stereotyping is apparent. Of Kubrick's five main female characters, three (Gloria Price, Sherry Peatty and Lolita) are treacherous trouble-makers, one (Varinia) is an ingenue, and one (Charlotte Haze) is a sex-hungry dope.

The domestic scene is one that does not interest Kubrick dramatically. Most of his characters, as well as functioning outside conventional society, are domestically dispossessed. Charlotte Haze and the Peattys are virtually the only characters to be seen at home; one would certainly not count the dingy temporary apartments of *Killer's Kiss* and the rooms of the other characters in *The Killing* as homes. As far back as Kubrick's first film, *Fear and Desire*, the line occurs: "We spend all our lives seeking our real selves, our permanent addresses." Pretentious perhaps in its context, it reverberates through all Kubrick's subsequent work, especially *2001: A Space Odyssey*.

Kubrick is not much concerned with women in his films except as the conventional props of femme fatale and ingenue. But one feels that he is in any case more in his element when not obliged to explore even male character in any depth. This is less a criticism than a definition of his method, which eschews exploration of character in favour of *deployment* of characters within certain prescribed or developing mutual interest/mutual conflict situations. His films are most successful when the fairly schematic characterisation gels with the operational content. The oddballs and fanatics of *Dr. Strangelove* inhabit a world in which too much psychologising or subtle nuancing would be fatal to the artistic design; while the space travellers of *2001* are, convincingly, people selected for their very lack of emotional complexity. *Napoleon* is the first military subject to offer Kubrick the chance to explore in detail the personality of a single central protagonist. In this respect *Napoleon* represents a great artistic challenge.

We have noted that Kubrick's main characters tend to be dispossessed male outsiders, living close to danger. They are professional dealers in violence – boxers, gladiators, gangsters, soldiers. The prototype, to which Kubrick returns time and time again, is the soldier. Of his ten film subjects to date (including *Napoleon* and *A Clockwork Orange*) five are concerned with military combat.

Kubrick himself was rejected for military service, so he has no personal experience of warfare other than what he might have obtained on photo-story assignments for *Look* magazine. But as a boy, he preferred war films above all others, and he developed an early passion for chess.

Chess is, of course, the War Game par excellence, involving strategic deployment of pieces whose movements are defined according to a strict hierarchy of power. The game offers a rich variety of possibilities within the security of its system of rules. Naturally, defeat is contingent upon every victory; the only alternative is stalemate. I am not, of course, implying that Kubrick has a morbid taste for violence. Rather, his love of chess, his distinctive working methods, his thematic concerns, and his predominant subject matter of men in war all consistently express his preoccupation with the exercise, strategy and problems of power.

While making *Paths of Glory*, Kubrick said that he found criminals and soldiers fascinating because they are "doomed from the start" and because of the cinematic possibilities inherent in their violent black-and-white confrontations. Militarism is only the most extreme example of a type of social organisation geared to exercising power through violence. And to function efficiently all social relations within this system must be depersonalised. Thus the military milieu aptly provides the paradigm for the Machine and for the warring elements in the human psyche.

We have noted that machines function in Kubrick's films as dramatic metaphors for the repressive, "rational" elements in the psyche. But it is also true that in the modern technological state real machines are concrete projections of that rationality, an attempt to order and control the environment with maximum efficiency to make life "easier." The attempt perversely creates new problems of its own: a new species has come into being, and hence a new species of relationship.

Kubrick has sometimes been accused of revealing antagonism – "ambivalently laced with a kind of morbid fascination," as *The New Yorker* puts it – towards machines and automation. But he himself denies this: "I'm not hostile towards machines at all; just the opposite in fact. There's no doubt that we're entering a mechanarchy, however, and that our already complex relationship with our machinery will become even more complex as the machines become more and more intelligent."[34] And again: "There's no doubt that there's a deep emotional relationship between man and his machines, which are his children. The machine is beginning to assert itself in a very profound way, even attracting affection and obsession. There is a sexiness to beautiful machines. The smell of a Nikon camera. The feel of an Italian sports car, or a beautiful tape recorder. We are almost in a sort of biological machine society already. We're making the transition towards whatever the ultimate change will be. Man has always worshipped beauty, and I think there's a new kind of beauty afoot in the world."[35] These sentiments pervade every shot of *2001*. How can anyone have thought the space-ballet in the film to be satirical?

Certainly Kubrick is fascinated by machines, especially recording instruments of all kinds. When Jeremy Bernstein, his *New Yorker* interviewer, visited him in New York at the time of making *2001*, he found that Kubrick owned a large collection of cameras, tape-recorders and hi-fi sets. "There was also a short-wave radio, which he was using to monitor broadcasts from Moscow, in order to learn the Russian attitude towards Vietnam."[36] Kubrick's interest in machines has also led him to take up flying. As a licensed pilot he logged about 150 hours until realising, he says, just how dangerous an activity it is. He now refuses to fly even in a commercial airliner. "I suppose," he says, "it comes down to a rather awesome awareness of mortality."[37]

For Kubrick, naturally enough, the machine which has a special potency is the camera. "Cameras, and the stories they can tell," he says, "have been my hobby, my life and my work." Cameras and photographs appear in several of his films, and are nearly always associated with violence or disaster. In *Killer's Kiss* the three central characters, all lonely and dispossessed, have photographs of their families pinned to the wall. In *Paths of Glory*, a photographer is in at the execution of the three soldier victims. In *Lolita*, the pernicious Quilty walks around with a camera, and Humbert gains an erection by gazing at a photograph of Lolita only to be told that Charlotte is sending her away. In *Dr. Strangelove*, the Russian, Ambassador de Sadesky, tries to take secret pictures of the War Room at the height of the crisis with a camera concealed in a toy clock – a miniature doomsday device. Mandrake says of the Japanese, "They tortured me, the swines. Funny. They make marvellous cameras." In *2001*, Dr. Floyd and his colleagues pose for a picture in front of the black monolith only to be dispersed by an unbearable cosmic howl. And the astronauts are constantly under observation by the arch-camera represented by HAL's system of fish-eye lenses – the Magic Eye incarnate.

Cameras clearly have menacing connotations in Kubrick's films. Don McCullin, a British photo-journalist who needs to photograph at least one war a year, refers to his own camera as a "toy" because "you can't kill anyone with it." And he speaks of the professional photographer as an invisible man who often makes people feel uncomfortable by invading their privacy. The camera, then, is an instrument of power. An invisible man who can so fix reality is powerful indeed. He shoots not to kill but to preserve things forever.

Eric Rhode has written of Kubrick: "By his own acknowledgment he is one of the most obsessive of directors, both drawn on by feelings of omnipotence and at the same time threatened by the possible consequences of this craving... an omnipotence that, for the most part, finds its symbolism in a fascination with, and fear of, the extended powers that machines have given to men."

While several critics have examined the theme of obsession running through Kubrick's work, no one has yet ventured to relate Kubrick's themes to his personality along the lines suggested by Rhodes's passing comment. This isn't too surprising, since information about Kubrick's early and private life is too sparse to mount any reliable theory to account for his personal preoccupations. Still, no one studying Kubrick's career can avoid being struck by certain consistent obsessive features: a rigorous perfectionism sought by the most comprehensive and exhaustive means; a capacity for self-effacement in the pursuit of his goals; a resentment of outside authority and desire to achieve absolute personal control over the environment; a love of order, discipline, organisation, symmetry and hygiene; and a preoccupation with mortality.

The personality with obsessive traits so organises his life to keep under control the subversive irrational forces which constantly threaten to engulf him. For him, life is precisely a battle between the powers of disorder and the repressive super-ego system that strives to keep the organism functioning and intact. There is a nagging sense of impending disaster, an anxiety that can only be allayed by a clearly-defined control system constantly monitoring the environment for danger signals. Such a personality, in the pursuit of absolute control, will tend to act out fantasies of omnipotence, to pre-empt for himself the very power, the very paternal authority, that might otherwise destroy him. Grasping the nettle as firmly as he must, such a man harnesses a strength and certitude that may equip him better than most to understand and deal with the genuine threats that assail a man's integrity, safety and freedom.

To identify Kubrick broadly with this personality pattern is in no way to reduce or disparage his achievements but only to hint very crudely at the psychological roots of his art, to suggest a possible identity of his films' basic themes and his own mental topography. Obviously one must make important qualifications. For several reasons it would be highly misleading to categorise this distinguished director and just leave it at that.

Firstly, we have seen that as thoroughly as Kubrick prepares his productions, he always leaves room for on-the-spot inspiration, even to the extent of encouraging improvisation from his actors when they are able to do it well. Hitchcock, for instance, leaves virtually nothing to chance. Secondly, Kubrick's films are infused with a saving humour. Thirdly, a perfectionist approach, if rare, is hardly unique among dedicated men – most artists of any accomplishment and originality have pursued their goals obsessively. As Kubrick has said: "A really great picture has a delirious quality in which you're constantly searching for meanings. It's all very elusive and very rich. There's nothing like trying to create it. It gives you a sense of omnipotence – it's one of the most exciting things you can find without being under the influence of drugs."

And finally, if one identifies certain obsessive traits in Kubrick's life and work, one does so in acknowledgment that we all share these characteristics to a degree; live, that is, in the same world of public and private anxieties, engage in our own battles – on differing fronts maybe – of balancing spontaneity and control in pursuit of our own forms of power. That is why we can respond so readily to Kubrick's films. That is why his best work, far from appearing too esoteric or too impersonal, can engage us deeply as social and political animals.

1. Kohler, Charlie. "Stanley Kubrick Raps," *Eye*, August 1968.
2. Wiseman, Thomas. "Stanley Kubrick," *Evening Standard*, 8 December 1960.
3. Walter, Renaud. "Entretien avec Stanley Kubrick," *Positif*, December 1968-January 1969.
4. Sigal, Clancy. "Slaughter Sugar-Coated," *Time and Tide*, 17 December 1960.
5. Gelmis, Joseph. *The Film Director As Superstar* (Doubleday & Co., Inc., 1970).
6. Kohler, "Stanley Kubrick Raps."
7. Agel, Jerome (editor). *The Making of Kubrick's 2001* (Signet, 1970).
8. ibid.
9. Kohler, "Stanley Kubrick Raps."
10. Kubrick, Stanley. "Words and Movies," *Sight and Sound*, Winter 1960/61.
11. Renaud, "Entretien avec Stanley Kubrick."
12. Bernstein, Jeremy. "How About a Little Game?" *The New Yorker*, 12 November 1966.
13. Agel, *The Making of Kubrick's 2001*.
14. Kubrick, Stanley. "How I Learned to Stop Worrying and Love the Cinema," *Films and Filming*, June 1963.
15. Gelmis, *The Film Director As Superstar*.
16. Haine, Raymond. "Bonjour Monsieur Kubrick," *Cahiers du Cinéma*, July 1957).
17. Gelmis, *The Film Director As Superstar*.
18. Renaud, "Entretien avec Stanley Kubrick."
19. ibid.
20. ibid.
21. Gelmis, *The Film Director As Superstar*.
22. Robinson, David. "Two for the Sci-Fi," *Sight and Sound*, Spring 1966.
23. Kohler, "Stanley Kubrick Raps."
24. Davis, Victor. "*2001*: the men who made tomorrow," *Daily Express*, 16, 17 and 18 April 1968.
25. Noble, Robin. "Killers, Kisses... and Lolita," *Films and Filming*, December 1960.
26. Gilliatt, Penelope. "*Dr. Strangelove*," *The Observer*, 2 February 1964.

27. Private correspondence.
28. Robinson, "Two for the Sci-Fi."
29. Kubrick, "Words and Movies."
30. Renaud, "Entretien avec Stanley Kubrick."
31. Uncredited. "*Spartacus*," *New York Times*, 2 October 1960.
32. Wilson, Colin. "They Say he is an Outsider, BUT," *Daily Express*, 6 December 1960).
33. Bernstein, "How About a Little Game?"
34. ibid.
35. Kloman, William. "In *2001*, Will Love Be a Seven-Letter Word?" *New York Times*, 14 April 1968.
36. Bernstein, "How About a Little Game?"
37. ibid.

BIBLIOGRAPHY

The bibliography is confined to items in English and French. It includes the most important books and articles, as well as minor articles and newspaper items to which I have referred in the text.

A. ARTICLES BY STANLEY KUBRICK

1. Kubrick, Stanley. "Words and Movies," *Sight and Sound* (London: Winter 1960/61). Translated into French in *Cinéma* 61 (Paris: July 1961). A short article on the adaptation of novels to the cinema.

B. MAJOR INTERVIEWS AND ARTICLES ADAPTED FROM INTERVIEWS WITH KUBRICK

2. Bernstein, Jeremy. "How About a Little Game?" *The New Yorker* (New York: 12 November 1966). A long article in the "Profile" series, based on various interviews with Kubrick, including visits to the set of *2001: A Space Odyssey*.

3. Haine, Raymond. "Bonjour Monsieur Kubrick," *Cahiers du Cinéma* (Paris: July 1957). Interviews with Kubrick and James B. Harris while shooting *Paths of Glory* in Germany.

4. Gelmis, Joseph. *The Film Director As Superstar,* Doubleday & Co., Inc. (New York: 1970) Interviews with various directors, including Kubrick.

5. Kohler, Charlie. "Stanley Kubrick Raps," *Eye* (New York: August 1968). An interview concentrating on *2001*.

6. Kubrick, Stanley. "How I Learned to Stop Worrying and Love the Cinema," *Films and Filming* (London: June 1963). Translated into French as "Kubrick et la bombe" in *Cinéma* 64 (Paris: May 1964). A statement on the origin of *Dr. Strangelove* and on some of the technical aspects of film-making. (Adapted from a tape-recorded interview with Robin Bean).

7. Norden, Eric. "Stanley Kubrick," *Playboy* (Chicago: September 1968). Long interview, mainly concerned with *2001* and Kubrick's speculations about the future.

8. Walter, Renaud. "Entretien avec Stanley Kubrick," *Positif* (Paris: December 1968 – January 1969). One of the most revealing of Kubrick's interviews, covering his film career in detail.

C. GENERAL ARTICLES ON KUBRICK'S CAREER

9. Alpert, Hollis. "Offbeat Director in Outer Space," *New York Times Magazine* (New York: 16 January 1966). Long article written while Kubrick was working on *2001*.

10. Burgess, Jackson. "The 'Anti-Militarism' of Stanley Kubrick," *Film Quarterly* (Berkeley, California: Fall 1964). An analysis of Kubrick's work, up to and including *Dr. Strangelove*, with a detailed discussion of *Fear and Desire*.

11. Ciment, Michel. "L'Odyssée de Stanley Kubrick," *Positif* (Paris: October 1968). Important article on Kubrick's career, with special emphasis on *2001*, and up-to-date filmography by Olivier Eyquem.

12. Johnson, Robert. "Kubrick's Obsession," *Screen Education* (London: January/February 1965). A schematic analysis of the recurrent theme of obsession in Kubrick's work.

13. Milne, Tom. "How I learned to stop worrying and love Stanley Kubrick," *Sight and Sound* (London: Spring 1964). A detailed

analysis of Kubrick's films with special emphasis on their dramatic structure and the characters' obsessions.

14. Noble, Robin. "Killers, Kisses... and Lolita," *Films and Filming* (London: December 1960). A detailed account of Kubrick's career up to *Paths of Glory*.

15. Russell, Lee (Peter Wollen). "Stanley Kubrick," *New Left Review* (Summer 1964). An attack on Kubrick at the time of *Dr. Strangelove*, cogently argued but neatly ignores contradictory evidence.

16. Stang, Joanne. "Film Fan to Film Maker," *The New York Times Magazine* (New York: 12 October 1958). A general account of Kubrick's career up to *Paths of Glory.*

17. Young, Colin. "The Hollywood War of Independence," *Film Quarterly* (Berkeley, California: Spring 1959). Article about the problems of young independent American film-makers: Martin Ritt, the Sanders brothers, and Stanley Kubrick.

18. Uncredited. "Talking about People: James Harris," *Film* (London: Winter 1962). Short article, based on an interview with Harris, who talks of his collaboration with Kubrick.

D. INDIVIDUAL FILMS

FEAR AND DESIRE

19. Owens, Iris. "It's movies for me," *Modern Photography* (New York: September 1953). A short, illustrated account of the making of *Fear and Desire*.

20. Tyler, Parker. "A Dance, a Dream and a Flying Trapeze?" *Theatre Arts* (New York: May 1953). A review of five films, including *Fear and Desire*.

21. Uncredited. *"Fear and Desire,"* *Motion Picture Herald* (New York: 4 April 1953). A review of the film.

KILLER'S KISS

22. Lambert, Gavin. *"Killer's Kiss,"* *Sight and Sound* (London: Spring 1956). A review of the film.

23. Uncredited. *"Killer's Kiss," Monthly Film Bulletin* (London: March 1956). A review of the film.

THE KILLING

24. Brien, Alan. *"The Killing," Evening Standard* (London: 26 July 1956). A review of the film.

25. Croce, Arlene. *"The Killing," Film Culture* (New York: Vol. II, No.3, 1956). A review of the film.

26. Kael, Pauline. *Kiss Kiss Bang Bang*, Little, Brown and Co. (Boston and Toronto: 1968). A collection of film criticism including a note on *The Killing* (in "Notes on 280 Movies") and comments on *Dr. Strangelove* (in her review of *Bonnie and Clyde*).

27. Lambert, Gavin. *"The Killing," Sight and Sound* (London: Spring 1956). A review of the film.

28. Tailleur, Roger. "Les Enfants de Huston," *Positif* (Paris: September 1958). A review of the film.

29. White, Lionel, *Clean Break*, E.P. Dutton and Co., Inc. (New York: 1955). Reprinted in paperback as *The Killing*, Tower Publications, Inc. (New York, 1964). The novel from which the film was adapted.

30. Uncredited. *"The Killing," Manchester Guardian* (Manchester: 28 July 1956). A review of the film.

31. Uncredited. *"The Killing," Time* (Chicago: 4 June 1956). A review of the film.

THE BURNING SECRET (screenplay only)

32. Zweig, Stefan. "The Burning Secret." Short story in *Kaleidoscope* (1936) (Cassell: London 1949). The short story, translated by Eden and Cedar Paul, from which Kubrick and Calder Willingham wrote an unfilmed screenplay.

PATHS OF GLORY

33. Alpert, Hollis. *"Paths of Glory," Saturday Review* (New York: 21 December 1957). A review of the film.

34. Atkinson, Brooks, "*Paths of Glory*," *The New York Times* (New York: 27 September 1935). A review of Sidney Howard's stage adaptation of Humphrey Cobb's novel.

35. Baumbach, Jonathan. "*Paths of Glory*," *Film Culture* (New York: February 1958). A review of the film.

36. Cameron, Ian and Shivas, Mark. "Interview with Richard Lester." *Movie* 16 (London: Winter 1968-69). Lester comments in passing on *Paths of Glory*.

37. Cobb, Humphrey. "*Paths of Glory*," William Heinemann (London: 1935). Reprinted in paperback by Corgi Books (London: 1966). The novel from which the film was adapted.

38. Crowther, Bosley. "*Paths of Glory*," *The New York Times* (New York: 26 December 1957). A review of the film.

39. Gish, Lillian, with Pinchott, Ann. *The Movies, Mr. Griffith, And Me*, W.H. Allen (London: 1969). Includes a reference to filming on the front-line.

40. Hill, Derek. "*Paths of Glory*," *Tribune* (London: 3 January 1958). A review of the film.

41. Hughes, Robert (editor). *Film: Books 2 – Films of Peace and War*. Grove Press, Inc. (New York: 1962). Includes several references to *Paths of Glory*.

42. Kubrick, Stanley. "*Paths of Glory*," *L'Express* (Paris: 5 March 1959). A letter from the director, protesting against the French reaction to his film.

43. Lambert, Gavin. "*Paths of Glory*," *Sight and Sound* (London: Winter, 1957-58). A review of the film.

44. Lefèvre, Raymond. "Les Sentiers de la Gloire," *Image et Son* (Paris: April 1962). An invaluably detailed feature spread on the background and critical reaction to *Paths of Glory*.

45. Lovell, Alan. "Study Unit 2: War on the Screen" (London: revised Autumn 1963). Some short notes, with comments on *Paths of Glory*, for a series issued by the Education Department of the British Film Institute.

46. de Ville, Bernard-Luc; et al. "Les Sentiers de la Gloire," *Cinéma* 58 (Paris: May 1958). A sequence of three articles, including a translation of Gavin Lambert's review of the film (see ref. 43)

47. Uncredited. "French Acquit 5 Shot for Mutiny in 1915; Widows of 2 win Awards of 7 Cents each," *The New York Times* (New York: 2 July 1934). A news despatch.

48. Uncredited. "'Glory' Runs into Many Troubles in Brussels," *Variety* (New York: 9 April 1958). A despatch from Paris concerning the Brussels furore over *Paths of Glory*.

49. Uncredited. "Military Bans 'Glory' from U.S. Armed Forces," *Variety* (New York: 16 July 1958). Despatch from Heidelberg on German and U.S.A.F. reaction to *Paths of Glory*.

SPARTACUS

50. Barr, Charles. "*Spartacus*," *Granta* (Oxford: 28 January 1961). A detailed review of the film.

51. Château, René. "Entretiens avec Michael Wilson et Dalton Trumbo," *Positif* (Paris: August/September, 1964). Trumbo's interview includes comments on *Spartacus*. The same issue of *Positif* carries some notes on the film.

52. Cutts, John. "*Spartacus*," *Films and Filming* (London: January 1961). A review of the film.

53. Dyer, Peter John. "*Spartacus*," *Sight and Sound* (London: Winter 1960-61). A brief, sceptical review of the film.

54. Fast, Howard. *Spartacus*, The Bodley Head (London: 1952). Reprinted in paperback by Panther Books (London: 1959). The novel from which the film was adapted.

55. Gill, Brendan. "*Spartacus*," *The New Yorker* (New York: 15 October 1960). A review of the film.

56. Knight, Arthur. "The Many Faces of Sir Laurence," *Saturday Review* (New York: 1 October 1960). Includes comments by Olivier on *Spartacus*.

57. Laing, Nora. "£3,500,000 Film Is Wrapped Up After 115 Days' Shooting." *Evening News* (London: 11 September 1959). A short news item.

58. Legrand, Gerard. "La Gloire et ses Chemins," *Positif* (Paris: May 1962). A pretentious article on the film.

59. Mann, Anthony. "A Lesson in Cinema," *Cahiers du Cinéma* in English (New York: December 1967). An interview with Anthony Mann, in which he briefly comments on his association with *Spartacus.*

60. Miller, Claude. "*Spartacus,*" *Télécine* (Paris: December 1961).

61. Schumach, Murray. "U.I. is Pondering Credit to Trumbo," *New York Times* (New York: 22 February 1960). News item.

62. Schumach, Murray. "Trumbo Will Get Credit for Script," *New York Times* (New York: 8 August 1960). News item.

63. Sigal, Clancy. "Slaughter Sugar-Coated," *Time and Tide* (London: 17 December 1960). An excellent review of the film.

64. Torok, Jean-Paul. "*Spartacus,*" *Positif* (Paris: January 1962). A review of the film.

65. Wilson, Colin. "They Say he is an Outsider, BUT," *Daily Express* (London: 6 December 1960). A review of the film by the author of *The Outsider.*

66. Uncredited. "Olivier to Act in Film of Spartacus," *The Times* (London: 23 May 1958). Short news item.

67. Uncredited. "Gladiators' Role Tony Curtis nixed, He'll do for Bryna," *The Hollywood Reporter* (Hollywood: 25 July 1958). News item concerning Brynner-Bryna rivalry over the *Spartacus* subject.

68. Uncredited. "Credit to Trumbo Disputed by Fast," *The New York Times* (New York: 23 February 1960). News item.

69. Archer, Eugene. "Hailed in Farewell," *The New York Times* (New York: 2 October 1960). A revealing short interview with Kubrick.

70. Uncredited. *"Spartacus,"* The Hollywood Reporter (Hollywood: 7 October 1960). A review of the film.

71. Uncredited. *"Spartacus,"* *Monthly Film Bulletin* (London: January 1961). A review of the film.

LOLITA

72. Archer, Eugene. "M-G-M to release *Lolita* in Spring," *The New York Times* (New York: 14 February 1962). Short news item.

73. Burch, Stanley. "Lolita's Saucy Sue will stick to script," *Daily Mail* (London: 29 September 1960). News item.

74. Coleman, John. "Qu'il t'y," *New Statesman* (London: 7 September 1962). A review of the film.

75. Croce, Arlene. *"Lolita,"* *Sight and Sound* (London: Autumn 1962). A review of the film.

76. Davies, Michael. "Lolita Fiasco," *The Observer* (London: 17 June 1962). A dispatch on the New York premiere.

77. Evans, Peter. *Peter Sellers: The Mask Behind the Mask*, Prentice-Hall Inc. (New Jersey: 1968). A showbiz biography of Sellers, touching upon his work in *Lolita* and *Dr. Strangelove*.

78. Hopkirk, Peter. *"Lolita*: Now It's Going on Celluloid," *Daily Express* (London: 6 July 1960). News item.

79. Kael, Pauline. *I Lost It at the Movies*, Jonathan Cape (London: 1966). Reprinted in paperback by Bantam Books (New York: 1966). A collection of film reviews, including one of *Lolita*, scorning attempts to compare the film with the novel.

80. Kauffmann, Stanley. *A World of Film*, Harper and Row (New York: 1966). A collection of film articles first published in *The New Republic*. It includes a review of *Lolita*, comparing it unfavourably to the novel (2 July 1962), and enthusiastic reviews of *Dr. Strangelove* (1 February and 21 March 1964).

81. Kubrick, Stanley. *"Lolita* Fiasco," *The Observer* (London; 24 June 1962). A letter replying to a hostile review (see ref. 76).

82. MacDonald, Dwight. *On Movies*, Prentice-Hall, Inc. (New Jersey: 1969). A collection of reviews, including reviews of *Lolita* and *Dr. Strangelove*.

83. Nabokov, Vladimir. *Lolita*, The Olympia Press (Paris: September 1955). The novel from which the film was adapted.

84. Nathan, David. "*Lolita* film men to meet censor," *Daily Herald* (London: 5 November 1960). News report on the arrival of Kubrick and Harris to film *Lolita*.

85. Marcorelles, Louis. "*Lolita*," *Cahiers du Cinéma* (Paris: March 1963). A review of the film.

86. Rhode, Eric. "*Lolita*," *The Londoner* (London: 20 September 1962). A review of the film.

87. Schiff, William; et al. "Gamesmanship," *Sight and Sound* (London: Spring 1963). Ingenious if far-fetched letter suggesting identifications in the film of Kubrick with Quilty and Nabokov with Humbert Humbert.

88. Shorter, Eric. "*Lolita*," *Daily Telegraph*. (London: 5 September 1962). A review of the film.

89. Spiller, David. "Putting on the Style," *Screen Education* (London: September-October 1968). A brief examination of *Lolita* in a general article on adapting novels to the screen.

90. Wiseman, Thomas. "Stanley Kubrick," *Evening Standard* (London: 8 December 1960).

91. Zec, Donald. "Lolita and the Lollipop," *Daily Mirror* (London: 17 May 1962). News item about Sue Lyon.

92. Uncredited. "Lolita and Friends," *Daily Mail* (London: 5 November 1960). Interview with Kubrick and Harris about *Lolita*.

93. Uncredited. "Plea to Stop Showing of *Lolita* film," *The Times* (London: 13 May 1961). News item.

94. Uncredited. "*Lolita*," *Monthly Film Bulletin* (London: October 1962). A review of the film.

DR. STRANGELOVE OR: HOW I LEARNED TO STOP WORRYING AND LOVE THE BOMB

95. Archer, Eugene. "How to learn to love world destruction," *The New York Times* (New York: 26 January 1964).

96. Beaton, Leonard. "Stop Worrying and Ignore the Bomb, The Answer to *Dr. Strangelove*," *The Guardian* (London: 4 February 1964). An article on the film.

97. Bryant, Peter (pseud. of Peter Bryan George). *Two Hours to Doom*, T.V. Boardman and Co. (London and New York: 1958). The novel on which the film was based, published in the U.S. under the title *Red Alert*.

98. Buchan, Alastair. "Basis of a Film," *The Times* (London: 31 January 1964). A letter about the film.

99. Bull, Peter. *I Say, Look Here!* Peter Davies (London: 1965). Pages 110-117 of the actor's autobiography deal with *Dr. Strangelove*.

100. Burdick, Eugene and Wheezer, Harvey. *Fail-Safe*, Dell Publishing Co., Inc. (New York: 1962). A novel on the same theme as *Dr. Strangelove*.

101. Burgess, Jackson. "*Dr. Strangelove*." *Film Quarterly* (Berkeley, California: Spring 1964). An excellent review of the film.

102. Chamberlain, William. "Red Alert," *Saturday Evening Post*. (New York: 21 May 1955). A short story set in a SAC base.

103. Cohn, Bernard. "Cent mille soleils au dollar," *Positif* (Paris: No. 64-65, 1964). A review of the film.

104. Fay, Gerard. "Kubrick's Strange Love," *The Guardian* (London: 5 June 1963). A short article based on an interview with Kubrick.

105. Forbes, Bryan. "*Dr. Strangelove*," *Films and Filming* (London: February 1964). A review of the film.

106. George, Peter. *Dr. Strangelove or: How I Learned to Stop Worrying and Love the Bomb*, Corgi Books and Bantam Books

(London and New York: 1963). A paperback novelisation of the film, written under the original author's real name.

107. Gilliatt, Penelope. "*Dr. Strangelove,*" *The Observer* (London: 2 February 1964) A review of the film.

108. Goldberg, Joe. "Dr. Kubrick," *The Seventh Art* (New York: Spring 1964). A sympathetic article on the film.

109. Hudson, Roger. "Putting the Magic in It," *Sight and Sound* (London: Spring 1966) An article, including comments by Anthony Harvey on editing *Dr. Strangelove.*

110. Hudson, Roger. "Three Designers," *Sight and Sound* (London: Spring 1964). An article including comments by Ken Adam on designing *Dr. Strangelove.*

111. Kubrick, Stanley. "Ten questions to nine directors," *Sight and Sound* (London: Spring 1964). Kubrick's answers to a brief questionnaire on production details of *Dr. Strangelove.*

112. Macklin, F. Anthony. "Sex and Dr. Strangelove," *Film Comment* (New York: Summer 1965) An article prefaced by a brief comment from Kubrick.

113. Mallone, Ronald S. "Message of Dr. Strangelove." *Sunday Telegraph* (London: 9 February 1964). A letter concerning U.S.A.F. accidents.

114. Milne, Tom. "*Dr. Strangelove,*" *Sight and Sound* (London: Winter 1963-64). A review of the film.

115. Mumford, Lewis. "*Dr. Strangelove,*" *The New York Times* (New York: 1 March 1964) A letter in defence of the film.

116. Narboni, Jean. "Homo Ludens," *Cahiers du Cinéma* (Paris: May 1964). A review of the film.

117. Piler, Jack. "Dr. Strangelove or how Stanley Kubrick and Peter Sellers are making a nightmare comedy about The Bomb," *Scene* (Philadelphia: 23 March 1962). An article about the film.

118. Price, Stanley. "Hot Line on Dr. Strangelove." *Town* (London: January 1964). A well-illustrated article on the making of the film.

119. Rhode, Eric. *Tower of Babel: Speculations on the Cinema.* Weidenfeld and Nicolson (London: 1966). A book of film essays, including a brief reference to *Dr. Strangelove* and *Metropolis.*

120. Taylor, Stephen. *"Dr. Strangelove," Film Comment* (New York: Winter 1964). A review of the film.

121. Worsthorne, Peregrine. *"Dr. Strangelove," Daily Telegraph* (London: 2 February 1964). A right-wing reaction to the film.

122. Uncredited. "Manhattan Comment," *Variety* (New York: 27 February 1963). News item concerning Columbia suing over alleged *Fail-Safe* plagiarisation.

123. Uncredited. *"Dr. Strangelove," Monthly Film Bulletin* (London: February 1964). A review of the film.

124. Uncredited. "Missile Guards had Mental Trouble," *The Guardian* (London: 18 August 1968). News item concerning dangerous missile base incident.

2001: A SPACE ODYSSEY

125. Agel, Jerome (editor). *The Making of Kubrick's 2001.* A Signet paperback for New American Library, Inc. (New York: April 1970). A source book on the film, including a selection of critical essays.

126. Adler, Renata. "The Screen: *2001* Is Up, Up and Away," *The New York Times* (New York: 4 April 1968). An unfavourable review of the film.

127. Adler, Renata. "Astronauts, Maoists – and Girls," *The New York Times* (New York, 21 April 1968). A second opinion on the film.

128. Austen, David. *"2001," Films and Filming* (London: July 1968). One of the more detailed and perceptive reviews of the film.

129. Allen, John. *"2001," Christian Science Monitor* (Boston: 10 May 1968) A review of the film.

130. Barker, Cliff. "Is *2001* worth seeing twice?" *Cineaste* (New York: Summer 1968).

131. Baker, Russell. "Observer: A Machine for All Seasons," *The New York Times* (New York: 7 April 1968). An article stressing the alleged anti-human, pro-machine elements in the film.

132. Baxter, John. *Science Fiction in the Cinema.* Tantivy Press (London 1970). Includes a disparaging section on *2001.*

133. Decker, Michael. "2004?" *Cineaste* (New York: Summer 1968).

134. Campbell, John Ramsey. "*2001*: Before the Rebirth," *Stardock* (London: No.2, April 1969). Occasionally overstated article on the sexual motifs in *2001.*

135. Clarke, Arthur C. *Expedition to Earth*, Sidgwick and Jackson (London: 1954). Reprinted in paperback by Sphere Books (London: 1968). A book of short stories, including "The Sentinel," the story used as a basis for the film, originally published in 1950.

136. Clarke, Arthur C. *2001: A Space Odyssey*, Hutchinson & Co., Ltd. (London: 1968) Reprinted in paperback by Arrow Books (London: 1968). A novel based on the screenplay by Stanley Kubrick and Arthur C. Clarke.

137. Clarke, Arthur C. "The Mind of the Machine," *Playboy* (Chicago: December 1968). An article on computers.

138. Clarke, Arthur C. *The Coming on the Space Age*, Victor Gollancz Ltd., (London: 1967). Reprinted in paperback by Panther Books (London: 1970). An anthology edited by Clarke, which includes Wernher von Braun's "Reminiscences of German Rocketry," reprinted from the *Journal of the British Interplanetary Society* (London: May, 1956).

139. Clarke, Arthur C. "The Myth of *2001*," *Cosmos* (Ilford, Essex: No.1, April 1969). Valuable article on some of the thematic elements in the film.

140. Conford, Christopher. "Old Vienna and the Infinite," *Kultur* (Royal College of Art newsletter) (London: 4 November 1968). A review of the film.

141. Crowdus, Gary. "A Tentative for the Viewing of *2001*," *Cineaste* (New York: Summer 1968).

142. Davis, Victor. "*2001*: the men who made tomorrow," *Daily Express* (London: 16, 17 and 18 April 1968). A report on the making of the film.

143. Fremont-Smith, Eliot. "Outward Bound," *The New York Times* (New York: 5 July 1968). A review of Clarke's novel, comparing it to the film.

144. Gasser, Mark H. "*2001: A Space Odyssey*," *Cineaste* (New York: Summer 1968). A review of the film.

145. Gelmis, Joseph. "The Message of Kubrick is non-verbal," *Newsday* (New York: 4 June 1968).

146. Gentleman, Wally. "Inside *2001*," *Take One* (Montreal: May-June 1968). An interview with a special effects supervisor who worked on the early stages of the film.

147. Gilliatt, Penelope. "After Man," *The New Yorker* (New York: 13 April 1968) A review of the film.

148. Graham, Colin. "Two Thousand and One: An Appreciation." *Supernatural Horror Filming* (Bournemouth: No.1, January 1969). Crude, over-awed article on the film.

149. Hofsess, John. "The Mind's Eye," *Take One* (Montreal, Vol. 1, No. 11). A review of the film.

150. James, Clive. "*2001*: Kubrick vs. Clarke," *Cinema* (Cambridge, No. 2, March 1969). An article veering between the perceptive and the obtuse.

151. Jeffries, Michael. "A Good Astronaut Gets on With His Father," *Evening Standard* (London: 19 November 1968). Part II of a series on space travel, "The Moon and Beyond."

152. Kloman, William. "In *2001*, Will Love Be a Seven-Letter Word?" *New York Times* (New York: 14 April 1968). Short interview with Kubrick concentrating on *2001*.

153. Kloman, William. "*2001* and *Hair* – Are They the Groove of the Future?" *The New York Times* (New York: 12 May 1968). A short feature included in the Sunday supplement on the arts.

154. Koch, Stephen. "Fiction and Film: A Search for New Sources," *Saturday Review* (New York: 27 December 1969). General article including comments on *2001*.

155. Kubrick, Stanley and Clarke, Arthur C. *2001: A Space Odyssey*, Filmscripts Ltd., Rayant Studios, Bushey, Herts. Unpublished early screenplay dated July 1965.

156. Kubrick, Stanley and Clarke, Arthur C. *2001: A Space Odyssey*, Filmscripts Ltd., Rayant Studios, Bushey, Herts. Unpublished intermediate screenplay, dated October 1965 - February 1966.

157. Lightman, Herb A. "Filming *2001: A Space Odyssey*" and "Front Projection for *2001*," *American Cinematographer* (Hollywood: June 1968). Two very detailed accounts of the technical side of *2001*.

158. Mailer, Norman. "The Mind of an Astronaut," *The Observer* (London: 19 April 1970). An extract from Mailer's book on the Apollo 11 voyage.

159. Martin, Marcel; et al. "*2001: L'Odyssées de l'espace*," *Cinéma* 68 (December 1968). A "table ronde" discussion by nine French film critics.

160. Mckee, Mel. "*2001*: Out of the Silent Planet," *Sight and Sound* (London: Autumn 1969). Article comparing *2001* to C.S. Lewis's *Ransom Trilogy*.

161. Nairn, Tom. "The Worst Trip Ever," *Oz* (London: No. 13, 1968). A review of the film.

162. Oakes, Philip. "Lift-off 65 One: Somebody up there likes me, I hope," *Sunday Times Magazine* (London: 3 October 1965). An article written before shooting of the film began.

163. Rhode, Eric. "Second Coming," *The Listener* (London: 9 May 1968). A review of the film.

164. Robinson, David. "Two for the Sci-Fi," *Sight and Sound* (London: Spring 1966). A report from the sets of *2001* and *Fahrenheit 451*.

165. Sand, Luce. "*2001, l'odyssée de l'espace*," *Jeune Cinéma* (Paris: November 1968). A review of the film.

166. Sarris, Andrew. "*2001: A Space Odyssey*," *The Village Voice* (New York: 11 April 1968). A review of the film.

167. Shatnoff, Judith. "A Gorilla to Remember," *Film Quarterly* (Berkeley, California: Fall 1968). Vividly argued, sceptical article, intent on cleverness but full of shafts of insight.

168. Sigal, Clancy. "2001: An informal diary of an infernal machine," *Town* (London: July 1966). A fatuous article on the making of the film.

169. Strick, Philip. "*2001: A Space Odyssey*," *Sight and Sound* (London: Summer 1968). A review of the film.

170. Taylor, John Russell. "On Seeing *2001* a Second Time," *The New York Times* (New York: 22 September 1968).

171. Thomas, David. "Critics Reviewed," *The Critic* (London: 3 May 1968). An assessment of English critical reaction to *2001*, followed by reprints of reviews from 13 British newspapers.

172. Trumbull, Douglas. "Creating Special Effects for *2001*," *American Cinematographer* (Hollywood: June 1968). An account by one of the technical effects supervisors of the film.

173. Weavers, Wally, "Visual Special Effects from *Things to Come* to *2001*," *Film and Television Technician*, April 1969.

174. Weiler, A.H. "Kazan, Kubrick and Keaton," *The New York Times* (New York: 28 April 1968). Article including comments by Kubrick on *2001*.

175. Youngblood, Gene. "Stanley Kubrick's *2001*: A Masterpiece," *Los Angeles Free Press* (Los Angeles, 19 April 1968). Reprinted in *The Village Voice* (New York: 2 May 1968). A detailed but facile review of the film.

176. Uncredited. "Facts for Editorial Reference," M-G-M Publicity Department (New York: 1968). A well-illustrated press hand-out on the film.

177. Uncredited. "*2001* Draws Repeat and Recant Notices, Also a Quasi-Hippie Public," *Variety* (New York: 15 May 1968). A news item.

178. Uncredited. "Stanley Kubrick," *L'avant-scène* (Paris: February 1969). Bio-filmography of Kubrick, plus short statement by the director concerning the origin of HAL's name, plus extracts from French newspaper reviews of *2001*.

179. Uncredited. "Kubrick's Stock Buy," *Variety* (New York: 28 February 1968). A news item.

180. Uncredited. "*2001: A Space Odyssey*," *Monthly Film Bulletin* (London: June 1968). A review of the film.

*

Discography

1. *2001: A Space Odyssey*, M-G-M Records. SIE-13 ST X Music from the Motion Picture Sound Track (1968).

2. *Music from Mathematics*. Played by IRM 7090 Computer. LAT 8523. Brunswick. Includes a recording of "Bicycle Built for Two" as "sung" by a computer (1965).

APPENDIX: TIMELINE

3 February 1969
David Austen, a journalist and film critic, presumably in response to an enquiry he sent, receives a brief letter from Stanley Kubrick in which he expresses interest in Austen's book project. Kubrick and Austen never meet, although Kubrick does submit replies to questions sent to him by Austen (material that appears to be lost). Austen falls ill and withdraws from the project.

6 May 1969
Neil Hornick signs a contract with Peter Cowie's Tantivy Press in London to deliver a book on the subject of "The Cinema of Stanley Kubrick" by 1 October 1969. Hornick's advance is £200 (approximately £3,000 today). The initial print run is to be 12,000 copies.

20 July 1969
Hornick meets Ray Lovejoy, assistant editor on Kubrick's *Dr. Strangelove* and the editor of *2001: A Space Odyssey* (and later *The Shining*). The same day, Hornick writes a letter to Kubrick, c/o Lovejoy at Boreham Wood Studios, explaining

that Austen has fallen ill and he has taken over the book project. He lays out his primary aims with the book: "to provide the reader with accurate factual information about your career and the circumstances in which each film was made; secondly, on the basis of this information to attempt a critical analysis of the films." Hornick encloses a list of questions with his letter, adding that they "are designed to clarify and settle many points of information, since I share your concern that the facts should be rigorously accurate. I should be delighted if you can spare time to check the chapters for factual errors. There are, of course, other questions which I should like to ask but I feel that they could be better put in an interview. It would be enormously helpful if you were free [to] discuss the book and your career at an early stage. I could record our conversation on tape or in writing as you prefer and of course would submit the written outcome of our talk for checking."

1 August 1969
After having spoken to Lovejoy, Cowie writes to Hornick: "In early September you should be able to meet Stanley Kubrick personally and put your questions to him during an interview. If all goes well and you can finish your manuscript as a result of this meeting by the first of second week in October, then the text should be delivered to Stanley for approval. Once he has read it, we can give it to the printers, and I am assured by Ray that he will set aside the time to check the manuscript very carefully – and in good time too." Hornick is given an extra month to complete the manuscript.

2 September 1969
David Norris, Kubrick's lawyer, writes to Cowie, explaining that in terms of his client making any desired changes to the manuscript of Hornick's book, "he cannot accept any strictness at [this] time since he himself, of course, is intensely involved with a major project [his film about Napoleon] which may well, from time to time, necessitate his 'working outside this country.'"

18 September 1969
Hornick resends his original letter to Kubrick.

1 October 1969
An agreement is signed between Kubrick and Cowie. Referencing the meeting between Cowie and Lovejoy on 1 August, Kubrick writes that he has "the right to read and examine the entire contents of the Book prior to its publication and to make such amendments and alterations thereto and deletions therefrom as I shall in my absolute discretion determine and you will not publish the Book and offer it for sale to the public until such time as its entire contents have been approved in writing by me." Crucially, the agreement states that to enable Kubrick to approve the contents of the book and make any necessary changes, "you will submit to me a copy of the Book in manuscript form and later in galley proofs (on the understanding that I shall return the galley proofs to you within 21 days of receipt) [,] the same being used to make up the book in its final form prior to publication and will not proceed thereafter to publish the same until I shall have approved the final text."

4 October 1969
Hornick sends his partial manuscript (he is still working on a couple of chapters, including a final summary chapter) to Kubrick. In his cover letter, he notes that there are questions of fact that he is uncertain about. "If we could meet, it would be of great help to me, both for clarifying doubtful points, and for exploring certain issues not, so far as I know, covered in previous published interviews with you… I must admit a certain apprehension with regard to the critical remarks I have made. Not because I lack confidence in my own opinions but because it is finally rather nerve-wracking to submit those opinions directly to their subject."

16 October 1969
Cowie writes to Hornick about his manuscript. He is complimentary about its contents, but notes: "It is possible, of course, that Kubrick may veto the book. I feel you are

straying onto dangerous ground when you start comparing him to HAL 9000 (although perversely, he may be flattered), and I anticipate your final chapter with some trepidation. For me, the book is almost good enough as it stands without further scrutiny of the man himself. However, if the worst comes to pass, I am so impressed with your work that I would be happy to commission another book from you if the subject was right – ideally, Elia Kazan."

24 October 1969
A letter from Kubrick's lawyer: "I have been asked by Stanley Kubrick to give you formal notice by means of this letter that he does not approve the contents of [your] book."

26 October 1969
Hornick writes to Lovejoy, expressing his disappointment and "upset," noting that it was "bewildering to receive news of his dissatisfaction in this way. I had understood that his legal agreement with the publisher, Peter Cowie, entitled him to ensure that the book was factually correct. I have always expected that a certain amount of rewriting would be necessary, but I didn't expect the whole book to be rejected, especially on the grounds of its general tone. I know that I am very critical of one or two of the films but my prevailing attitude towards Mr. Kubrick's work is one of respect and admiration. My final chapter, which I have been working to complete during the last couple of weeks, is an analytical summary of his work in general, expressing the highest regard." In the hope that Kubrick might change his mind, Hornick reiterates that he is "prepared to rewrite a considerable portion of the book in the interests of greater accuracy. As to the tone of the book, I would try to modify that too if it does not compromise the critical evaluations which must surely remain a matter of personal response and hence not within the scope of Mr. Kubrick's agreement with Peter Cowie."

27 October 1969
Cowie to Kubrick's lawyers: "We assume that a detailed explanation for this rejection will come from Mr. Kubrick soon."

11 November 1969
Cowie to Kubrick's lawyers: "We still do not know why Mr. Kubrick has rejected the manuscript of this book. In your letter of September 2 you said 'I am sure that we both appreciate that a man of Mr. Kubrick's intelligence and integrity can be relied upon to treat this matter responsibly.' Surely, therefore, we are entitled to some explanation of his attitude?"

27 November 1969
After meeting with Lovejoy, Cowie explains to Hornick in a letter that while Tantivy Press "was tied by the agreement with K, *you* were not and that we might have to release you from your contract so that the book could be launched by a firm not party to any agreement with K. Lovejoy assured me that in such an event, Kubrick would fight 'tooth and nail' with every legal means at his disposal to prevent distribution of the book. We agreed that the next positive move was for K to underline the passages he felt unacceptable, and return the MS to me. You and I would then confer, and on your behalf I said I felt confident that you would at least make some attempt – if not to eliminate your criticisms – at any rate to recast them tone-wise. My final impression is that K does not disapprove of the book as a whole and that he definitely wants to keep the lines open. His Napoleon project is not progressing happily, and this may account in some degree for his reactions at this time."

5 February 1970
Hornick writes to Lovejoy, explaining the situation as he understands it, "that Mr. Kubrick was in process of examining the manuscript for factual errors and false emphases, and would return the manuscript to me or the publisher, Peter Cowie, in reasonable time for appropriate

revisions to be made. But I've heard nothing further either from you or from Mr. Kubrick. I am afraid that the longer publication is delayed the more dated is the book likely to become. I am disturbed that Mr. Kubrick has not found it possible to communicate with me directly at any time. And, above all, I am worried that all the work I have put into this project will go completely to waste."

18 February 1970
Cowie exclaims to Hornick: "The outlook is gloomier with each passing week. It may be that Kubrick, his mind preoccupied with this new picture that has been announced [*A Clockwork Orange*], has conveniently shelved the book and the correction thereof. I feel that you should now write to him direct with a final plea – for the return of the manuscript (which is your legal property) at the very least. Although we have had the covers printed and laminated at considerable expense, I realise that Tantivy cannot proceed to set the book up in type without Kubrick's consent, and it may be that if you could interest another publisher, not bound by the agreement that we have with Kubrick, we could come to an amicable arrangement to release you from your contract."

22 February 1970
Hornick writes to Kubrick, explaining that Cowie has agreed to release him from his contract and that he is exploring other publishing options. "I must therefore ask you to return my property to me at once. If there is still the slightest chance of it being published, with appropriate corrections and modifications as suggested by yourself, by Peter Cowie, I would naturally prefer it. But both Peter Cowie and myself are naturally sceptical."

22 February 1970
Hornick writes to Penelope Houston, gatekeeper of the British Film Institute's Cinema One series, asking if she would be interested in reading the manuscript.

26 February 1970
Kubrick's lawyers write to Cowie and Hornick stating that "Mr. Kubrick has already made it clear that he will not approve the publication of the work in the form submitted to him. He has already made known his objections and it is unnecessary to enumerate them further beyond repeating that they are too broad to make feasible any editing on his part. Our Client would be prepared to consider a re-edited draft of the manuscript if one were re-submitted. If, however, any attempt were to be made by yourself or any other publisher to publish the existing manuscript without his approval our Client will have no alternative but to accept our advice to take all steps as are open to him to prevent such publication and to seek redress for damages suffered."

8 March 1970
Harvey Teff, a friend of Hornick's and a Professor of Law at Durham University, weighs in, noting that the easiest course of action is to take the manuscript to another publisher, adding that if Hornick does "wish to continue with Cowie, he would have to show that the agreement [with Kubrick] is not a legally binding contract. Briefly, the main argument he could put forward is that there is no true bargain i.e. Kubrick is merely promising to let him do what he could have done in any event i.e. publish a book about Kubrick. In law, an agreement is only binding if both sides provide something of economic value. A debatable point is whether Kubrick's agreement to vet the book could be considered as his part of the bargain (the law is not concerned with the respective value of each party's contribution). Presumably this would have been so if the original interview-type format had been retained. But as things stand, is Kubrick making any contribution at all?"

15 March 1970
Hornick writes to Kubrick, citing the letter dated 26 February, and insisting that no specific objections, as detailed by Kubrick, were ever made known to him. Kubrick's complaints "apparently lie precisely in that area

of 'criticism' as distinct from 'fact' which your solicitors, in a letter to Mr. Cowie of 2nd September 1969, strongly imply will not cause you to withhold your consent to publication." Hornick notes – as stated in his letter to Kubrick of 4 October and to Lovejoy on 26th October – that he was always willing "to reconsider and revise the book in the light of your indications." Hornick requests that Kubrick return his manuscript immediately.

25 March 1970
Penelope Houston writes to Hornick explaining that "after considerable discussion and with considerable regrets," his book isn't suitable for the Cinema One series. It is, she explains, too long. Moreover, "on the later films more than the earlier ones, I do get a general feeling that critically you are circling around – talking about points of detail, performances, explaining connections and so on, but sometimes leaving the film itself rather lost in the middle of all this."

31 March 1970
In response to a letter of enquiry from Hornick, publisher Ian Cameron of November Books writes: "Thank you for letting me read your manuscript on Kubrick. I'm sorry to say that I do not wish to take it on for a variety of reasons, of which the legal difficulties are by far the least important. For my taste it ploughs much too laboriously through the background and the script aspects without offering a sufficiently strong treatment of what is surely the important thing: Kubrick's directorial personality. Although I think it is a perfectly publishable book on Kubrick, it is not the book of Kubrick which I would wish to publish. Nevertheless, thanks for letting me see it."

20 April 1970
Kubrick's lawyers write to Hornick, making clear that Kubrick will return the manuscript only after Hornick promises that he will not attempt to publish his book anywhere other than Tantivy.

20 May 1970
After taking legal advice, Cowie writes to Hornick, explaining that he would prefer not to release Hornick from his contract "for the primary reason that by so doing we might lay both ourselves and you open to legal action from Kubrick. Apparently, while it might prove difficult for Kubrick to prove any damage caused him by the book, it would not be necessary for him to prove that the material was defamatory to show damage, for what is fair comment as far as libel is concerned may nonetheless be damaging to his career as a film director. In Counsel's opinion, the prudent course would be for us to pay you £100 in advance when you give us a copy of the manuscript and hope that in the not too distant future Kubrick may change his mind – he might suffer a couple of screen setbacks and suddenly be anxious for a book on his work, he might find that the book Alexander Walker is allegedly preparing is impossible to place with a publisher, he might consider 'a re-edited draft of the manuscript if one were re-submitted' ([lawyer's] letter to Tantivy of February 26, 1970), or we might be able to keep the door open through Lovejoy or other acquaintances of Kubrick we might come into contact with."

2 July 1970
After discussing the matter with Kubrick's lawyer, Cowie's lawyer explains that "the reasons why Mr Kubrick had retained Mr Hornick's manuscript were that he could not accept some of the criticisms in the manuscript and had he deleted such criticisms only two thirds of the manuscript would have remained. In the normal course Mr. Kubrick would have been prepared to have spent some considerable time re-writing the other one third of the manuscript which he could not accept but due to his commitments this is not a possibility."

6 September 1970
Hornick considers his options: to leave the book with Tantivy Press and retain his £200 advance, or end his agreement with Tantivy and return his advance in order to freely offer the

book to other publishers. He chooses the latter course and his legal agreement with Tantivy is formally severed.

13 October 1970
A representative of Methuen Publishers writes to Hornick, apologising for not having responded sooner: "I am afraid we have decided not to make you an offer for publication. It does seem to us that this is a book best suited to inclusion in a series of accounts of the work of modern film directors. We do not, as you know, publish such a series and have as yet no firm plans for doing so. We do not feel that we could publish your book successfully outside such a context."

November 1970
Hornick approaches a literary agency to see if they can place his book with a publisher. Several publishers reject the book, including Rupert Hart-Davis (September 1971), Faber (November 1971), University of California Press (December 1971) and Lorrimer (December 1971).

October 1971
Alexander Walker's book *Stanley Kubrick Directs* is published in the United States.

March 1972
Stanley Kubrick Directs is published in the United Kingdom.

20 March 1972
Hornick writes to Alexander Walker, letting him know that "last week I placed the manuscript of my book in the library of the British Film Institute, together with an introduction summarising the history of the book's suppression (my Kubrick correspondence file offers more ample detail). As I know that you are interested in Kubrick's work it may be that you'd like to glance at my own effort to analyse it. It will certainly be fascinating to read your own account, especially as I enjoyed your previous film books."

December 1990
Richard Gollner, a literary agent friend and associate of Hornick's, gets wind of the book and encourages Hornick to resubmit the book in the form of a proposal and sample chapters. "I see no reason why a revised and updated version couldn't be undertaken," Hornick responds. "The four films Kubrick has made since *2001: A Space Odyssey* seem to me consistent with the general analysis I offer in my final chapter." Hornick names the chapters he will add to the book: "The Old Ultra-Violence: *A Clockwork Orange*," "Picturesque Picaresque: *Barry Lyndon*," "Labyrinth of Solitude: *The Shining*" and "Back to the Front: *Full Metal Jacket.*" There are no takers.

ABOUT THE AUTHOR

Neil Hornick was born in London in 1939. He studied Psychology at University College London and, after a period travelling abroad, earned a post-grad Certificate in Drama with Distinction at Bristol University in 1965-6. He was artistic director of The Phantom Captain performance company for 36 years, and from the mid-1980s he also ran a literary consultancy, Reading & Righting, under his pen-name, Robert Lambolle. Still resident in London, he is married and has a son and daughter. He believed he was retired until Paul Cronin dusted him off and put him to work on resurrecting his once-suppressed book about film director Stanley Kubrick. His complete professional and personal archives were acquired by the British Library in 2022.

INDEX